WHAT DOG?

WHAT DOG?

Second Edition

A GUIDE TO HELP NEW OWNERS SELECT THE RIGHT BREED FOR THEIR LIFESTYLE

Amanda O'Neill

BARRON'S

Second edition for North America published in 2015 by Barron's Educational Series, Inc. First edition for North America published in 2006 by Barron's Educational Series, Inc.

Second edition published in Great Britain in 2015 by Interpet Publishing, Vincent Lane, Dorking
Surrey RH4 3YX
England

All inquiries should be addressed to:
Barron's Educational Series, Inc.
250 Wireless Boulevard
Hauppauge, NY 11788
www.barronseduc.com

ISBN: 978-1-4380-0591-1

Library of Congress Control No.: 2014955139

Editor: Philip de Ste. Croix
Designer: Philip Clucas MSIAD
Production Management: Consortium, Suffolk
Print Production: 1010 Printing International Ltd., Hong Kong

Printed in China

9 8 7 6 5 4 3 2 1

The information and recommendations in this book are given without any guarantees on behalf of the author and publisher, who disclaim any liability with the use of this material.

The Author

Amanda O'Neill has written more than 20 books including *The Best-Ever Book of Dogs* and *Cats and Dogs* and was editor of *The Complete Book of the Dog*. She is a regular contributor to a number of dog magazines in the U.K. She is now enjoying retirement in the West Country with her family and two eccentric dogs.

Dedication

For Gary Cook and Harry Penfold, with love from Tabitha and Franklin.

A Note on Pronouns

Many dog lovers feel that the pronoun "it" is not appropriate when referring to a beloved pet. For this reason, dogs are referred to as "he" throughout this book unless the topic specifically relates to female dogs. No gender bias is intended by this writing style.

Throughout the book, silhouettes of the selected breeds are shown in relation to the profile of a Wire-haired Fox Terrier (above), which stands around 15 in (38 cm) tall at its withers. This is to allow the reader to get an impression of the relative sizes of the dogs being described. It should be understood that the sizes given in the data tables are averages and that inevitably, some dogs will grow to be smaller or larger than this at maturity. The sizes are for general guidance only. Where breed standards stipulate a height, allowance has been made beyond this to include the sizes of typical pets.

Contents

Introduction

No animal comes in such varied shapes and sizes as the dog, nor with such a wide range of temperaments. Big or small, shaggy or bald, placid or dynamic, there are hundreds of breeds from which to choose the one that will best suit your own personality, circumstances, and lifestyle.

Before you choose a breed, ask yourself the following questions:

How much exercise (truthfully) will you give your dog? Are you content with a stroll round the park, do you enjoy long walks every day, wet or dry, or do you prefer short walks during the week and long country walks on weekends or in nice weather? Different breeds have different needs. Owners who love walking can pick from a wide range—even some of the Toy breeds thoroughly

enjoy regular ten-mile hikes or more. Couch potatoes should look specifically at less active breeds—a dog that needs lots of exercise and is denied this will be unfit and unhappy, and will usually find something potentially destructive to do with his spare energy.

Do you really, really enjoy grooming? If not, pick a short-coated breed. If you don't mind some grooming, consider a medium coat. Only aquire a long-coated do if you want to spend time daily with a brush and a comb. Some long-coated breeds nowadays have enormous coats that need hours of care and, if neglected, mat and tangle beyond redemption. Heavy-coated dogs like Poodles and Old English Sheepdogs are often passed on to rescues in pitiful states simply because their owners failed to consider their grooming needs.

Do you have young children living in, or regularly visiting, your home? If so, choose a calm, sensible, reliable breed. If said children are not well behaved or will be left alone and unsupervised with the dog, buy them a video game instead—no dog, however good-natured, should be expected to put up with ill-treatment.

Do you have the experience and strong personality to enjoy a challenging, dominant dog, or would you be happier with a gentler dog that is eager to please? It is important to make the right choice here. Most breeds fall into the middle range between dominant and submissive, the ideal temperament for a pet. Strong-minded dogs (often working breeds) are best suited to equally strong-minded owners who know how to be pack leader without bullying and who have plenty of time for training. Dominant breeds like Rottweilers and Pit Bulls can be wonderful dogs in the right hands, but the increasing number of news reports of dog attacks on humans reflects what happens when they have owners unwilling or unable to commit to their training. At the opposite extreme, "soft" breeds like the Maltese lack nothing in personality, are great fun, and certainly a better choice for the novice.

Are you house-proud? If heavy shedding or a dog that carries in a lot of mud and water would be a problem, you will need to think carefully about the type of coat you are looking at. Be aware that some short-coated breeds shed hairs even more profusely than some long-coated breeds.

Do you want a watchdog? You don't need to narrow your choice down to guard breeds such as Dobermans and Bullmastiffs—these certainly make great protection dogs, but are best with experienced handlers who can keep their guarding instincts under control. Most people don't actually need a guard breed for this purpose—even small dogs are very effective burglar deterrents, and most dogs, however gentle, will defend their owners if a threat arises.

● *National crime statistics show that small dogs like this Shih Tzu deter burglars just as well as bigger breeds.*

Breed standards are guidelines, not absolutes.
Generally speaking, the standard of each breed tells
you what to expect in terms of appearance and
temperament. However, bear in mind that many
standards (and breed books) are written by people
who love that particular breed and may emphasize its
virtues without, perhaps, preparing you for its particular
demands and difficulties. If you like what you have read
or heard about a breed, go and meet as many
examples as possible and talk to their owners before
making a decision.

● *As a show dog, this Brussels Griffon must conform to
a stipulated size; pet dogs may be bigger or smaller.*

Size at withers: Dog 9-10 in. (24-26 cm) Bitch 8-9 in. (22-24 cm)

TERRIER **e.g. Parson Russell Terrier,** **Cairn Terrier**	Lively, bossy, busy, wilful; fun dogs with lots of character; strong hunting drive; can be fiery with other dogs; often great diggers and escapologists.
SIGHTHOUND **e.g. Greyhound, Whippet**	Gentle, affectionate; strong hunting and chasing drive, need opportunities to run; not particularly obedient and may not be trustworthy off leash; often escape artists.
SCENTHOUND **e.g. Basset Hound, Beagle**	Friendly, stubborn; strong hunting drive; need lots of exercise; not usually very obedient and usually hard to recall from a scent; often strong "houndy" smell.
GUNDOG (Sporting dog) **e.g. Labrador Retriever,** **Cocker Spaniel**	Good-natured, intelligent, highly trainable; need lots of exercise; generally good with children. European all-around breeds generally stronger willed.
HERDER **e.g. Border Collie,** **German Shepherd Dog**	Highly intelligent and need lots of mental and physical exercise; very trainable; strong chasing drive; often very sensitive and need early socialization.

Dogs are individuals. A breed standard outlines what dogs of that breed should be like, but that still leaves room for a lot of variation. Even within the same litter, puppies will show differences in character (the bold one, the timid one, the inquisitive one, and so forth) and even in looks (the big one, the one with funny ears, or an unusual tail carriage). In terms of both physical appearance and temperament, much depends on the breeder's goals. Breeders who are aiming for the show ring will produce dogs that look as much like the show standard as possible, whereas breeders who want working dogs generally value performance over appearance. In some breeds (e.g., English Setters), working strains and show strains are quite different.

Nonetheless, breed standards are very useful guidelines, making it clear that most Border Collies are intelligent workaholics, most Basset Hounds will follow a scent instead of coming back when called, and so on.

A useful starting point when considering breeds is to look at their origins and function. Hounds have been bred for centuries to hunt, terriers to go down holes and kill, and sheepdogs to herd. A pet hound, terrier, or sheepdog that is not required to carry out his ancestral tasks will still have these instincts. So if you want a calm, gentle, laid-back dog, you don't want a terrier; if you want a dog that will leave an interesting scent the moment you call him, you don't want a hound.

GUARD **e.g. Rottweiler, Doberman Pinscher**	Strong-willed and need confident, experienced owner; highly trainable in the right hands; protective drive needs to be controlled; socialization essential.
TOY **e.g. Pomeranian, Yorkshire Terrier**	Need lots of love and cuddles; despite small size, generally much more of a "real dog" than reputation suggests and most Toys enjoy long walks, opportunity for training, and so on.
SPITZ (Northern dogs) **e.g. Norwegian Elkhound, Keeshond**	Active, energetic, often noisy; tend to be independent and stubborn — not for obedience enthusiasts; need close relationship with owner, and dislike being left alone.
SLED BREEDS **e.g. Alaskan Malamute, Siberian Husky**	Active, not geared to obedience; need lots of exercise; strong prey drive and rarely to be trusted off leash; destructive if bored; great escapologists.
BULLY BREEDS **e.g. Bulldog, Staffordshire Bull Terrier**	Strong-minded dogs of fighting ancestry but not generally aggressive nowadays—although most will not back down if challenged, smarter than reputation suggests.

Buy a puppy from a reputable breeder.
Backyard and commercial breeders ("puppy mills")
whose only interest is making money will be looking at
quantity rather than quality. They may buy litters too
young to leave their mothers or breed from unhealthy
and ill-kept bitches to churn out puppies that may
never recover from their bad start in life. Also, a
breeder who doesn't care where the puppies end up
is unlikely to have gone to much trouble raising them.
The most ideal situation would be for the puppy to go
directly from his birth home to his permanent home
without going through the trauma of a middleman.

Questions to ask the breeder:
• Have the puppies been raised in the house or in
  a kennel?
• What socialization have they had? (Have they
  been exposed to everyday household noises and
  activities? If not, they are poorly prepared for their
  new home.)
• What are the parents' temperaments and
  personalities like?
• Have appropriate health checks for the breed been
  carried out, such as hip or eye testing? (If the
  breeder says these don't matter, go elsewhere.)

● *Puppies need a good start in life to grow into healthy dogs.*

• At what age can the puppies leave their mother?
  (Caring breeders won't let them leave too early.)

● *Puppies grow up fast. The progression from helpless
pup to confident adult takes about two years.*

● *Puppy socialization: This pup is starting to learn that cats are part of the family, too.*

that you can offer a good, and permanent, home. Most responsible breeders will insist that the pup be returned to them if at any stage you are unable to keep him.

Don't buy a puppy if:

- You can't see his mother and assure yourself that she is fit, healthy, and of good temperament.
- You can see the mother and/or father and they are badly cared for or have poor temperaments.
- The breeder has multiple breeds and multiple litters—this suggests a money-making venture rather than a caring breeder.
- The puppy's environment is dirty and squalid, suggesting a poor level of care.
- The breeder is ignorant or dismissive of health issues in the breed.

• What paperwork is provided? This should include American Kennel Club (AKC) registration, pedigree, vaccination, and worming records, and in some breeds, certification for puppy or parents for hip scores or eye tests. Caring breeders will usually provide a nutrition sheet and offer after-sale advice.

Good breeders know their pups as individuals and will try to match each pup to the right owner. They will also care where their pups are going and be unwilling to sell you a puppy until they are satisfied

Time spent choosing the right breed and the right breeder is never wasted. You are picking a companion who may be with you for the next ten or twenty years —for his sake as well as your own, choose wisely.

Dogs from rescue organizations

You may prefer to adopt a dog from a rescue organization. In addition to general rescue organizations, there are breed-specific rescues for almost every breed, from Great Dane Rescue to Chihuahua Rescue groups (details available from the American Kennel Club). Dogs come into rescue for all sorts of reasons. Some are cruelty cases, some have been abandoned, some are homeless through the death or changed circumstances of the owner, and many are passed on to rescue because their owners did not realize when they bought a cute puppy what it would turn into. Rescue workers are used to explanations ranging from "I didn't expect my Wolfhound puppy to grow so big" to "The kids are too rough for my Chihuahua."

Some rescue dogs have been much loved pets and need only to adapt to a change of home; others carry a lot of emotional baggage or even physical problems,

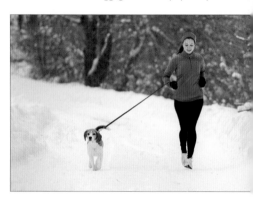

● *Rescue workers will try to ensure that families with active lifestyles are matched up with suitably energetic, fun-loving dogs*

but with loving care they can become wonderful companions. Good rescue organizations aim to know each case as an individual before matching dogs to the right new owners.

Most rescues are run by dedicated volunteers. Single-breed rescues tend to be run by people who know the breed well, can advise you on any problems that may arise and will provide backup after you

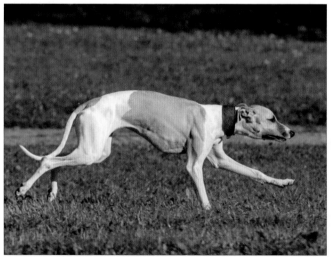

● *Former racing greyhounds are always available for rehoming. They make excellent pets, as they are friendly, gentle, and undemanding—and are most appreciative of home comforts.*

take your dog home. Sadly, a few groups are less than ideal, so be prepared to ask questions and assess the environment and people affiliated. A good rescue roup will interview you to stablish your suitability for ne of their dogs, and will sually pay a home visit to nsure that you have a uitable environment. Don't e offended by tough uestioning: It is the rescue vorkers' responsibility to nsure that a dog who has ready lost one home is oing to find a permanent, oving residence.

● *Before bringing your new dog home, make sure everything is ready for him, and try to make the journey as unstressful as possible.*

● *Dogs adapt amazingly well to owners' different lifestyles, but it pays to spend time on one's choice of breed.*

Most rescues do charge for their dogs, in the form of a set donation to help keep the organization running—the amounts vary from rescue to rescue. You are unlikely to find a puppy of your chosen breed via rescue—many of the dogs will be adults. Good rescues will be open about any behavioral problems of individual dogs—and eager to tell you about their virtues, which may be many. In some cases, old dogs may be guaranteed free medical treatment in exchange for a home for their twilight years, and such senior citizens can be very rewarding companions.

Rehoming a rescue dog may mean that you miss out on the fun of a puppy. However, many wonderful dogs are found through rescue, and you have the added satisfaction of having saved a life.

Before you bring your dog home, get everything ready for him.

Yards need to be dog-proofed—check fencing, and look out for danger spots like ponds or sheds where chemicals are stored. Indoors, look out for hazards like trailing electrical cords or wires, or accessible upstairs windows that a dog might jump through. You may want to put up safety gates across doorways or stairs so that you can control access until your new dog knows the ropes.

A comfortable bed gives your dog a place that he knows is his own, as well as a place to sleep.

gradually switch to whichever type of food you favor: fresh, canned, or dry foods are all suitable for most dog

Your dog's grooming needs will depend on h breed, but if in doubt start out with a soft bristle brush. Puppies don't need much grooming, but if you accustom them to being brushed from day one they will be much easier to groom as adults. Groomin is important to keep the coat healthy, but also a way of showing affection, an opportun to carry out health checks, and a means of showing a bossy dog who is in charge.

The type of collar and leash also depends on the breed. In general, puppies are best started out with sof puppy collars. Adults are usually most comfortable with

You will need to buy basics such as a bed, food and water bowls, grooming kit, collar and leash, and toys. A wide range of products is available in pet stores, but a new dog's needs are quite simple.

Decide where your new dog is going to sleep. He needs a comfy, easily cleaned bed in a secure, draft-free corner. You may want to train your dog to sleep in a crate, where he can be safely secured when necessary, or you may prefer an open bed. Puppies who are being housetrained are often best suited to a crate of appropriate size, which can be replaced by a comfy bed when they have been successfully housebroken (and can be trusted not to chew it up!).

Food and water bowls should be of an appropriate size and easily cleanable—hygiene matters for dogs just as much as for people. Responsible breeders will provide an age-appropriate nutrition chart, and you should always stick to the breeder's food for the first few weeks to avoid stomach upset. Later on, you can

● *Providing toys for your dog makes it easier to teach him not to borrow your belongings for play sessions!*

a buckled leather collar; some breeds do better with a harness. Don't forget to add an address tag—this is a legal requirement in many places as well as a safety measure. The once-popular choke chain is not recommended, as it is all too easy to damage a dog's neck with this type of collar unless you really know what you are doing. Adults that pull on the leash may do better with a head halter, which gives you more control.

● *A dog is for life, not just for Christmas—a long-term, demanding but rewarding commitment.*

Plan your new dog's social life and check out local training classes before you bring him home. For the first week or so (in the case of a puppy, until his vaccinations are complete), his new family and new environment will be enough for him to cope with. Once he is settled in, socialization is important. Puppies will benefit from meeting sensible visitors as well as from puppy socialization classes to accustom them to other dogs. For adult dogs, a weekly obedience class or similar activity will help you to build up a good relationship. Before you acquire your dog is also the best time to locate a good neighborhood veterinarian—don't leave it until you need one in a hurry.

How to use this book

This book aims to provide useful information for any-one who wants to choose the best companion breed for him/herself. It is not a guide to show standards. If you specifically want a show dog, you will need to look much more closely into details of colors, exact heights, grooming requirements, and so on.

Breed attributes given are those of an average dog of that breed, and individual dogs will vary according to their upbringing. For example, "attitude toward other dogs" will be affected by socialization (or lack of it). So where a breed is listed as being good with other dogs, a dog of that breed who has never mixed with other dogs will lack confidence with them and may be aggressive through fear. Similarly, "ease of training" will depend to some extent on the trainer (some breeds listed as "poor" in this area have produced obedience champions in the right hands). "Quietness" or "destructiveness" will depend on environment (most dogs can be noisy or destructive if neglected). "Protective behavior" (the likelihood of the dog sounding the alarm when he hears something unusual and barking at intruders) can be developed or partly repressed by an owner. Essentially, this guide aims to show you the raw material with which you will be working: It is up to you to develop your dog's potential.

Small Dogs

Don't underestimate small breeds. Little dogs are as loving, intelligent, and energetic as their bigger cousins. They enjoy exercise, make great watchdogs, and have lots of personality. Small size has practical advantages too: Little dogs need less space and cost less to maintain than big ones, and they also have longer life spans.

Chihuahua

The world's smallest breed, the Chihuahua is nonetheless all dog and not a mere fashion accessory. Certainly it is the ideal lapdog, content to soak up affection and return it in kind. But, it is also a lively and playful little animal that enjoys country walks and outings. Alert, loving, and intelligent, it likes to be the center of attention and receive plenty of cuddles. Its small size and low exercise requirements suit this breed well for apartment life, but it still needs company and mental stimulation.

The Chihuahua is an all-American breed, originating in medieval South and Meso-America, where it is said to have been sacred to the Aztecs. In the 19th century, it was introduced to the U.S. and subsequently worldwide. The popularity of the breed today means quality is variable—choose a breeder carefully to find a pet that is physically and temperamentally sound.

WHAT colors?

All colors acceptable, including red, cream, gold, fawn, sable, chocolate, blue, bi-color, tri-color, and black and tan. Merles (a sort of marbled effect distinguished by the presence of irregular dark blotches against a lighter background of the same basic pigment) are a recent introduction to the breed not universally approved.

WHAT grooming does the coat need?

Both types of coat are easy care. Smoothcoats require minimal grooming—just an occasional combing to remove dead hair. Longcoats need a little more time, but a weekly check for tangles and a gentle brushing will keep them looking and feeling good.

HOW suitable are they as family dogs?

Highly suitable—for the suitable family. They do tend to pick a favorite person, which is why many families end up with more than one Chihuahua. However, they are not recommended for households with very young children, as their small size makes them vulnerable. In any case, they prefer to be the baby of the family themselves.

WHAT type of home?

These are essentially companion dogs which need company in order to thrive. So long as they can be with their owner, they can be just as happy in town or country. Apartment dogs will benefit from daily access to a park to provide both physical and mental stimulation, but they can exercise themselves quite well indoors playing with their owners.

WHAT type of owner?

Chihuahuas need affection and attention so they need owners who are prepared to give, and receive, plenty of it. They make ideal companions for the housebound elderly, but can also enjoy a moderately robust family life with older, sensible children. This is not a suitable breed for part-time owners, as they crave company.

HOW compatible with other pets?

Chihuahuas enjoy the company of other pets (especially other Chihuahuas) if properly socialized in puppyhood. However, early socialization is essential to accustom them to bigger dogs—and also to control their hunting instincts toward smaller pets.

Character Trait	Poor	Average	Good	Excellent
Attitude toward other dogs				
Quietness				
Not destructive				
Protective behavior				
Not likely to stray				
Good with children				
Ease of training				

Original purpose: Companion; possibly edible; possibly sacred
Male height: 6-9 in (15-23 cm)
Female height: 6-9 in (15-23 cm)
Weight: not to exceed 6 lb (1-2.8 kg)
Lifespan: 14-18 years

HOW much exercise?

Chihuahuas can thrive on little exercise, but will also enjoy as much as you can offer. A healthy adult can walk quite happily for miles, and the breed also enjoys mini agility events.

HOW easy to train?

Chihuahuas don't rank high on the trainability scale—perhaps partly because owners of these mini dogs are rarely obedience enthusiasts. In fact, this breed responds surprisingly well to gentle, consistent training, but don't expect too much of them.

WHAT good points?

Devoted, responsive, non-aggressive, playful, alert, and low-maintenance in terms of exercise and food requirements, easily transported.

WHAT to be aware of?

Not the easiest breed to housetrain. Can be yappy if untrained, and also can be fussy eaters if encouraged. Dislikes the cold.

● *A long coat will require a little more time for grooming.*

Small dogs

WHAT medical problems?

Chihuahuas are generally hardy little dogs. Possible problems include open molera (an opening at the top of the skull, like that of a newborn baby), leaving the head vulnerable; slipping kneecaps; and heart problems.

Pekingese

Imperious and self-assured, the Pekingese has been termed an "honorary cat," and he has both a cat's dignity and a cat's playfulness. He is a dog of great personality, devoted to his owner and naturally good-mannered, but among the most stubborn and self-opinionated of all breeds. Despite his lapdog appearance, he is a sporty little dog who hates being left out of any activities. Sadly, modern show trends have exaggerated his foreshortened face and heavy coat so that he can no longer be as active a companion as he would wish, and his health and grooming needs are too much for many pet owners.

Recent genetic research shows that the Peke is among the oldest dog breeds. He originated in China, where he was the favorite of the imperial court and was unknown in the West until the mid-19th century. Today a glamorous showdog, he remains an enchanting companion.

WHAT colors?

Any color except liver or albino. Popular colors include red, fawn, brindle, black, white, parti-color. Solid colors usually have a black muzzle or mask.

WHAT grooming does the coat need?

The dense coat needs grooming daily, working right down to the skin with a bristle brush and comb, with special attention to the thick fur behind the ears and in the armpits. Grooming sessions must include checking and cleaning the facial wrinkle and checking the breeches for soiling. Many modern Pekes have so much coat that pet owners may prefer to clip it short, both for their own convenience and for their dog's comfort.

HOW suitable are they as family dogs?

Pekes tend to attach themselves most strongly to one person, but if brought up in a family they will have plenty of affection to spare for the whole household. They are not recommended for homes with young children because they are vulnerable to rough handling, but they thoroughly appreciate having considerate older children to play and socialize with.

WHAT type of home?

Large house, condo, or apartment, a Peke will fit in anywhere as long as he has his owner with him. He does enjoy a yard where he can fill his coat with mud and burrs before settling down to enjoy the process of being brushed clean again.

WHAT type of owner?

Pekes need loving owners with plenty of time for them, and they are wasted on anyone who does not share their sense of fun. They are perhaps not for the house-proud, as they cover carpets and furniture with shedded fur and can carry in astonishing amounts of mud and water on their coats.

HOW compatible with other pets?

Pekes are great with other animals, though like all dogs they need to be introduced carefully to small pets. They should not be encouraged to play with boisterous breeds, as their eyes are vulnerable to injury. On country walks, watch out for livestock, as most Pekes consider themselves hunting breeds and will chase sheep if they have not been taught not to do so.

HOW much exercise?

The Peke enjoys walks and outings, but his heavy coat and breathing

Character Trait	Poor	Average	Good	Excellent
Attitude toward other dogs				
Quietness				
Not destructive				
Protective behavior				
Not likely to stray				
Good with children				
Ease of training				

Original purpose: Lapdog and status symbol
Male height: 6-9 in (15-23 cm)
Female height: 6-9 in (15-23 cm)
Weight: 6-12 lb (2.75-5.5 kg)
Lifespan: 12-14 years

difficulties make it hard for him to go far. Daily walks at his own pace and for his own choice of distance will help to keep him healthy; but he should never be exercised in hot weather, as he overheats easily.

HOW easy to train?

Pekes are intelligent and quick learners, but prefer to train their owners rather than be trained; as the saying goes, "Nine out of ten Pekingese are disobedient; the tenth is really deaf." However, they are usually prepared to be cooperative if they believe their owner has a reason for asking them to do something. They do like showing off, and some individuals have even taken successfully to competitive obedience work for that reason.

● *The massive coat is only a crowning glory if you are prepared to spend time on daily grooming.*

WHAT good points?

Devoted, entertaining, intelligent, stable, dignified, alert, mischievous, playful, loving, sensitive, gentle.

WHAT to be aware of?

Heavy grooming requirements. Shortened nose leads to breathing difficulties. Pekes snore, wheeze, and tend to sneeze in your face.

WHAT medical problems?

Pekes are prone to breathing difficulties, over-heating, eye injuries, and back problems. They may also suffer from dis-location of the kneecaps (patellar luxation), tear gland defects, and soreness in their nose wrinkles.

Small dogs

Yorkshire Terrier

The Yorkie is a terrier in lapdog's clothing—a glamorous miniature version of his ratting ancestors. Despite his small size and decorative coat, he retains the true terrier spirit—busy, bustling, and full of bounce. Devoted to his owner, he is an enthusiastic (sometimes overenthusiastic) watchdog, a keen hunter given the chance, and a lovable, if demanding, companion.

Don't make the mistake of seeing him as a lapdog. He needs mental and physical activity if he is not to become bored and frustrated. He refuses to acknowledge his small size and can be aggressive toward bigger dogs if not socialized from puppyhood. This is a small dog with a big personality.

There is considerable variation between show and pet Yorkies, both in size and in coat. Those bred as pets are often larger, and the extravagant coat of the show ring, with its silky tresses decked with bows, is unlikely to be achieved by a family pet.

WHAT colors?

Dark steel-blue body with golden-tan head, chest, and legs. Puppies start out black with tan points, gradually fading to the clear blue color and extending the tan areas —a process that may take up to three years.

WHAT grooming does the coat need?

The fine, silky coat needs daily brushing and combing to prevent tangles, and the hair over the eyes should be trimmed or tied back. Many pet owners prefer to keep the coat clipped short. In any case, the full flowing show coat is achieved only by hours of labor, and is preserved between shows by being tied up in tissue paper.

HOW suitable are they as family dogs?

The Yorkie really comes into his own as a companion for adults, but he can be a great family pet with sensible older children. He is not recommended for younger children, as his small size makes him vulnerable and he can become snappy in self-defense if teased.

WHAT type of home?

Small enough for apartment life, and tough enough for the country, a Yorkie can fit in anywhere. As a country dog, he will need supervision to keep him out of mischief and rabbit holes. As a city dog, he will need access to a park or yard for exercise and an owner sensible enough to recognize that little dogs are easily trodden on in the street.

WHAT type of owner?

A devoted and demanding companion, the Yorkie needs an owner with plenty of time for him. He is an ideal pet for an active, older owner, providing encouragement to remain fit and active, but he can also be a fun dog for a sensible family. A non-shedding coat means this is a breed that can be suitable for asthmatics and others who are sensitive to dog hair.

HOW compatible with other pets?

Like most terriers, Yorkies will live happily with other animal members of their own household once properly introduced, but should probably never be trusted with small prey animals such as mice and hamsters. They also need to be accustomed to strange dogs in puppyhood to prevent the onset of interdog aggression.

HOW much exercise?

Two short walks a day will keep your Yorkie healthy, but he will enjoy as much exercise as you are able to offer. This breed has a low boredom threshold, so the more activity available for them, the better.

Character Trait	Poor	Average	Good	Excellent
Attitude toward other dogs	■	■	■	
Quietness		■		
Not destructive	■	■	■	
Protective behavior	■	■	■	
Not likely to stray	■	■	■	
Good with children	■	■		
Ease of training	■	■	■	

Place of origin: **Britain**

Original purpose: Small vermin hunting
Male height: 8-9 in (20-23 cm)
Female height: 8-9 in (20-23 cm)
Weight: not to exceed 7 lb (3.2 kg)
Lifespan: 14-16 years

HOW easy to train?

The Yorkie is intelligent and a quick learner as far as basic companion dog training goes, but he can be stubborn and is usually too independent and easily distracted to be an ideal candidate for competitive obedience. However, his energy and enthusiasm can make him a star at mini agility.

WHAT good points?

Intelligent, lively, playful, alert, affectionate, adaptable in terms of exercise, long-lived, hypoallergenic coat, easily transported.

WHAT to be aware of?

High grooming needs. Can be yappy if untrained, and can become snappy if teased or undersocialized. Males can be oversexed (usually resolved by neutering). As with all highly popular breeds, beware of commercial breeders who may produce physically and temperamentally unsound pups.

WHAT medical problems?

Generally a healthy breed. Reported problems include dislocation of elbow and kneecap, malformation of spinal vertebrae, Legg-Calvé-Perthes disease (affecting the hip joint), cataracts, epilepsy, heart murmurs.

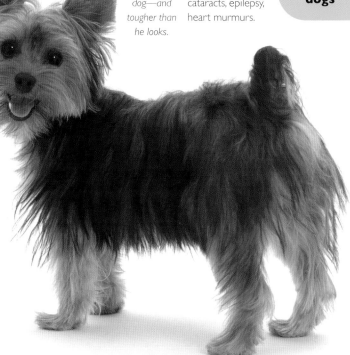

● *A lively dog—and tougher than he looks.*

Small dogs

Dachshund *Other names: Teckel*

Originally bred as a hunter to pursue badgers (his name means "badger dog"), foxes, and rabbits underground, the Dachshund has made a successful career change to become a popular companion. A wilful, self-opinionated charmer, he is a pet with personality plus. Despite his short legs, he is a sporting little character, active, playful, and always ready for a walk or a game, or to set off hunting—but also perfectly capable of being quiet and sensible when necessary. He is an affectionate and devoted companion who wants to be close to his owner. One word of caution: His long back makes him vulnerable to spinal injuries.

Dachshunds come in two sizes, the ever-popular Miniature and the more substantial Standard, each of which has three coat varieties, Smooth, Longhaired, and Wirehaired. All have the same happy temperament although Longhairs may be slightly more easygoing and Wirehairs a little more extroverted.

WHAT colors?
Red or black and tan are the most common colors, but Dachshund also come in chocolate and tan, cream, dapple (known as merle in other breeds), and brindle.

WHAT grooming does the coat need?
Smoothhairs need little maintenance: a weekly brush to remove dead hairs will suffice. Longhairs and Wirehairs need brushing and combing two or three times a week to prevent matts and tangles. Wirehairs need their coats hand stripped two or three times a year to keep them under control.

HOW suitable are they as family dogs?
Dachshunds make delightful family dogs, who will fit in with a wide range of lifestyles. As long as they are not ignored, they are equally happy to join in activities or just enjoy being cuddled. Children must be taught how to pick up a Dachshund carefully to avoid the

● Time for a walk. To neglect exercise is to risk back trouble.

risk of back injury. This breed is better in households with older, sensible children, as they can be jealous and may nip if teased or mishandled.

WHAT type of home?
Although they were bred for a sporting life in the country, Dachshunds can be just as happy in the city. Miniatures in particular make ideal apartment dogs, provided they have enough exercise.

WHAT type of owner?
Dachshunds are great companions for the elderly, and equally well suited to a lively young family. However, they are not for those who want a placid, malleable pet. Potential owners should be prepared for a feisty, stubborn, comical, loving little dog—and should be fairly strong-willed themselves, or they will find themselves at the bottom of the pack hierarchy!

HOW compatible with other pets?
Generally sociable and outgoing, Dachshunds usually get along well with other dogs and enjoy having a canine playmate in the same household. They do have a strong hunting drive, and if they are to share a home with cats or small pets such as rabbits, they need to learn early on that these are also family members and not prey animals to be chased.

HOW much exercise?
Dachshunds need regular exercise; allowing them to become unfit is asking for back trouble. Two half-hour walks a day is all that is

Character Trait	Poor	Average	Good	Excellent
Attitude toward other dogs				
Quietness				
Not destructive				
Protective behavior				
Not likely to stray				
Good with children				
Ease of training				

Original purpose: Hunting
Height (Standard): 8-10 in (20-25 cm)
Height (Miniature): 5-6 in (13-15 cm)
Weight (Standard): 16-32 lb (7.2-14.5 kg)
Weight (Miniature): 9-11 lb (4-5 kg)
Lifespan: 12-14 years

needed, but they will enjoy surprisingly long country hikes if that is their owner's choice. However, they should be discouraged from jumping, again because of their vulnerability to back injury.

HOW easy to train?

Smart and strong-willed, the Dachshund will ride roughshod over an owner who lets him. Given an owner who can establish firm but kind leadership, he is perfectly trainable, though not a natural for formal obedience. Training should be positive, consistent, and reward-based to encourage him to learn.

WHAT good points?

- *Short legged but sporting: a loving but feisty pet.*

Intelligent, lively, courageous, faithful, versatile, good-tempered, playful, entertaining, adaptable, determined, brave; an alert watchdog.

WHAT to be aware of?

Tendency to bark—and they have a big bark for their size. Can be difficult to housetrain.

WHAT medical problems?

Dachshunds are prone to back problems. Other conditions to watch out for include elbow malformation (dysplasia), dislocation of the kneecap (patellar luxation), epilepsy, eye problems (cataracts and progressive retinal atrophy), diabetes, and epilepsy.

Small dogs

Maltese

Ornamental and gentle, the Maltese has been considered the ultimate lapdog for centuries. His tiny size and luxurious snow-white tresses clearly identify him as a breed designed to be a lady's "comforter," and he has the sweet nature and happy temperament to match. Loving, playful, and responsive to his owner's moods, he makes an enchanting companion. He is also an intelligent little dog who benefits from training and enjoys walks just as much as cuddles. His coat takes a lot of care, so this is a breed only for those who enjoy grooming.

The Maltese is a toy breed of some antiquity with no traces of descent from any working breed —breed historians trace his origins back to Roman times. First exhibited in the U.K. in 1864 and in the United States in 1877, he is today equally successful as a glamorous show dog and as a delightful companion.

WHAT colors?

Pure white is the only color in this breed, although pale lemon markings are acceptable. Other colors were accepted at one time, but the colored strains died out altogether in the early years of the 20th century.

WHAT grooming does the coat need?

Daily grooming with a bristle brush is essential to keep the luxurious white tresses in good condition, and the facial hair needs tying back from the eyes. Pet Maltese are probably happier with the coat clipped down to a puppy trim, but it will still need careful brushing daily to avoid mats and tangles.

HOW suitable are they as family dogs?

Good-tempered and reliable, they can be excellent family pets, although their small size makes them unsuitable for households with young or rough children. Older, sensible children will appreciate their sweet nature, playfulness, and love of attention. They do need training as well as pampering, or they can become overdependent and clingy.

WHAT type of home?

These are essentially companion dogs that need company in order to thrive. So long as they can be with their owner, they can be just as happy in city or country, and are small enough to fit in an apartment. They love country walks and hunting in hedgerows but can be perfectly content trotting around the block—though their flowing coats will pick up dirt anywhere, making daily grooming even more important.

WHAT type of owner?

The Maltese needs an affectionate and sensitive but sensible owner who will appreciate his desire for around-the-clock company and attention, but also recognize that he is a dog, not an ornament, and requires proper training, exercise, and socialization. This is a high-maintenance breed not suitable for busy owners.

HOW compatible with other pets?

Maltese are friendly and gentle, and will get along well with other household pets if brought up with them. Their small size means that they do need supervision with bigger dogs to prevent accidental injury. Small pets such as hamsters need careful introduction. Despite his cuddly appearance the Maltese does retain all of a dog's natural hunting instincts.

HOW much exercise?

This is a breed that will adapt to the owner's requirements. A daily stroll

Character Trait	Poor	Average	Good	Excellent
Attitude toward other dogs				
Quietness				
Not destructive				
Protective behavior				
Not likely to stray				
Good with children				
Ease of training				

Original purpose: Lapdog and status symbol
Male height: 9-10 in (23-25 cm)
Female height: 9-10 in (23-25 cm)
Weight: 4-6 lb (2-3 kg)
Lifespan: 12-14 years

around the park will suffice, but a fit adult Maltese will also enjoy surprisingly long country walks. Don't forget, however, to allow time after the walk to clean up your pet's coat, which will pick up an amazing amount of dirt on each outing.

HOW easy to train?

This is a bright, little dog who is eager to please and who responds well to gentle training. Treat him like a toy, and he is likely to become demanding, clingy, and overdependent. Treat him like the intelligent creature he is, providing him with plenty of mental stimulus, and he will be a delight to live with.

● *His flowing tresses need considerable care.*

Many Maltese have achieved excellent results in competitive obedience and agility.

WHAT good points?

Small dogs

Sweet-tempered, lively, intelligent, affectionate, gentle, friendly, sensitive, alert, playful; hypoallergenic coat suitable or allergy sufferers.

WHAT to be aware of?

Time-consuming grooming needs. Prone to separation anxiety when left alone too much. Often hard to housetrain, and prone to barking.

WHAT medical problems?

Maltese are generally a healthy breed. Known problems include dislocation of kneecaps (patellar luxation), eye infections, lack of glucose in the blood (hypo-glycemia), teeth and gum weaknesses, and liver shunt (an inherited defect whereby the liver does not get a proper blood supply and does not function properly).

Havanese
Other names: Bichon Habanero, Bichon Havanais, Havanese Silk Dog

Barely known outside his native Cuba until the 1990s, the Havanese has come from nowhere to win hearts with his silky coat and sweet nature. A natural companion breed, he is bright, affectionate, playful, and devoted to his family. Although a toy breed, he is far from fragile and sturdy enough, both physically and mentally, to make a great children's playmate. Havanese are sociable and outgoing.

They like people and get along well with other pets. Gentle, responsive, and willing to please, they are thoroughly endearing little characters. The downside is the heavy grooming requirements: The soft flowing coat that gave them their earlier name of "Havanese Silk Dog" needs loving daily attention.

A member of the Bichon family, the Havanese was taken to Cuba by Spanish settlers and developed there as a distinct breed. By the 1950s they had become rare, but are now enjoying a well-earned revival in their popularity.

WHAT colors?
Any color or combination of colors, including black, white, chocolate, gray, silver, apricot, gold, champagne, sable, parti-color and tri-color.

WHAT grooming does the coat need?
The silky coat needs daily grooming with a soft bristle brush and wide-toothed comb to remove dead hair and prevent tangles. The long hair above the eyes needs to be clipped, braided, or tied back to keep it out of the eyes. A neglected coat will mat into a disastrous mess and lead to skin problems and extreme discomfort. Show dogs are shown in full coat; pets can be clipped short for convenience, but still need to be brushed every day.

HOW suitable are they as family dogs?
Havanese were made to be family dogs. They are happiest in a family atmosphere, and have a natural affinity with children—especially children old enough to treat them sensitively, who will find them tireless playmates. As with any dog, young children must be supervised to prevent unintentional mistreatment of the pet.

WHAT type of home?
Robust enough for life in the country and compact enough for a city apartment, these undemanding dogs are at home wherever their family is.

WHAT type of owner?
Only those who enjoy grooming should consider a Havanese.

Other than that, he makes great companion for any loving owner, whether a single senior in need of friendship or a lively family with a vacancy for another playmate. He is not suitable for people who work full-time and would have to leave him alone a great deal, nor for insensitive owners who are not interested in giving and receiving affection.

HOW compatible with other pets?
Havanese are as friendly toward other pets as they are toward people. They mix well with other dogs and live happily with cats or even smaller pets. If they are not accustomed to cats in puppyhood, however, they cannot be expected to understand that cat chasing is not an acceptable game.

HOW much exercise?
Most of a Havanese's exercise needs will be met by play in the house and yard: an hour's walking a day, broken up into two or three

Character Trait	Poor	Average	Good	Excellent
Attitude toward other dogs			X	
Quietness			X	
Not destructive			X	
Protective behavior		X		
Not likely to stray			X	
Good with children				X
Ease of training				X

Original purpose: Lapdog
Male height: 8-11 in (20-28 cm)
Female height: 8-11 in (20-28 cm)
Weight: 7-13 lb (3-6 kg)
Lifespan: 12-16 years

brisk outings, will suffice. On the other hand, they have plenty of energy and stamina and will thoroughly enjoy long walks if that is what their owner's lifestyle requires of them.

HOW easy to train?

In the past, Havanese were popular circus dogs because they enjoy learning and showing off what they have learned. Bright and eager to please, they are among the easiest of toy breeds to teach. Training should be positive, gentle, and sensitive, as they are discouraged by harsh treatment and can be quite distressed if scolded.

WHAT good points?

Friendly, lively, outgoing, playful, gentle, affectionate, responsive, sensitive, intelligent, long-lived.

WHAT to be aware of?

Above average coat care. Quite a dependent breed that may suffer from separation anxiety if left alone for long periods.

WHAT medical problems?

Havanese are hardy little dogs with few inherited disorders reported. Possible conditions include eye problems (cataracts, progressive retinal atrophy, and tear duct defects), lack of thyroid hormone (hypothyroidism), kneecap dislocation (patellar luxation), and liver shunt (an inherited defect whereby the liver does not get a proper blood supply and does not function properly).

Small dogs

Papillon
Other names: Continental Toy Spaniel, "Butterfly Dog"

As early as the 14th century, the Papillon's ancestors were the favorite lapdogs of European courts. Bred for generations to be a decorative and charming companion. He is sweet, playful, devoted and makes a delightful pet. For all his dainty appearance, he is one of the most trainable of the toy breeds, competing successfully against bigger breeds in obedience, agility, and tracking. He is a very adaptable little dog who can be calm and restful or playful and energetic as required, as long as he can enjoy the company of his owner. He does, however, deserve an owner who has time to devote to him and who will stimulate hi intelligence and keep him busy.

The Papillon takes his name from the French word for "butterfly," his wide-set erect ears resembling a butterfly's wings. There is also a drop-eared version known as the Phalène (French for "moth"), which is considered to be the original type but is less common today.

WHAT colors?

White with patches of any color other than liver, red, black or sable being most common. Tri-colors are white with black patches; tan spots over the eyes; and tan inside the ears, on the cheeks, and under the root of tail. Show dogs are required to have symmetrical facial markings.

WHAT grooming does the coat need?

The fine, silky coat is easy to keep in good condition, provided one is prepared to spend a few minutes each day with brush and comb to prevent tangles from forming—paying particular attention to ear fringes. Footpads may need trimming to keep the feet sound.

HOW suitable are they as family dogs?

Best for families with older children. Papillons are generally good with children, but younger children are often not so good with Papillons. These are quite fragile little dogs,

● *The pretty butterfly shape of the ears is the origin of this breed's name.*

especially in puppyhood, and unsuited to the rough and tumble of hectic family life. Their tendency to be possessive with their toys may also lead to problems with young children.

WHAT type of home?

These are essentially companion dogs that need company in order to thrive. As long as they can be with their owner, they can be just as happy in city or coun They do need a securely fenced yard, as they can squeeze through tiny gaps and are also great jumpers.

WHAT type of owner?

Papillons are ideal companions fo the elderly and ideal dogs for fam with older children. Their main function in life is to give and recei affection, so they need owners w are fully committed to spending t with them. A gentle, sensitive owr who enjoys making use of a dog's intelligence will bring out the best this breed.

HOW compatible with oth pets?

These friendly, gentle little dogs g along well with other pets, especi cats and small dogs. They do need supervision with bigger dogs, as t are quite unaware of their size an can irritate larger animals by bein bossy. Most are keen hunters of s prey and need careful introducti to small pets such as hamsters.

Character Trait	Poor	Average	Good	Excellent
Attitude toward other dogs			■	
Quietness		■		
Not destructive			■	
Protective behavior		■		
Not likely to stray			■	
Good with children			■	
Ease of training				■

Original purpose: Lapdog and status symbol
Male height: 8-11 in (20-28 cm)
Female height: 8-11 in (20-28 cm)
Weight: 4-9 lb (1.8-4.1 kg)
Lifespan: 12-15 years

HOW much exercise?

Papillons don't need a great deal of exercise, and short walks will suffice. On the other hand, they will cope equally well with an energetic lifestyle, and a healthy adult can walk for miles. They will also benefit from active playtime, and many breeders recommend having two Papillons who can play together.

HOW easy to train?

Generally considered the most trainable of all toy breeds, the Papillon often excels at obedience work. In fact, this breed responds surprisingly well to gentle, consistent training, but don't expect too much of them.

WHAT good points?

Lively, friendly, alert, playful, adaptable, highly intelligent and trainable, eager to please, neither shy nor aggressive, long-lived.

WHAT to be aware of?

This little dog's loving nature can lead to overprotectiveness or separation anxiety if he is over-coddled in puppyhood. He can also be possessive with toys and an over-enthusiastic barker, so needs his owner's time and sensible training in puppyhood to prevent these problems from arising.

WHAT medical problems?

Generally a healthy and long-lived breed. Known problems include kneecap dislocation (patellar luxation) and eye problems (progressive retinal atrophy).

Small dogs

● *Alertness and intelligence on display.*

Pomeranian *Other names: Dwarf Spitz, Loulou*

This little ball of fluff looks like a child's toy, but he has a larger-than-life personality, and is active, inquisitive, extroverted and self-important. Tiny and decorative, he is also full of himself, interested in everything that is going on, and determined to be involved. He is one of the most independent of the toy breeds, intensely loyal and protective toward his owner but tends to be bossy. For those who want a big character in a little package, and who enjoy grooming, he makes an enchanting companion.

It is understandable that the Pom should consider himself a big dog, as the breed was not miniaturized until Victorian times. The original Pomeranian was a larger dog, about 30 lb (13.6 kg), until a fashion for tiny specimens led to the creation of the modern Pom. His larger cousins are now known as German Spitz and come in a variety of sizes.

WHAT colors?

All colors acceptable, including orange, orange sable, cream, wolf sable, black, chocolate, beaver, blue, and parti-colors. Merles (a sort of marbled effect distinguished by the presence of irregular dark blotches against a lighter background of the same basic pigment) are a recent introduction to the breed not universally approved.

WHAT grooming does the coat need?

Don't consider this breed if you don't enjoy grooming. The thick coat requires daily attention, using a stiff bristle brush to work through the fluffy undercoat and long straight topcoat. Show dogs are delicately trimmed to emphasize the rounded shape.

HOW suitable are they as family dogs?

Highly suitable—for the suitable family. Their tiny size and high energy

● *Toylike in appearance—but the Pom displays remarkable energy.*

level makes them unsuitable for households with very young children, but they make great companions for older children and adults. He does need plenty of attention to keep him out of mischief, so he may not be ideal for a busy family.

WHAT type of home?

A Pom will fit in anywhere, from apartment to mansion. As long as he can be with his owner, he can be just as happy in city or country. Apartment dogs will benefit from daily access to a park to provide both physical and mental stimulation, but they can exercise themselves quite well indoors through playing with their owners.

WHAT type of owner?

Poms need affection and attention, but they also need training. An over-indulgent owner can turn this bossy little dog into a household tyrant. Given an owner who is prepared to spend time on gentle but firm and consistent training, he makes an ideal companion for the housebound elderly, but can also enjoy a moderately robust family life with older, sensible children.

HOW compatible with other pets?

Poms are sociable little dogs that generally get along well with other household pets, though if kept with bigger dogs they run the risk of accidental injury. They do need sensible socialization in puppyhood

Character Trait	Poor	Average	Good	Excellent
Attitude toward other dogs				
Quietness				
Not destructive				
Protective behavior				
Not likely to stray				
Good with children				
Ease of training				

Original purpose: Lapdog (but his ancestors were herders)
Male height: 8.5-11 in (22-28 cm)
Female height: 8.5-11 in (22-28 cm)
Weight: 3-7 lb (1.4-3 kg)
Lifespan: 12-15 years

to curb their natural desire to chase strange cats and bully strange dogs.

HOW much exercise?

The Pom's exercise requirements are minimal. He can obtain all the exercise he needs running around a small yard or simply playing indoors. Having said that, he enjoys walks just as much as bigger breeds, and a healthy adult should be able to walk for miles.

HOW easy to train?

This breed responds surprisingly well to gentle, consistent training, but don't expect too much of them. They are intelligent and quick to learn; but they are also quite stubborn and mischievous, so not the breed for obedience enthusiasts.

WHAT good points?

Extroverted, vivacious, intelligent, active, loving, gregarious, good watchdogs, low maintenance in terms of exercise and food requirements, easily transported.

WHAT to be aware of?

Poms like the sound of their own voices, and need sensible training to prevent them from being noisy. They shed profusely, so you will need a good vacuum cleaner. Watch out for unscrupulous breeders who may produce stock with untypical poor temperaments.

WHAT medical problems?

Like other toy breeds, Pomeranians may suffer dislocation of the kneecaps (patellar luxation). Other disorders occurring in the breed include tracheal (windpipe) collapse, inward-turning eyelids (entropion), cataracts, and skin disease causing loss of hair.

Small dogs

Bichon Frise

Few breeds look as much like a fluffy toy as the Bichon, a cuddly white snowball with jet black eyes and nose. This is one of the liveliest of toy breeds, a playful extrovert with a great enthusiasm for life and affection for people. A delightful companion, he demands attention and is happy to reciprocate. He is tougher than he looks, and with an active owner can enjoy long country walks or agility. He does take a lot of grooming, and is a strong-willed little dog who can be manipulative and stubborn (and, if spoiled, a positive household tyrant), so sensible training in puppyhood is absolutely essential.

The Bichon's history displays his adaptability. He was an aristocratic lapdog in 17th-century France and Spain, later earning his living as the performing dog of street performers and circuses. In the mid-20th century, he emerged from obscurity as a highly popular show dog and companion, a status this happy, affectionate, and intelligent dog well deserves

WHAT colors?

Always white. Puppies under 18 months may show faint cream or apricot markings.

WHAT grooming does the coat need?

A lot — daily brushing and combing, regular baths, and clipping every four to six weeks. The face needs special attention to avoid brown tear stains and stains around the mouth. The natural coat (preferred in Europe) is a mass of soft loose curls, but in the U.K. and U.S. the coat is trimmed to a sculptured shape. Pet owners often find a puppy clip more manageable.

HOW suitable are they as family dogs?

The Bichon's happy, people-loving nature makes him a great family dog in a household where there is plenty of time for him. He is not ideal for families with very young children, as he likes to be the center of attention himself. He is likely to compete for toys and affection and is also vulnerable to toddlers who cannot distinguish between stuffed toys and sensitive living creatures.

WHAT type of home?

Equally suited to city or country living, mansion or apartment, the Bichon can fit into most lifestyles as long as he has exercise and attention. Given the choice, he would prefer to have a yard so he can play outdoors.

WHAT type of owner?

A Bichon needs attention, attention, and attention—he is not a part-time dog. He needs an owner who can be with him most of the time. He is best suited to a lively owner who will enjoy playing with him, who is loving but firm, patient enough not to allow this little charmer to turn into a spoiled brat and who is happy to spend a fair amount of time on grooming.

HOW compatible with other pets?

This good-natured breed generally gets along well with other dogs and with cats in the same household. Puppyhood socialization is importa to ensure that he knows how to behave with larger breeds. He may need supervision with strange cats, and also with other small pets, whic he may see as toys.

HOW much exercise?

Bichons are very adaptable. They don't need a lot of exercise, but w enjoy plenty if it is offered. They have lots of energy, which they can burn off in play and by racing arou the house. A couple of short walks day will keep them fit, or they will enjoy longer walks if on a regular basis—but they may need a bath after a muddy country expedition.

Character Trait	Poor	Average	Good	Excellent
Attitude toward other dogs			●	
Quietness		●		
Not destructive			●	
Protective behavior	●			
Not likely to stray			●	
Good with children			●	
Ease of training		●		

Place of origin: **Mediterranean**

Original purpose: Companion
Male height: 9.5-11.5 in (24-29 cm)
Female height: 9.5-11.5 in (24-29 cm)
Weight: 7-12 lb (3-5.5 kg)
Lifespan: 12-15 years

HOW easy to train?

The Bichon's natural liveliness can be a challenge. Like many toy breeds, they can be strong-willed and stubborn, but will respond to training as long as their interest is caught and maintained. Training needs to be gentle but firm, patient and persistent. This breed can be slow to mature, so don't expect rapid results.

WHAT good points?

Happy, lively, very friendly, affectionate, playful, outgoing, vivacious, intelligent, nonaggressive, companionable.

WHAT to be aware of?

A demanding little dog who may be too exuberant for owners who want a gentle lapdog temperament. Heavy grooming commitment. Can be noisy.

WHAT medical problems?

This is generally a healthy breed, but slipping kneecaps and hip malformation (dysplasia) can occur, as can hemophilia and heart defects. Progressive retinal atrophy (degeneration of the light receptor cells in the eyes) has been recorded in the U.S. and Australia.

● *They look like fluffy toys, and are almost as good-natured.*

Small dogs

Lhasa Apso

His name means "hairy barking dog," and the Lhasa Apso is indeed a keen watchdog covered with flowing hair. Beneath the abundant coat is a hardy little dog full of personality, who loves human company, is very attached to his owner, and will adapt to a range of lifestyles. Despite his glamorous appearance, he is no lapdog but an assertive character with the independence typical of Oriental breeds and a definite mind of his own. He will give you his heart, but don't expect him to obey your every command. As a companion, he is playful, affectionate, and attuned to his owner's mood—and requires a serious commitment to grooming.

Lhasa Apsos were developed in Tibetan monasteries as companions, sentinels, and "good luck dogs." Introduced to England in the late 19th century as "Lhassa terriers," they achieved KC recognition (the Kennel Club in England) in 1902 and subsequently were recognized by the AKC in 1935.

WHAT colors?

Golden, sandy, honey, dark grizzle, slate, smoke, parti-color, black, white, or brown.

WHAT grooming does the coat need?

This is a high-maintenance coat needing thorough daily grooming with a firm brush and combing right down to the skin, paying special attention to the face and underparts. Although the hair is usually allowed to fall over the eyes, it can be tied back for comfort. The coat can be cut down to a puppy clip every four to six weeks, although some daily grooming is still needed. A neglected coat mats and tangles, causing skin problems and real discomfort.

HOW suitable are they as family dogs?

Playful and affectionate, the Lhasa makes a great family dog as long as his needs are understood. He is very good with sensible children, but dislikes rough handling and may snap if teased or accidentally stepped on. Not recommended for households with children too young to be gentle. He does like to be the baby of the household himself, and busy families may find that they do not have enough time for him.

WHAT type of home?

This adaptable little dog can be happy in the city or in the country. He would prefer a yard to play in, but if none is available can make do quite happily with three or four brief but interesting walks every day.

WHAT type of owner?

Lhasa owners should appreciate an independent, manipulative little dog and have plenty of time for grooming, play, and cuddles. He can be equally happy as sole companion to a senior or with a lively family—his main need is to be loved. Owners who don't actively enjoy grooming should probably look elsewhere, as this is a major commitment with the breed.

HOW compatible with other pets?

Early socialization is essential to ensure good relationships with other dogs: Lhasas are naturally suspicious of strangers, and that includes strange canines. Males in particular can be aggressive toward other male dogs. They are usually good with cats and other small pets in their own household, but often consider chasing strange cats as great fun.

HOW much exercise

Lhasas are very adaptable. They don't need a great

Character Trait	Poor	Average	Good	Excellent
Attitude toward other dogs	▓	▓		
Quietness	▓	▓		
Not destructive	▓	▓	▓	
Protective behavior	▓	▓	▓	
Not likely to stray	▓	▓	▓	
Good with children	▓	▓	▓	
Ease of training	▓	▓		

Original purpose: Companion, watchdog
Male height: 10-11 in (25-28 cm)
Female height: 8-10 in (20-25 cm)
Weight: 13-15 lb (6-7 kg)
Lifespan: 12-14 years

Small dogs

● *Very obviously this is a high-maintenance coat.*

deal of exercise and can stay fit with daily short walks; but they can thoroughly enjoy longer walks if that is your lifestyle.

HOW easy to train?
Moderate. Lhasas are smart little dogs who can learn anything they want; the trick is making them want to learn. Formal obedience is not their style, but good behavior needs to be taught. Training should start early and be firm, fair, consistent, and above all fun.
Food rewards appeal to most Lhasas; a forceful approach will get you nowhere.

WHAT good points?
Merry, assertive, alert, steady, hardy, energetic, loyal, affectionate in nature, intelligent.

WHAT to be aware of?
Heavy grooming commitment. Can be difficult to housetrain.

WHAT medical problems?
Generally a healthy and long-lived breed, with some occurrence of progressive retinal atrophy; also rare juvenile kidney disease.

Australian Terrier

Affectionately nicknamed the "Little Terror," the Aussie is a classic short-legged, shaggy terrier born to hunt vermin and to be a lively companion. He is a busy little dog, full of spirit and fun, needing an active family who will enjoy his energy. Highly affectionate, he wants to be involved in family life and is unsuited to being left alone for long periods. For those who appreciate terrier high spirits, he is a wonderful pet, sometimes mischievous but also very responsive to his owner's moods. The breed is generally healthy and long-lived, with an easy-care coat and happy temperament. Although not a yappy dog, he is a keen watchdog who will announce visitors.

Developed in the Australian outback from ancestral British terrier breeds, the Aussie was imported to the U.K. in 1906 and recognized in the U.S. in 1960. Slow to achieve popularity, his virtues have now won wider recognition, both as a lively and affectionate family pet and as a show dog.

WHAT colors?

Blue and tan (blue, steel blue, or dark gray blue with rich tan on face, ears, underbody, lower legs, feet, and around the vent), solid sandy, solid red.

WHAT grooming does the coat need?

This is an easy-care coat. Unlike many terriers, the pet Aussie does not require stripping, although show dogs are tidied up with a stripping knife. A weekly brushing with a bristle brush to remove dead hairs will suffice, plus trimming the hair between the eyes for comfort. Particular attention needs to be paid to flea control, as allergies are common in this breed.

HOW suitable are they as family dogs?

The Aussie makes an excellent family pet. He is generally very good with children, although (as with any small dog) supervision with toddlers is essential. For sensible children he is the ideal fun-loving and tireless companion, as well as a protective guard.

WHAT type of home?

Equally suited to city or country living, as long as they have plenty to do these little terriers can fit into most lifestyles. They are not meant for kennel life, for they need involvement with their human family and plenty to do—otherwise they might engage in destructive behavior. They will appreciate a yard, but secure fencing is a must to prevent unwanted solo hunting excursions.

WHAT type of owner?

If you like the spunky terrier temperament, you'll love the Aussie. If you prefer a more placid pet, look elsewhere. Like all terriers, he needs an owner with a firm, consistent approach to training, plenty of time for him, and a reasonably active lifestyle.

HOW compatible with other pets?

Terriers are naturally bossy little dogs and can be aggressive toward strange dogs—particularly big ones. They will accept dogs (and cats) that are members of the same household, although rivalry between adult males may be a problem. Small pets like rabbits and hamsters are best kept well out of the way of these enthusiastic hunters.

HOW much exercise?

This little terrier needs a great deal of exercise to keep him fit and to ward off boredom. Despite his

Character Trait	Poor	Average	Good	Excellent
Attitude toward other dogs				
Quietness				
Not destructive				
Protective behavior				
Not likely to stray				
Good with children				
Ease of training				

Original purpose: Vermin control
Male height: 10-11 in (25-28 cm)
Female height: 10-11 in (25-28 cm)
Weight: 12-14 lb (5.4-6.5 kg)
Lifespan: 12-14 years

short legs, he can run for miles. Particular attention needs to be paid to teaching him the recall, as his hunting instincts remain keen and he is not easily deflected from chasing anything that moves.

HOW easy to train?
Like most terriers, the Aussie can be willful and has a low boredom threshold, so training needs to be firm, consistent, and fun. Keep training sessions short, with plenty of rewards (treats, toys, or verbal praise) to maintain his interest, and he is a quick learner. This breed has been trained to high levels of competitive obedience.

WHAT good points?
Friendly, extroverted, high-spirited, alert, adaptable, fun-loving, affectionate, loyal, full of character, hardy, good watchdog.

WHAT to be aware of?
Males can be aggressive toward other dogs and have the terrier tendency to take on much larger opponents. If left alone for long periods, they may become destructive or noisy. They are born diggers—not an ideal choice for dedicated gardeners.

WHAT medical problems?
The Aussie is generally a healthy breed. Disorders that have been noted include diabetes and thyroid disorder, some predisposition to skin allergies, dislocation of the kneecap (patellar luxation), Legg-Perthes disease (a degenerative hip condition).

Small dogs

● *Although shaggy, the "Little Terror's" coat does not require great attention. Weekly grooming should suffice.*

Border Terrier

One of the most sensible and good-natured of the terriers, the Border is a smart, functional little dog. He was bred to keep up with hounds and horses over a long day's hunting, and he retains all the stamina, speed, and agility this required. However, nowadays it is his friendly nature that is most valued, and he has come into his own as a companion and family pet.

This is a dog with all the terrier virtues, games, and love of family and fun, but without the aggressive edge of some terriers. He does need time, attention, and exercise for both mind and body to keep him out of mischief.

Borders love a close involvement with family life and hate being left alone all day—and a lonely, bored Border is likely to be noisy and destructive. In a loving home, however, this breed can be one of the best family dogs available, since he has the reputation of being very good with children.

WHAT colors?

There are four approved colors: red, wheaten, grizzle and tan (the grizzle hairs being of agouti coloring with each hair banded in three colors), and blue and tan. White markings on the chest are acceptable.

WHAT grooming does the coat need?

The harsh, weatherproof coat is relatively low maintenance, needing a good brush through, say, twice a week. To keep the coat looking good, it needs to be hand stripped two or three times a year, plucking dead hairs from the coat with finger and thumb—your pup's breeder can teach you the technique.

HOW suitable are they as family dogs?

The Border is an ideal family pet. He is generally very good with children, although (as with any small dog) supervision with youngsters is essential. He won't tolerate being

● Smart and alert, the Border is gentler than most terriers.

teased or ill treated, but he is the ideal fun-loving and tireless companion for sensible children.

WHAT type of home?

As long as a Border has reasonable exercise and plenty to interest him, he will be just as happy in the city as in the country. He will appreciate a yard, which needs to be securely fenced—most of this breed are champion escapologists who won't hesitate to scramble over or under obstacles in quest of adventure.

WHAT type of owner?

This is a great dog for active owners and families who want a lively, good natured dog and have time for play and exercise—and who have no small pets that might be risk. If you enjoy a busy, stimulating pet who wants to participate fully in family life, and are prepared to put time into puppy socialization and training, the Border could well be the dog for you.

HOW compatible with other pets?

Borders are sociable creatures that usually get along well with other dogs and with cats within their own household—but probably not with other people's cats. They have strong hunting instincts, and should not be trusted with smaller animals such as hamsters or guinea pigs.

HOW much exercise?

This active breed will take all the exercise you can offer. A daily stroll once around the block is not enough to keep a Border fit and happy—a fit adult can run for miles. He needs regular, brisk walks,

Character Trait	Poor	Average	Good	Excellent
Attitude toward other dogs				
Quietness				
Not destructive				
Protective behavior				
Not likely to stray				
Good with children				
Ease of training				

Original purpose: Vermin control
Male height: 10-11 in (25-28 cm)
Female height: 10-11 in (25-28 cm)
Weight: 11.5-15.5 lb (5-7 kg)
Lifespan: 12-15 years

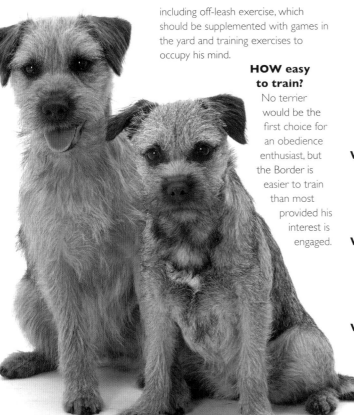

including off-leash exercise, which should be supplemented with games in the yard and training exercises to occupy his mind.

HOW easy to train?

No terrier would be the first choice for an obedience enthusiast, but the Border is easier to train than most provided his interest is engaged.

However, his strong streak of independence means that he is likely to obey in his own time rather than instantly. Keep training sessions short, challenging, reward-based, and fun for best results.

Small dogs

WHAT good points?

Sensible, affectionate, active, devoted to owner, sweet-natured, alert, playful, good-natured with strangers, gentle for a terrier.

WHAT to be aware of?

Like most terriers, has a tendency to bark excessively and, if left to his own devices, will dig up the yard. Strong instinct to chase anything that moves.

WHAT medical problems?

Generally a healthy breed without significant health problems. Occasionally reported are dislocation of the kneecap (patellar luxation), eye problems including glaucoma and cataracts, and skin problems.

Miniature Pinscher

The "King of the Toys" is a smart, elegant little dog with clean lines, a classy high-stepping gait, and dainty, even fragile appearance. In temperament, however, he is far from fragile. More terrier than lapdog in character, this is an alert, bossy, and dynamic character. He is highly active, energetic, fearless and inquisitive, an enthusiastic watchdog, and a loving companion. This busy little dog is perhaps not suitable for the novice, as he is strong-willed and, given the chance, can become a household tyrant. He needs socialization to prevent his innate suspicion of strangers from escalating into overt aggression, exercise and mental stimulation to keep him happy, and constant supervision to keep him out of mischief.

The Min Pin dates back to at least the 16th century. Despite the name, he has no connection with the Dobermann Pinscher, although they share the same stylish build—on a different scale.

WHAT colors?

Black and tan, chocolate and tan, blue and tan, or solid red. Slight white marking on chest permissible but not desirable.

WHAT grooming does the coat need?

The easy-care coat needs only weekly brushing to remove dead hairs and the occasional polish with a soft cloth.

HOW suitable are they as family dogs?

The Min Pin makes a great addition to a family who want a little dog with a big character. He is very loving, good with sensible children who treat him with respect, and enjoys participating in family activities. He is not recommended for households with young children, as he is too fragile to withstand rough handling and may nip if teased.

WHAT type of home?

This compact little dog makes an ideal apartment pet, but he can be just as happy burning off energy in the country. Min Pins are great escapologists who need secure fencing and screens on windows and doors: They will take advantage of any opportunity to run out and investigate the world outside. With their fine coats, they feel the cold and need a warm home.

● "Let's play," suggests an energetic Miniature Pinscher.

WHAT type of owner?

Min Pins do best with experienced, confident owners who appreciate a high-energy breed and can cope with a dog with the attitude of an adventurous toddler who is into everything. They need firm but gentle handling by owners who are neither harsh nor overindulgent, and they should not be left alone for long periods, as they need company and supervision.

HOW compatible with other pets?

Like terriers, Min Pins are bossy little dogs descended from

Character Trait	Poor	Average	Good	Excellent
Attitude toward other dogs			●	
Quietness	●			
Not destructive		●		
Protective behavior				●
Not likely to stray		●		
Good with children		●		
Ease of training		●		

Original purpose: Small vermin hunting
Male height: 10-12 in (25-30 cm)
Female height: 10-12 in (25-30 cm)
Weight: 8-10 lb (3.5-4.5 kg)
Lifespan: 12-14 years

generations of ratters. They are usually fine with cats and dogs within their own household, but can be dominant and aggressive with strange dogs and will chase strange cats. They are unlikely to be safe with small pets like rabbits, guinea pigs, and hamsters.

HOW much exercise?

Min Pins are adaptable. They don't need a lot of exercise, but will enjoy as much as is offered. Ideally they should have a good walk every day and burn off the rest of their energy in play. This breed really feels the cold and will need a warm coat for winter walks.

HOW easy to train?

Training the Min Pin is not easy, but can be achieved with time, patience, and persistence. He has a short attention span and a low boredom threshold, so training needs to be firm, consistent, and fun. Keep training sessions short, with plenty of rewards to maintain his interest. A sense of humor is vital, as this breed loves to play the clown.

WHAT good points?

Loyal, loving, alert, excellent watchdog, fearless, animated, curious, active, entertaining, sound, intelligent, convenient size.

WHAT to be aware of?

Can be difficult to housetrain and likes the sound of his own voice. His curiosity can lead him into trouble, so care needs to be taken to pinscher-proof the home—he can jump onto furniture and steal hazardous items such as medication, as well as being able to run through the smallest of gaps. The yard, too, should be secure.

WHAT medical problems?

This is generally a healthy breed, with occasional kneecap dislocation (patellar luxation) the only real concern.

Small dogs

Pug

Supremely dignified on the outside and a natural clown on the inside, the Pug is a custom-built companion for less active owners. He is far from sedentary himself, but a busy, curious little dog full of personality who loves to play and requires plenty of interaction with his owner. However, he is a low-maintenance dog needing relatively little exercise or grooming. Sociable, equable, and affectionate, he will adapt to most lifestyles as long as he has his owner's company. The breed does have quite a few health and breathing problems, and needs special consideration in hot weather.

Pugs originated in China in ancient times and reached the West by trade in the 16th or 17th century to become great favorites in Holland and later England, reaching the height of their popularity in the 18th century. Although Pugs have been out of fashion for some time, they are now enjoying a well deserved comeback.

WHAT colors?

Silver, apricot, fawn, or black. The lighter colors have a dark mask, ears, thumb mark or diamond on forehead, and trace (a line down the back from head to tail).

WHAT grooming does the coat need?

The short, smooth coat requires regular brushing to remove dead hairs —Pugs shed a surprising amount. In addition, the facial wrinkles need checking and cleaning daily; if this task is neglected, they may become damp, smelly, and even infected.

HOW suitable are they as family dogs?

The Pug is an ideal dog for a family whose lifestyle does not revolve around long walks. He tends to regard himself as one of the children, and his even temperament and playful nature make him a wonderful choice for children old enough to understand how to handle a living creature. However, preschool children are likely to be too rough for a small dog.

WHAT type of home?

Any home that has a Pug-lover will suit a Pug. He is compact enough for a small apartment and sturdy enough to prosper in the country. He would not be happy kenneled often, however, as he needs to be with people.

WHAT type of owner?

This is a wonderful breed for anyone who wants a close, affectionate relationship with a dog and will appreciate a lively, demanding little character. Pugs won't suit owners who want a dog to go for long, energetic walks or to work at competitive obedience, but they are adaptable and can adopt a wide variety of lifestyles.

HOW compatible with other pets?

Pugs will happily extend their friendship to other animals of all kinds—but be careful with kittens or aggressive cats, as the Pug's bulging eyes are vulnerable to scratches.

HOW much exercise?

Pugs have boundless energy, but will use most of it up in play and don't need a great deal of exercise. However, two brisk walks a day are recommended to keep them fit— and if your lifestyle includes regular exercise, a fit adult Pug will enjoy accompanying you for several miles.

*Place of origin: **China***

Character Trait	Poor	Average	Good	Excellent
Attitude toward other dogs				
Quietness				
Not destructive				
Protective behavior				
Not likely to stray				
Good with children				
Ease of training				

Original purpose: Lapdog
Male height: 10-11 in (25-28 cm)
Female height: 10-11 in (25-28 cm)
Weight: 14-18 lb (6.5-8 kg)
Lifespan: 12-15 years

This breed should never be walked in hot weather, as they overheat easily.

HOW easy to train?

If you want an obedience champion, look elsewhere. Pugs are strong-minded little dogs who can be taught good behavior reasonably easily but have little interest in responding quickly to commands. However, they are intelligent and can learn if they wish—individuals have performed well at obedience, flyball, agility, and even as support dogs for disabled owners, carrying out tasks like fetching the telephone and unloading the washing machine.

WHAT good points?

Friendly, affectionate, tolerant, good-tempered, lively, playful, entertaining, sociable, intelligent, loads of personality, adaptable.

WHAT to be aware of?

Snorting, snuffling, wheezing, snoring, and flatulence. Susceptibility to overheating.

Constant heavy shedding. May be hard to housetrain.

WHAT medical problems?

Breathing problems associated with the short face, including elongated soft palate; hip malformation (dysplasia); kneecap dislocation (patellar luxation); Legg-Perthes disease (lack of blood supply to the top of the femur resulting in bone death); hemivertebrae (congenital spinal deformity); eye problems (cataracts,

● *His flat face and bulgy eyes have great charm.*

ulcers, vulnerability to injury) and inward-turning eyelids (entropion); tendency to aquire mast-cell skin tumors.

Small dogs

● *The Pug's facial wrinkles should be checked every day.*

Shih Tzu

China's "Chrysanthemum Dog," with his flowerlike face and cascade of fur, looks like a glamorous toy, but he is a sturdy little dog bursting with personality. The Shih Tzu is a merry extrovert, playful, highly sociable, and affectionate without being clingy. The independent character typical of Oriental breeds makes him a great companion but a poor choice for obedience fanatics. He is highly adaptable, happy to rest on a pillow or enjoy country walks. His only real disadvantage is his flowing coat, which requires a lot of time and an owner who sincerely enjoys grooming.

One of the Oriental "lion dogs" representing the lion of Buddha in canine form, the Shih Tzu developed in China from Tibetan lion dogs presented to the Emperor. Reaching the West in the early 20th century, he was initially identified with Tibet's Lhasa Apso; recognized as a distinct breed in the 1930s, he rapidly achieved popularity.

WHAT colors?

All colors are allowed, including gold, black, gray, silver, brindle, and parti-color.

WHAT grooming does the coat need?

A major commitment, half an hour every day brushing down to the skin, combing face furnishings, and tying up the topknot to keep hair out of the eyes. Regular baths are also needed, monthly or even every two weeks depending on the environment. The coat can be cut down to a puppy clip every four to six weeks, although some regular daily grooming is still needed. A neglected coat inevitably tangles and mats causing skin problems and real discomfort.

HOW suitable are they as family dogs?

Sturdy, good-tempered, and playful, the Shih Tzu is an ideal choice for a family who appreciate his willful charm, are prepared to involve him in all family activities, don't expect obedience, and enjoy grooming. He is good with children, and a fun playmate, as long as they are good with dogs. Not recommended for households with children too young to be gentle; parents of little ones may not have enough time for grooming and attention.

WHAT type of home?

This adaptable little dog is ideal for city life but can live anywhere. He would prefer a yard for outdoor games, but if none is available can make do quite happily with three or four daily walks around the block.

WHAT type of owner?

The Shih Tzu is an ideal breed for anyone who wants a playful, entertaining companion, and who enjoys grooming. He needs an affectionate but sensible owner, strong-minded enough not to allow a small dog to become a household tyrant, and with time for socialization and play.

HOW compatible with other pets?

If well socialized in puppyhood, the Shih Tzu is normally friendly with other animals of all species.

HOW much exercise?

This very adaptable breed will fit in with his owner's requirements. He can enjoy lengthy hikes, but is equally happy with short outings and plenty of time for active play in the yard. If confined to an apartment, think in terms of four walks a day to keep him healthy.

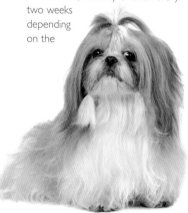

● *Delightful to look at and an ideal companion dog in town or country.*

Character Trait	Poor	Average	Good	Excellent
Attitude toward other dogs				
Quietness				
Not destructive				
Protective behavior				
Not likely to stray				
Good with children				
Ease of training				

Original purpose: Lapdog
Male height: 8-11 in (25-28 cm)
Female height: 8-11 in (25-28 cm)
Weight: 9-16 lb (4.1-7.3 kg)
Lifespan: 11-14 years

HOW easy to train?

Moderate. With a firm, kind, consistent approach, the Shih Tzu is perfectly ready to cooperate and learn good behavior. However, he is a strong-minded, wilful little dog, and formal obedience is not his natural style. Training for fun rather than for competition is well worthwhile to keep him entertained, otherwise he may find less acceptable ways of amusing himself.

• These lovely locks require a lot of maintenance, thirty minutes of grooming each day plus regular baths.

WHAT good points?

Playful, happy, friendly, loving, loyal, attentive, active, full of character, small but not fragile, adaptable, good with children.

Small dogs

WHAT to be aware of?

Heavy grooming commitment. Can be difficult to housetrain. Prone to eye injuries.

WHAT medical problems?

Generally a healthy, long-lived breed, the Shih Tzu may suffer from heart conditions, kidney problems, inter-vertebral disc disease, certain blood disorders, and a number of eye problems including ulcers and conjunctivitis.

Pembroke Welsh Corgi

Among the smallest working breeds, the Pembroke originated as a cattle dog, driving livestock by "heeling" (nipping cows' heels to keep them moving)—a task that required an active, strong-minded dog. Although a convenient size for modern homes, he is a "big dog in a small body," a cheerful companion, and an enthusiastic watchdog who likes to keep busy. Bossy, and often excitable, he needs sensible handling and an outlet for his intelligence and energy. Corgis often perform well at obedience, agility, and herding trials, but above all they need an active sense of involvement in family life.

The Corgi's origins are obscure, possibly dating back to the Dark Ages. In 1934, the different types from north and south Wales were separated into two breeds, Pembroke and Cardigan. The Pembroke, the smaller and more extroverted, is the more popular, probably because of its adoption by the British Royal Family.

WHAT colors?

Red, sable (red with black-tipped hairs) or fawn, with or without white markings on legs, brisket, neck, head or foreface, or tri-color (mostly black, with tan and white markings).

WHAT grooming does the coat need?

This is an easy-care coat, needing only weekly brushing (daily during the twice-yearly molt) to remove dead hairs.

HOW suitable are they as family dogs?

Pembrokes enjoy family life and are fun companions for older, sensible youngsters, though often too excitable to be recommended for young or very boisterous children. Nipping the heels of livestock was once their profession, and as youngsters they often need to be taught not to nip ankles or this can become a habit.

● *An appealing trio of Cardigans.*

WHAT type of home?

A country home is ideal, but the Pembroke will adapt to city life provided he has enough activity. He should have access to a yard where he can burn off some energy, and preferably a park.

WHAT type of owner?

The Pembroke is a good choice for anyone who likes big dogs but doesn't have room for one. He needs a fairly strong-minded owner, or he can take over the household. Corgis fare best with active owners who enjoy walking, training, and play and can keep them busy—it is a shame to let their intelligence go to waste.

HOW compatible with other pets?

Pembrokes generally get along well with other dogs, and with cats in their own household, subject of course to early socialization. Males from some bloodlines can be aggressive toward dogs of the same sex. Take care with small pets such as rabbits and hamsters: Corgis were originally farm dogs and natural ratters, and have not lost their innate prey drive.

HOW much exercise?

Moderate. These short-legged dogs do not need as much exercise as most working breeds and can keep fit with a daily walk in the park, but they have plenty of stamina and will enjoy long walks, free running, and active play.

HOW easy to train?

Given an owner who can establish

Character Trait	Poor	Average	Good	Excellent
Attitude toward other dogs		■		
Quietness	■			
Not destructive		■		
Protective behavior		■		
Not likely to stray		■		
Good with children			■	
Ease of training			■	

Original purpose: Herding
Male height: 10-12 in (25-30 cm)
Female height: 10-12 in (25-30 cm)
Weight: 20-26 lb (9-12 kg)
Lifespan: 11-13 years

Small dogs

kind but firm leadership, this intelligent dog is easily trained—but also easily bored. As a working dog, he was expected to use his initiative rather than follow commands blindly, and he sees little point in repetitive exercises. Reward-based training techniques work best to motivate him. Get him interested, and his desire to show how clever he is will take him the rest of the way.

WHAT good points?

Outgoing, alert, friendly, active, people oriented, playful, energetic, long-lived, hardy, good watchdog.

WHAT to be aware of?

Can be noisy. Tendency to nip ankles if not discouraged from this bad habit in puppyhood. Watch out for a tendency to put on weight, which can put too much strain on his long back.

WHAT medical problems?

Corgis are generally a healthy and long-lived breed. Short legs and a long back make them vulnerable to back problems, and occasional inherited defects include hip malformation (dysplasia), von Willebrand's disease (a bleeding disorder), and progressive retinal atrophy (degeneration of the light receptor cells in the eyes).

In the U.S., Welsh Corgis almost always have cropped tails.

West Highland White Terrier

One of the most popular breeds, the Westie has taken his transformation from working terrier to household pet in stride. This is a busy, merry little dog and probably the only breed whose standard calls for him to be "possessed of no small amount of self-esteem." Less fiery and hyperactive than some terrier breeds, he makes a great companion who is prepared to enjoy almost any lifestyle, equally successful as a city dog or country companion. He has a great sense of fun and, like all terriers, likes to keep busy. This is an affectionate and adaptable breed, friendly and extroverted. He is hardy and relatively easy to care for, although his trademark white coat requires attention to keep it neat.

The Westie originated from the same stock as the Cairn and other Highland terriers. He was recognized as a distinct breed in 1907, and he has never looked back.

WHAT colors?
White only.

WHAT grooming does the coat need?
Brush with stiff bristle brush at least twice a week to prevent tangles from forming. The coat needs stripping about every four months, a task probably best left to a professional. Show dogs have the coat sculpted into a stylized shape with a stripping knife; pets can be left shaggy, but may need the hair around eyes and ears trimmed for health and comfort.

HOW suitable are they as family dogs?
These fun-loving little dogs enjoy family life and want to be involved in family activities. They are generally great companions for sensible children who treat them with respect, although they won't tolerate being teased or otherwise mistreated.

WHAT type of home?
The Westie is highly adaptable. He is perfectly happy as a city dog,

● *The Westie: A truly fun dog.*

provided that he has regular walks (not just quickly around the block). He will also thoroughly appreciate country life, where his sporting instincts and love of exploration will thrive.

WHAT type of owner?
A fun dog for a lively family, the Westie can also be an ideal companion for an active, older owner, providing encouragement to remain fit and active. Best for those who appreciate the busy, enthusiastic, loving, and sometimes maddening terrier character, he needs an owner who can apply a firm, consistent approach to training and has time for play, exercise, and cuddles.

HOW compatible with other pets?
Generally good with other animals, the Westie is nonetheless a terrier, with strong hunting and chasing instinct and a tendency to be bossy with other dogs. Sensible early socialization is important, and other pets should be introduced with care and plenty of supervision.

HOW much exercise?
These active little dogs love exercise and long country walks, but they are quite adaptable and can burn off a lot of energy playing in the yard. City dwellers should think in terms of two or three good walks a day, preferably including time off-leash in the park

Character Trait	Poor	Average	Good	Excellent
Attitude toward other dogs				
Quietness				
Not destructive				
Protective behavior				
Not likely to stray				
Good with children				
Ease of training				

Original purpose: Vermin control
Male height: 10-11 in (25-30 cm)
Female height: 9-10 in (23-28 cm)
Weight: 15-21 lb (6.8-9.5 kg)
Lifespan: 12-14 years

Work on the recall is important: This is a dog who will disappear over the horizon in pursuit of an interesting scent once his hunting instincts are aroused.

HOW easy to train?

No terrier would be the first choice for an obedience enthusiast, and Westies are as obstinate and willful as any. With firm, consistent, reward-based training he will become a well-behaved household pet, but training needs to start early to establish who is in charge. Keep training sessions short, challenging, and fun to retain his interest.

WHAT good points?

Affectionate, loyal, active, hardy, versatile, fun-loving, curious, friendly, plenty of personality, convenient size.

Small dogs

WHAT to be aware of?

Overpopularity has made this breed a target for puppy mills: buy from reputable breeders or risk health and temperament problems. Regular coat care is an ongoing commitment.

WHAT medical problems?

Most Westies are healthy, but (as with other white breeds) chronic skin problems are not infrequent. Other disorders include Legg-Perthes disease (hip problems), hernias, liver disease, and craniomandibular osteopathy ("Westie jaw"), a painful bone deformity in puppies.

● *Early socialization will be important when training these young Westie puppies.*

Cavalier King Charles Spaniel

An absolute winner in the toy dog category, the Cavalier has a gentle and courteous nature that seems utterly appropriate to its history as the favorite dog of King Charles II of England. His ancestors may have originated in the East, making their way by the Middle Ages to Europe, where they were crossed with spaniels. In the 16th century they reached England, to develop there into today's toy breed.

Part of the secret of this breed's success underlies the reason why it was so popular as a ladies' lap dog. He dotes on his owner and will repay the care you lavish on him with absolute devotion. But this is no living room wimp—the sporting ancestry and typical spaniel energy ensure that Cavaliers are also lively and playful companions who are just as much fun to be with outdoors. Graceful and balanced in movement and possessing a charming docile expression, this is an ideal family dog—good-spirited, polite and friendly, and full of enthusiasm!

WHAT colors?

Black and tan, ruby, Blenheim (rich chestnut markings, well broken up, on pearly white ground), tri-color.

WHAT grooming does the coat need?

The coat is long, silky, and free from curl. A slight wave is permitted by the breed standard, and there is plenty of feathering. This breed is a delight to groom and does not require a lot of attention. Ten minutes or so a day working with a slicker brush and comb, paying particular attention to the areas that are heavily coated, should be quite sufficient.

HOW suitable are they as family dogs?

A great choice as a family pet, Cavaliers are some of the nicest and best-mannered toy dogs available. They get along well with children, are easy to handle, and make loving companions for the elderly, being good-natured and affectionate.

WHAT type of home?

These sturdy and appealing little dogs are very adaptable and suit a variety of lifestyles. While their size and nature mean that they can be treated as lapdogs by people who lead their lives predominantly indoors, they are also happy running vigorously after scents in the wide open and so are well adapted to country dwellers.

WHAT type of owner?

This breed in many ways offers the best of both worlds—it is a toy-sized dog that enjoys the social life of a family but also embodies the virtues of a sporting breed with a good nose and hunting instinct. So the Cavalier King Charles can be equally at home with a large, energetic family as with a single owner, whatever his/her age. Sometimes called a "people's dog," Cavaliers enjoy human company of all kinds. The owner must be prepared to let the dog participate in family life and enjoy the companionship of people—it would be cruel to own a Cavalier King Charles and leave him locked up on his own for long periods.

HOW compatible with other pets?

Cavaliers generally mix well with other pets, rarely showing signs of possessiveness or jealousy. But take care when introducing them to large dogs as their tolerant, gentle nature means they can be overwhelmed by the rough and tumble of bigger breeds. Two or more Cavaliers will usually live happily together.

HOW much exercise?

While a Cavalier loves snoozing in comfort at home, his sporting

Character Trait	Poor	Average	Good	Excellent
Attitude toward other dogs				
Quietness				
Not destructive				
Protective behavior				
Not likely to stray				
Good with children				
Ease of training				

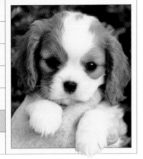

Original purpose: Lapdog
Male height: 10-12.5 in (25-32 cm)
Female height: 9-12 in (24-30 cm)
Weight: 12-18 lb (5.5-8 kg)
Lifespan: 9-14 years

ancestry means that he does need to get outside and run off excess energy at least once day. A regular walk around the park or a play session in the yard will be enough to keep a Cavalier in good condition. If you have a chance to enjoy a longer walk in the country, the dog will remain eager to keep you company.

HOW easy to train?

This breed ranks somewhere around the middle of the rankings for trainability and working intelligence, so you will not find him the fastest to learn and respond. But he is at his best as a family companion, so owners do not generally look to the breed to star in high-level agility and obedience tests.

WHAT good points?

Friendly, nonaggressive, fun-loving, sporting, active, fearless, charming, and gentle expression.

WHAT to be aware of?

Has a tendency to become distracted by scents when out on a walk, so you need to keep an eye on a dog that may wander off; little road sense so keep on a leash in public places; while not "yappy," will tend to bark at strangers. However, his friendly nature means that he is not a good watchdog.

WHAT medical problems?

While generally vigorous and fit dogs that can

sometimes to live to 14 years of age, Cavaliers can be susceptible to a hereditary heart condition—mitral valve disease. Other typical health problems include malformation of the hip (dysplasia). and eye problems like cataracts and retinal atrophy.

Small dogs

Cairn Terrier

The Cairn takes his name from the rocky outcrops (cairns) of the Scottish Highlands where his ancestors dug out foxes, badgers, and other predators. Although today his primary role is as a companion, this is one terrier breed that has not been prettied up for the show ring and retains the appealingly scruffy, workmanlike appearance of his forebears. As a companion, he is ideal for those who want a small, active dog who will walk for miles. A true terrier, bossy, busy, and happy, he will never be content to be a mere couch potato and needs exercise for both mind and body. Provided he is kept occupied, he makes a great household pet who is devoted to his family.

While retaining all the terrier courage and assertiveness, the Cairn is less dog aggressive and more amenable to training than many terrier breeds and can perform well in obedience events.

WHAT colors?

Cairns come in a variety of colors including cream, wheaten, light or dark red, gray, and nearly black. Brindling (black hairs mixed with the base color) is acceptable in any of these colors.

WHAT grooming does the coat need?

The harsh, weatherproof coat is relatively low maintenance, needing perhaps ten minutes a day with brush and comb or a more thorough session once a week. Cairns should never be clipped but hand stripped, plucking dead hairs from the coat with finger and thumb—your pup's breeder will be happy to teach you the technique.

HOW suitable are they as family dogs?

The Cairn makes an excellent family pet. He is generally very good with children, although (as with any small dog) supervision with toddlers is essential. He won't tolerate being teased or ill-treated, but for sensible children he is the ideal fun-loving and tireless companion, as well as a protective watchdog.

WHAT type of home?

The Cairn will adapt to most lifestyles. He is in his element in the country, with hedges and ditches to explore, but will be just as happy bustling about the city. He will appreciate a yard, which needs to be securely fenced—a bored terrier won't hesitate to scramble over or under obstacles in search of adventure.

WHAT type of owner?

This is a great dog for an active owner who enjoys country walks and who is prepared to maintain a firm, consistent approach to training. If you enjoy a busy, stimulating pet who wants to participate fully in family life, and are prepared to be "pack leader," the Cairn is a great choice—but if you prefer a more placid companion, look outside the terrier group.

HOW compatible with other pets?

Cairns will get along with other pets in the household better than some terrier breeds, but need careful introduction. They have strong chasing instincts, and should not be trusted with smaller animals such as hamsters or rabbits.

HOW much exercise?

This active breed needs a fair amount of exercise for its size. A daily stroll once around the block is not enough to keep a Cairn fit and happy—a fit adult can run

Character Trait	Poor	Average	Good	Excellent
Attitude toward other dogs		■		
Quietness	■			
Not destructive		■		
Protective behavior			■	
Not likely to stray			■	
Good with children			■	
Ease of training		■		

Original purpose: Vermin control
Male height: 11-12 in (28-30.5 cm)
Female height: 11-12 in (28-30.5 cm)
Weight: 14-16 lb (6.5-7.25 kg)
Lifespan: 13-14 years

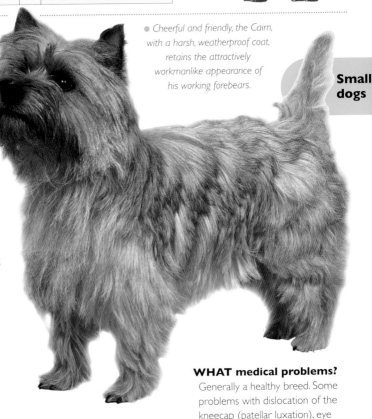

● *Cheerful and friendly, the Cairn, with a harsh, weatherproof coat, retains the attractively workmanlike appearance of his working forebears.*

Small dogs

for miles. He needs regular brisk walks, including off-leash exercise, which should be supplemented with games in the yard and training exercises to occupy his mind.

HOW easy to train?

No terrier would be the first choice for an obedience enthusiast, but Cairns respond better than most to firm, sensible, reward-based training to become well-behaved household pets. Training sessions should be short, challenging, and fun to retain his interest. It is vital to start training at an early age to ensure that your Cairn knows who is in charge.

WHAT good points?

Cheerful, friendly, intelligent, lively, resourceful, confident, small yet tough, a keen watchdog, not a heavy shedder.

WHAT to be aware of?

Like most terriers, has a tendency to bark excessively and, if left to his own devices, will dig up the yard. Can be possessive of food and toys.

WHAT medical problems?

Generally a healthy breed. Some problems with dislocation of the kneecap (patellar luxation), eye problems including glaucoma and cataracts, and skin problems.

Chinese Crested

The Chinese Crested is a hairless dog with decorative trim—flowing crest, "socks," and plumed tail setting off a bare body. Although some find the idea of a bald dog offputting initially, he is an attractive little dog, elegant, graceful, and reminiscent of a miniature pony with flowing mane and tail. His skin is soft and warm to the touch, lacking any "doggy" odor and ideal for many allergy sufferers. Gentle, playful, and absolutely devoted to his owner, this breed was designed to be a lapdog. He also comes in a "powder puff" variety that is very hairy, veiled in a long, silky coat. Both types can appear in the same litter.

The breed was common in China in the 1880s, when it came to the attention of the Western world. Its origins are obscure, although it may be connected with the hairless dogs of Africa and Central America.

WHAT colors?

Any color or combination of colors. The skin of hairless dogs may be lilac, blue, gold or pink, often spotted or dappled, and tends to darken in summer and lighten again in winter. Spotted specimens are usually born plain pink, developing the spots after the first week.

WHAT grooming does the coat need?

Hairless dogs need the same skin care as a child, cleansing and moisturizing, and the protection of sunblock in summer. Like teenagers, they can suffer from acne and blackheads if the skin is neglected. Powderpuffs need daily grooming of the soft coat to prevent tangles, and often have the face clipped to show the sweet expression.

HOW suitable are they as family dogs?

Ideally suited for life with a considerate family, this breed actively enjoys the company of children. He loves play and cuddles, and is devoted to family members. However, he is physically dainty and not suited to rough games and temperamentally too gentle to be happy in a rowdy family.

WHAT type of home?

Home is where the heart is for this loving little dog, and he will adapt to any environment as long as he has his owner's company. His compact size makes him suitable for apartment life. He does need protection from extremes of temperature—a warm coat in winter and sunblock in summer are essential.

WHAT type of owner?

The Chinese Crested can be a wonderful companion for a single person, or happy in the heart of the family. He needs a sociable, affectionate owner who is willing to provide plenty of companionship and to receive devotion in return. Owners of this vivacious breed should make time for play and affection, as well as for the important daily skin care.

HOW compatible with other pets?

This breed is generally very good with other pets, although, like other breeds, he needs to be properly socialized with them while young.

HOW much exercise?

Like most toy breeds, the Crested can thrive on minimal exercise but will relish a surprising amount of activity. Short, frequent walks will keep him happy and interested, but he will enjoy walking for a good few miles if that is his owner's preferred lifestyle.

Character Trait	Poor	Average	Good	Excellent
Attitude toward other dogs			▓	
Quietness	▓			
Not destructive		▓		
Protective behavior		▓		
Not likely to stray	▓			
Good with children			▓	
Ease of training		▓		

Original purpose: Lapdog
Male height: 11-13 in (28-33 cm)
Female height: 9-12 in (23-30 cm)
Weight: Under 12 lb (2.3-5.5 kg)
Lifespan: 13-15 years

● A contrast: hairless and "powder puff."

HOW easy to train?

Intelligent but not always easy to train—aim for cooperation rather than strict obedience. He has a mind of his own and tends to be stubborn. However, he does need directing toward good behavior from an early age to prevent him from becoming a household tyrant.

WHAT good points?

Affectionate, intelligent, loyal, happy, playful, gentle, entertaining, friendly, alert, good watchdog, no "doggy" odor.

WHAT to be aware of?

Regular skin care is a must, and protection from chills and sunburn is important. Can be yappy, and has a tendency to high-pitched "singing" that some find endearing, others off-putting.

Small dogs

WHAT medical problems?

As a breed extremely healthy and hardier than they look. Recorded problems include dislocating kneecaps, Legg-Perthes disease (crippling hip disorder), and skin allergies.

French Bulldog *Other names: Bouledogue Francais*

This bat-eared, frog-faced charmer is about as far removed from his big, fierce, bull-baiting ancestors as a Bulldog can be. A sweet-natured clown, he was made for the role of companion and entertainer. He fits well into modern lifestyles, being compact in size, lively without being boisterous, naturally quiet, and has an easy-care coat and low exercise requirements. He is a highly sociable, very loving dog who needs company and hates being left out of family activities. More energetic than he looks, he is nonetheless not built for a very active lifestyle. Over-exertion or overheating causes breathing difficulties because of his foreshortened face.

Despite his name, the Frenchie originated in Britain as an unwanted by-product of mid-19th century bulldog breeding programs. It was left to the French to recognize the potential of this comical little dog, which became a fashionable pet in Paris—and subsequently across Europe and the U.S.

WHAT colors?

Brindle, fawn, or pied (predominantly white with brindle markings).

WHAT grooming does the coat need?

This is an easy-care coat, needing only occasional (weekly) brushing to remove dead hairs. However, the face should be cleaned daily with a damp cloth, paying particular attention to the area around the eyes. The short coat has the advantage of minimal shedding.

HOW suitable are they as family dogs?

The Frenchie certainly has the temperament to be an ideal family pet, a role he enjoys as long as children are old enough to respect his needs. He makes a truly fun companion for sensible children. Physically, however, he is unsuitable for a very active family, and his vulnerability to overheating can be a problem in summer.

WHAT type of home?

This adaptable breed can be happy in city or country as long as he has his owner's attention. He appreciates a yard to play in, but always needs shade in summer. Wherever he lives, care must always be taken to protect him from extremes of temperature.

WHAT type of owner?

This is a breed that needs human companionship, so he must have an owner who can spend time with him—an ideal choice for retirees or people who can take their dog to work with them. He is unsuited to energetic types who love long walks or to obedience fanatics, but is perfect for gentle, affectionate owners who value character and a sense of humor in a dog.

HOW compatible with other pets?

Puppyhood socialization is important, as Frenchies can be very possessive of their owners and regard other dogs as competitors. Some dominant males can be very territorial. Having said that, they are good-natured and will generally get along well with other pets in their own household, although they may find it amusing to chase cats.

HOW much exercise?

Although the Frenchie's exercise needs are very moderate, he does need regular outings, about half an hour twice daily. Avoid exercise in hot weather, as this breed overheats very easily. The adult Frenchie can easily become a couch potato, which will not do his health any good. Puppies are generally

Place of origin: **Britain/France**

Character Trait	Poor	Average	Good	Excellent
Attitude toward other dogs			■	
Quietness		■		
Not destructive			■	
Protective behavior		■		
Not likely to stray		■		
Good with children			■	
Ease of training			■	

Original purpose: Lapdog
Male height: 11-13 in (28-33 cm)
Female height: 11-13 in (28-33 cm)
Weight: 24-28 lb (11-12.5 kg)
Lifespan: 9-11 years

very lively, and walks should be built up gradually from about six months.

HOW easy to train?

Quite easy, as long as you don't expect Collie-style formal obedience. Frenchies think life should be fun. If training sessions are treated

as a game they will learn quickly. Several of this breed have even succeeded in competitive obedience trials.

Small dogs

WHAT good points?

Vivacious, deeply affectionate, intelligent, affectionate, sociable, great sense of fun, adaptable, well suited to city life.

WHAT to be aware of?

Like all short-faced dogs, Frenchies may have breathing difficulties when exposed to heat or overexertion, and are liable in any case to snort, snuffle, wheeze, and snore. They also have a tendency to flatulence.

WHAT medical problems?

Breathing problems are inevitable with short-faced breeds: Avoid overheating and overexertion. Other problems include spinal disc trouble, hip malformation (dysplasia), and cataracts in the eyes.

Miniature and Toy Poodles

The two smaller Poodle breeds look like fluffy toys, but they are no mere fashion accessories. The Miniature and Toy are smaller versions of the Standard Poodle, originally a working water retriever of great intelligence and versatility. They share his brains, energy, and sense of fun. Overpopularity has led to puppy mills churning out specimens (Toys in particular) that are physically and temperamentally unsound, but a well-bred Poodle is capable of a great deal. Lively, loving, and extroverted, they make endearing companions and are highly trainable. They do need a great deal of coat care, and are not dogs who thrive without plenty of company.

Poodles date back to at least the 15th century, and the smaller versions were certainly known by the 18th century and possibly well before that time. Miniatures (then called Toys) were formally recognized in 1907, while Toys had to wait until 1957 for recognition.

WHAT colors?

Any solid color, including white, cream, brown, apricot, black, silver, and blue. Parti-colors occur but are not recognized by the AKC.

WHAT grooming does the coat need?

The thick, curly coat does not molt and keeps growing if not clipped. Daily grooming with slicker brush and wide toothed comb is essential to prevent the coat from matting, and it needs clipping every six to eight weeks. Show dogs are presented in an elaborate lion clip that requires a great deal of maintenance; pets are usually more comfortable with a practical short trim (lamb or puppy clip).

HOW suitable are they as family dogs?

Toys are vulnerable to rough handling by children, and are happier as the companion of adults. Miniatures are sturdier and make great family dogs as long as they are treated as a member of the family and not denied attention. Most Minis love children and make great playmates. However, they are sensitive, excitable, and easily stressed, and not well suited for a noisy, rowdy household.

WHAT type of home?

Miniatures are particularly adaptable and can be happy in city or country. Toys are ideal for city life and make great apartment dogs, although they will do just as well as their bigger cousins in a country home, enjoying walks and exploring hedges and ditches with unbounded enthusiasm.

WHAT type of owner?

These little Poodles need owners who recognize that they are more than fashion accessories and can provide affection, attention, and mental stimulation. They are fun dogs with a lot to offer. Miniatures in particular thrive on more exercise than they are often offered. Owners do need to be committed to grooming or, at the very least, to regular trips to a groomer.

HOW compatible with other pets?

These friendly little dogs usually get along well with other animals, especially any that can be persuaded to join them in a game. They remain very puppyish throughout life and, like children,

Fancy haircuts are not compulsory!

Character Trait	Poor	Average	Good	Excellent
Attitude toward other dogs				
Quietness				
Not destructive				
Protective behavior				
Not likely to stray				
Good with children				
Ease of training				

Original purpose: Lapdog
Miniature height: 11-15 in (28-38 cm)
Toy height: Under 10 in (25 cm)
Miniature weight: 26-30 lb (12-14 kg)
Toy weight: 4-8 lb (1.8-3.6 kg)
Lifespan: 12-14 years

can become overexcited and annoying to older, calm pets if not reminded of their manners.

HOW much exercise?
Moderate. Miniatures should have at least half an hour's walk every day and plenty of active play; Toys don't need a great deal of exercise, but they can walk a great deal farther than one might expect and will benefit both in mind and body.

HOW easy to train?
Miniature and Toy Poodles are bright dogs whose capacity to learn should not be wasted. They can be excitable, so training needs to be calm, gentle, and sensitive, but they are quick learners and keen to please. Handlers need a sense of humor: Poodles are easily bored by repetition and often have a creative approach to obedience.

WHAT good points?
Intelligent, good-tempered, obedient, eager to learn, affectionate, reliable, lively, sensitive, adaptable, fun-loving, nonaggressive, convenient size.

WHAT to be aware of?
Above-average coat care requirements.

Tends to enjoy the sound of his own voice. Some bloodlines can be very high strung and oversensitive. Choose breeder with care.

Small dogs

WHAT medical problems?
Inherited disorders include kneecap dislocation (patellar luxation), Legg-Perthes disease (degeneration of the head of the thighbone due to insufficient blood supply), epilepsy, and progressive retinal atrophy (degeneration of the light receptor cells in the eyes). There is also some occurrence of other eye problems, and Toy bitches occasionally suffer from a malformed ureter, causing incontinence. If grooming is neglected, skin problems may arise.

● The dense curly coat lends itself to sculpturing.

Italian Greyhound *Other names: Piccolo Levrieri Italiani*

Daintiest of all breeds, this miniature greyhound has all the grace of his full-size cousin plus the charm of a true toy dog. Mini-greyhounds have been treasured pets since at least Roman times, so they have been bred for generations to specialize in the role of loving companion. Gentle, affectionate, and entertaining, they need to be with their owner as much as possible and cannot have too much attention. They are highly dependent, even clingy, and need plenty of gentle socialization to give them confidence. Properly brought up, however, they are lively, playful, and often mischievous.

Despite their delicate appearance, they are quite hardy, but puppies under 18 months old have fragile bones and need special care to protect them from the risk of breaking a leg. They have very little awareness of how small they are and are quite capable of leaping from a dangerous height and doing themselves damage.

WHAT colors?
Black, blue, cream, fawn, red, white, or pied (white with colored patches).

WHAT grooming does the coat need?
The fine, satiny coat sheds little and needs very little care, just an occasional brushing with a soft bristle brush or simply "polishing" with a piece of silk or velvet cloth.

HOW suitable are they as family dogs?
The Italian Greyhound can make a delightful pet for a quiet family with considerate older children. A busy, noisy household is not the right environment for him, and he is simply not safe with young or careless children, as he can easily be injured in rough play.

WHAT type of home?
The Italian Greyhound will be happy anywhere that suits his owner. His small size and low exercise requirements make him an ideal pet for an apartment.

However, he is just as much at home in the country, where he will walk miles, chase rabbits, and generally hark back to his sighthound ancestry.

WHAT type of owner?
This is a dog for quiet, gentle owners who want a constant companion and are prepared to lavish affection on him. He needs a lot of attention and consideration. A lover of warmth and comfort, he would prefer an owner who is willing to share a bed with him. Not for owners who want formal, prompt obedience, as this is not his style.

HOW compatible with other pets?
In general this charming little dog is prepared to be friendly with other animals of all kinds, but common sense needs to be applied. His sighthound heritage means that he can be tempted to chase cats or other small animals, and his fragility means that he is at risk of injury from boisterous larger dogs. Early socialization is important, or he may become timid.

HOW much exercise?
How much would you like? This is a truly adaptable little dog who can exercise himself playing in the house and yard or who can enjoy long country walks, depending on your lifestyle. Remember that, despite his size, he has all the instincts of a sighthound and will disappear into the distance if he spots a rabbit. Puppies under a year old should have restricted exercise to avoid the risk of injury to fragile bones.

Character Trait	Poor	Average	Good	Excellent
Attitude toward other dogs				
Quietness				
Not destructive				
Protective behavior				
Not likely to stray				
Good with children				
Ease of training				

Original purpose: Lapdog
Male height: 12-15 in (30-38 cm)
Female height: 12-15 in (30-38 cm)
Weight: 7-14 lb (3.2-6.4 kg)
Lifespan: 12-15 years

HOW easy to train?

Moderate. These are sighthounds, therefore they have a short attention spans and no predisposition toward formal obedience. However, basic training and lots of socialization are important to increase their confidence as well as to encourage good behavior. Training should be broken up into frequent short sessions and motivated by praise and treats.

Small dogs

WHAT good points?

Intelligent, affectionate, trusting, vivacious, sweet-natured, playful, good-tempered, devoted, entertaining.

WHAT to be aware of?

Very sensitive to the cold. Provide a snug bed, and a sweater for cold weather. Puppies are very fragile and can break a leg just wriggling out of your arms. No sense of heights, may recklessly jump out of a window or off a balcony.

WHAT medical problems?

Generally a healthy breed. Some epilepsy, hair loss (alopecia), and dislocation of kneecaps (patellar luxation) reported. Broken bones are the main hazard. These dogs should be supervised at all times to prevent injury.

● *Less fragile than his delicate appearance suggests, the Italian Greyhound makes one of the most loving canine companions imaginable.*

Miniature Schnauzer *Other names: Zwergschnauzer*

The smallest of the three Schnauzer breeds, the Miniature was a 19th-century creation intended to present the virtues of the versatile Standard Schnauzer in a conveniently sized package. Small but sturdy, he makes an excellent companion and family dog, adaptable to most lifestyles and very people oriented. He is an intelligent, active dog who needs company and attention and repays it with affection

and loyalty. Sometimes described as "a terrier without attitude," he has a terrier's liveliness and enjoyment of life but not the fire and aggression associated with many terriers. He can be quite bossy if allowed but is very responsive to training and benefits from the mental stimulation of obedience or agility.

Originating in Germany, the breed reached the United States in the 1920s and soon became popular there. In Britain, interest did not really take off until the 1960s, since then the Miniature Schnauzer has become very well established.

WHAT colors?

Black, black and silver (black with silver points), or pepper and salt (dark to light gray, the hairs being banded). In Europe, the Fédération Cynologique International has recently accepted pure white, but this color is not recognized in America.

WHAT grooming does the coat need?

This is quite a high-maintenance coat, needing at least weekly grooming (ideally ten minutes a day) with a stiff brush for the body and a comb for the whiskers and leg hair. The beard usually needs cleaning after every meal! Twice a year the coat should be hand stripped. Clipping is unacceptable for show dogs as it affects coat texture, but pet owners may find it simpler.

HOW suitable are they as family dogs?

The Miniature Schnauzer makes

an excellent family dog who is devoted to his family and wants to be fully involved in all their activities. He enjoys the company of sensible children who have been taught to treat him with respect, and he makes a fun playmate.

WHAT type of home?

This conveniently sized little dog fits in anywhere and is equally at home in city or country. He can adapt perfectly well to apartment life as long as he has regular exercise.

WHAT type of owner?

The Miniature Schnauzer needs a loving, responsible owner who appreciates a lively dog with character and has plenty of time for him—this breed is miserable if left alone for long periods. A good choice for someone wanting to take up obedience or agility with a small breed—as long as they are prepared to spend time on coat care.

HOW compatible with other pets?

Generally friendly with other animals in the same household, this cocky little dog can sometimes be a bit too bossy with strange dogs for his own good, so early socialization is recommended.

HOW much exercise?

This very adaptable breed will adapt to his owner's lifestyle. He can stay fit with quite moderate exercise—three brisk walks a day—or he can enjoy regular long country rambles. He has plenty of energy

Character Trait	Poor	Average	Good	Excellent
Attitude toward other dogs				
Quietness				
Not destructive				
Protective behavior				
Not likely to stray				
Good with children				
Ease of training				

Original purpose: Ratter and companion
Male height: 13-14 in (33-36 cm)
Female height: 12-13 in (30.5-33 cm)
Weight: 13-15 lb (6-7 kg)
Lifespan: 13-14 years

for play and is a suitable choice for obedience work or agility.

HOW easy to train?

Miniature Schnauzers are very trainable, given calm, firm, consistent handling. They do need to be persuaded that lessons are fun, and a reward-based approach will achieve best results. Quick to learn, they are equally quickly bored by repetition, so keep lessons short and stimulating.

WHAT good points?

Intelligent, active, versatile, adaptable, playful, alert, reliable, obedient, inquisitive, affectionate, responsive.

WHAT to be aware of?

Above-average grooming requirements. Tend to like the sound of their own voices.

WHAT medical problems?

This breed suffers from two hereditary eye disorders, cataracts and progressive retinal atrophy (degeneration of the light receptors cells in the eyes). All breeding stock should be eye tested. Otherwise this is generally a healthy breed, with occasional incidence of bleeding disorders (hemophilia and von Willebrand's disease), heart murmurs, diabetes, Legg-Perthes disease (degeneration of the head of the thighbone due to insufficient blood supply), and liver shunt (an inherited defect whereby the liver does not get a proper blood supply and does not function properly).

Small dogs

Parson Russell Terrier

The identity of the Parson Russell has been a source of confusion for some time. These merry little dogs originated as a strain of Fox Terrier, bred to keep up with hounds and horses and then to bolt the fox from its earth. Like Fox Terriers, their lively, fun-loving, and affectionate nature also made them popular pets. However, until recently they were not officially recognized by any kennel club, and the name "Jack Russell" was often applied to any mainly white mongrel terrier.

1997 saw the recognition of the original long-legged type (resembling the original Fox Terrier before it became a show dog) as the Parson Jack Russell (later Parson Russell). Short-legged specimens have since achieved recognition in some countries as a separate breed, the Jack Russell. Whatever the name, like most terriers, they are great, if energetic, companions who enjoy life and want to investigate every part of it.

WHAT colors?

All white or white with black, tan, or lemon markings, typically confined to the head and root of tail.

WHAT grooming does the coat need?

Parson Russells may have rough or smooth coats, but both are easy to groom, needing only a brisk weekly brushing with a stiff bristle brush. Show dogs are neatened up by careful hand stripping.

HOW suitable are they as family dogs?

These are great dogs for active families who will include them in all their activities. They can be a bit too fiery for the comfort of small children but are fun dogs for sensible older children, full of energy and never tired of playing. They do need a lot of supervision. If bored, they will certainly find some mischief to occupy themselves.

WHAT type of home?

These energetic dogs are ideal for country life, but will adapt to an urban lifestyle, even in an apartment, as long as they have a reasonable-sized yard and access to a local park for exercise. Yards must be securely fenced as, like most terriers, these are consummate escape artists always on the look-out for adventure.

WHAT type of owner?

Terrier enthusiasts only should apply! Parson Russells are best suited to active, experienced, strong-willed owners who expect a dog to be involved in all family activities, and will not allow a clever, bossy little dog to rule the household. Not suitable for owners who are out all day, as they will get into mischief if bored. Not recommended for avid gardeners: They dig!

HOW compatible with other pets?

Early socialization with other dogs is essential to prevent the natural terrier fire escalating into aggression. Parson Russells have very strong chasing and hunting instincts. They will usually be friendly with cats in their own household, but strange cats and small pets are definitely at risk.

HOW much exercise?

These active little dogs are very adaptable and will obtain a lot of exercise through play, but they benefit from a brisk walk at least twice a day plus time for free galloping. Their intense hunting

Character Trait	Poor	Average	Good	Excellent
Attitude toward other dogs	▓			
Quietness	▓			
Not destructive		▓		
Protective behavior			▓	
Not likely to stray	▓			
Good with children			▓	
Ease of training		▓		

Place of origin: **Britain**

Original purpose: Hunting vermin
Male height: 13-14 in (33-35.5 cm)
Female height: 12-13 in (30.5-33 cm)
Weight: 13-17 lb (5.9-7.7 kg)
Lifespan: 13-15 years

drive means that they should not be trusted off-leash in any place where they might start chasing, especially near roads.

HOW easy to train?

Moderate. Owners of these stubborn, active, and mischievous dogs need to be firm, patient, and consistent, prepared to respect the independent terrier spirit while insisting on reasonable standards of behavior. A Parson will never be the first choice for formal obedience work, but sensible training will produce a dog who is a pleasure to live with rather than a hooligan.

WHAT good points?

Active, lively, alert, friendly, forthcoming,

Socialization with other dogs [in] puppyhood is [cr]ucial for Parson Russells.

fearless, loving, playful, vigilant, convenient size, hardy.

WHAT to be aware of?

Excitable, stubborn, territorial; strong hunting instinct. Can be noisy, and can be dog aggressive.

WHAT medical problems?

Generally hardy and healthy, though some eye problems (primary lens luxation), deafness, dislocation of the kneecaps (patellar luxation), and Legg-Perthes (disease of the hip joints).

Small dogs

Beagle

The Beagle is the smallest of the pack hounds and was developed to hunt hares, with huntsmen following on foot. His convenient size and merry nature have also made him deservedly popular as a companion breed. Like all scenthounds, he has a strong hunting instinct and will follow a scent regardless of his owner's calls. He is more amenable than most of his kind and fits in well with family life. Lively and affectionate, he is friendly toward everyone and gets along well with children. As long as he has company and exercise, he is an easy dog to live with, sensible and well-behaved at home, low maintenance, and generally robust and healthy.

Dedicated hunter, loving companion, and smart show dog, the Beagle is a real all-around dog who is also employed worldwide as a sniffer dog, using his keen nose to detect anything from drugs or fire accelerants to termites.

WHAT colors?
Any accepted hound color, such as lemon and white, red and white, tri-color (black, tan and white), and mottled—never black and tan.

WHAT grooming does the coat need?
The short coat is easy care but benefits from regular brushing (at least once a week) with a hound glove or bristle brush to remove dead hairs. Grooming sessions should include checking that the floppy ears are clean to prevent infections.

HOW suitable are they as family dogs?
This is an ideal family dog for an active household. He loves to be part of the family and is generally very good with older children. His bounciness and tendency to mouth hands and clothes in play mean he may be too robust for the comfort of toddlers. In any case, few households with pre-school children will have the time

● *Born to run, the Beagle is most likely to flourish in a country setting.*

and energy to cope with the mischievous whirlwind that is a Beagle puppy.

WHAT type of home?
The Beagle is best suited to a country home, but can be just as happy living in a city provided his exercise needs are fulfilled. He is not a suitable apartment dog, as he should have access to a yard with a good, secure fence as he is quite an escapologist when bored.

WHAT type of owner?
This is a breed for an active, easy-going owner who wants an affectionate companion and enjoys long walks. Beagles are happy as part of a lively family or living alone with an active older person. Not a breed for those who are out at work all day, as they do not like being left alone for long periods, nor for those who want strict obedience.

HOW compatible with other pets?
These friendly dogs get along well with other dogs and with pets of different species within their own household. However, they were bred to chase, so expect them to do just that.

HOW much exercise?
Moderate. Beagles are built to run and can keep going for miles, but a couple of half-hour walks each day plus active playtime will keep them fit and happy. A stroll round the block is not enough! Without sufficient regular exercise, they easily become obese and unhealthy.

Character Trait	Poor	Average	Good	Excellent
Attitude toward other dogs				
Quietness				
Not destructive				
Protective behavior				
Not likely to stray				
Good with children				
Ease of training				

Original purpose: Hunting hares in packs
Male height: 13-15 in (33-38 cm)
Female height: Slightly smaller
Weight: 18-30 lb (8-14 kg)
Lifespan: c. 14 years

● *This Beagle is trim and in fine condition, but a tendency toward greediness can sometimes result in obesity.*

HOW easy to train?

Moderate. Training needs to start early and trainers need to be patient and persistent, as Beagles are naturally both stubborn and easily distracted if they pick up a scent. They respond well to reward-based training, but don't overdo the treats. Their strong chasing instinct means that extra attention must be paid to teaching the recall.

Small dogs

WHAT good points?

Intelligent, playful, loving, friendly, energetic, nonaggressive, happy, bold, even-tempered, physically very sound.

WHAT to be aware of?

May be hard to control off-leash. Tends to be greedy and prone to obesity. Some are very vocal. The short coat has a noticeable "doggy" smell and sheds surprisingly profusely over carpets, furniture, and clothes.

WHAT medical problems?

Generally free from major defects but epilepsy and seizures, eye problems, and "Beagle pain syndrome" (neck pain and fever in youngsters) have been reported.

Shetland Sheepdog *Other names: Sheltie*

The enchantingly pretty Shetland Sheepdog resembles a miniature Rough Collie and shares many of the virtues of that breed. Loyal, affectionate, and responsive, he requires sensitive handling to bring out the best in him. The Sheltie is naturally standoffish with strangers, and lack of proper socialization in puppyhood may allow this to develop into timidity. Like most herding breeds, he has a high intelligence and needs to be allowed to use this. If denied mental stimulation such as obedience training or agility, he can become neurotic, noisy, and destructive. In the right hands, however, he is an affectionate and rewarding pet, with a sweet temperament and a strong desire to please.

The Sheltie originated in the Shetland Isles, probably in the early 19th century, as a herder and general farm dog. Today the breed has become more elegant and more heavily coated in line with his cousin the Rough Collie.

WHAT colors?

Sable (from pale gold to mahogany), tri-color (black, tan, and white), and blue merle (a kind of two-toned marbled effect) are the most common colors, all with white markings that may include blaze, collar and chest, frill, legs, and tail tip. Less frequently seen are black and white or black and tan.

WHAT grooming does the coat need?

That glamorous coat needs regular, preferably daily, brushing and combing, paying special attention to the soft hair behind the ears, inside the thighs, and in the armpits, where it mats easily. Shelties molt heavily, once or twice a year, at which time the coat comes out in handfuls and is best tackled with a bath to remove as much dead hair as possible.

HOW suitable are they as family dogs?

Fantastic—with the right family, generally a calm family with sensible, older children. Shelties dislike boisterous play and loud noises and if harassed by children may be driven to nip. These highly sensitive little dogs react badly to a tense or hectic environment and need a peaceful home.

WHAT type of home?

A country home is probably every Sheltie's ideal, but this breed will adapt perfectly well to life in an apartment as long as they are given sufficient daily exercise to keep them active.

WHAT type of owner?

The Sheltie is a wonderful companion for calm, sensitive, affectionate owners who have time for the necessary exercise, training, and grooming. This is definitely not a "home alone" dog. Shelties need company and owners who will not leave them alone for long periods.

HOW compatible with other pets?

Shelties are gentle dogs who are generally good with other animals. They do have a strong instinct to chase (and sometimes nip) things that move, so may not be good with neighbors' cats.

HOW much exercise?

These are active little dogs that need at least a couple of walks a day in the park and plenty of playtime. It is advisable to seek a secure place for off-leash exercise because of their extreme sensitivity to loud noises, which may cause them to bolt if startled.

Character Trait	Poor	Average	Good	Excellent
Attitude toward other dogs			■	
Quietness		■		
Not destructive			■	
Protective behavior			■	
Not likely to stray			■	
Good with children			■	
Ease of training				■

Original purpose: Herder
Male height: 13-16 in (33-40.5 cm)
Female height: 13-16 in (33-40.5 cm)
Weight: 14-16 lb (6-7 kg)
Lifespan: 12-14 years

HOW easy to train?

Shelties are very intelligent, willing to please, and easy to train in the hands of a sensitive owner. This breed needs encouragement and reward-based training. Harsh training techniques and scoldings will be counterproductive, but gentle, patient, and consistent training will usually achieve admirable results.

● Since his days as a working dog in the Shetlands, the Sheltie has become more heavily coated and elegant. His coat now benefits from daily attention.

WHAT good points?

Gentle, very affectionate, responsive, alert, loyal, intelligent, nonaggressive, devoted to owner, good watchdog, eminently trainable and willing to please.

Small dogs

WHAT to be aware of?

Demanding in terms of coat care — and company. Early socialization vital to prevent shyness. Extreme sensitivity to stress. Can be very clingy. Not recommended for hectic homes or for homes with young children. Strong innate chasing instinct.

WHAT medical problems?

Eye problems including progressive retinal eye disease (PRA) and collie eye anomaly, for which puppies should be eye tested. Von Willebrand's disease (a blood disorder), hip malformation (dysplasia), kneecap dislocation (patellar luxation), epilepsy, heart valve defects, and thyroid disease also occur in this breed.

Shiba Inu

The Shiba is one of the more primitive breeds, meaning that his behavior is more like that of a tamed wild animal than a domesticated one. Despite his sweet appearance, he is no cuddly toy, but strong-willed, independent, and an avid hunter. He is loyal and devoted, but on his own terms, with a catlike aloofness. He is intelligent and a quick learner, but has no natural inclination for obedience. Agile and graceful, he can climb, jump, or dig his way out of anywhere. If you enjoy a dog with a mind of his own, he can be a delightful and entertaining companion, but he is not for the novice.

The smallest of Japan's "national monument" breeds, the Shiba developed as a hunter and guard. His origins date back into ancient history, but the Shiba as we know it was formally established in the early 20th century when the Japanese began to classify their native breeds, blending several local strains to create the standardized Shiba Inu.

WHAT colors?

Red, black and tan, and sesame (red with black tips), all with *urajiro* markings (white underparts, chest, and facial markings). White/cream is also accepted in the U.K. and some other countries, but not in the United States.

WHAT grooming does the coat need?

Minimal for most of the year—a weekly brushing will do. Twice a year, Shibas molt massively, needing a daily comb with a grooming rake to lift out dead hair.

HOW suitable are they as family dogs?

The right dog in the right home can become a great family dog, but the Shiba's high energy levels, strong hunting drive, unreliable recall, and aloofness do not make him the obvious choice for this role. If raised with well behaved children, he can be very good with youngsters, but tolerance of mishandling doesn't come naturally to him and he is not recommended with small children.

● *DNA analysis suggests that the Shiba is one of the oldest dog breeds, dating back to the 3rd century BC.*

WHAT type of home?

Think Fort Knox, or as near as you can manage, to keep this dog safe. Shibas believe in the right to roam, and can dash through doors or jump, climb, or dig their way out of yards. They can be city or country dogs, and adapt surprisingly well to apartment life, as long as their high energy and exercise needs are kept in mind.

WHAT type of owner?

The Shiba needs an owner who will respect his independent nature and work with him. Patience, persistence, and a sense of humor are essential. Potential owners must be prepared to commit a lot of time to socialization, training, exercise, and companionship—this is not a part-time dog.

HOW compatible with other pets?

These dedicated hunters are not safe with small furries or larger livestock. They can live with confident cats if raised from puppyhood with them, but neighborhood cats are still at risk. Shibas can also be dog aggressive, especially to the same sex, and need good socialization as puppies to prevent this.

HOW much exercise?

The active and energetic Shiba needs at least two hours of exercise a day, and is tireless on longer hikes. However, exercise should be on-leash in most

Character Trait	Poor	Average	Good	Excellent
Attitude toward other dogs	●			
Quietness			●	
Not destructive		●		
Protective behavior			●	
Not likely to stray	●			
Good with children		●		
Ease of training		●		

Original purpose: Hunter and guard
Male height: 14.5-16.5 in (36.8-41.9 cm)
Female height: 13.5-15.5 in (34.3-39.4 cm)
Weight: 17-23 lbs (7.7-10.4 kg)
Lifespan: 12-15 years

circumstances, as his strong hunting drive will always outweigh his recall training.

HOW easy to train?

Quick to learn, but slow to obey, the Shiba needs firm guidelines, positive and reward-based training, persistence, and consistency. Most Shibas like to have their own way, and training should start from day one to prevent them from training you. Avoid any form of force training—firm but kind is definitely the right way to go.

WHAT good points?

Loyal, intelligent, athletic, independent, naturally clean, easily housetrained, good watchdog, generally quiet.

WHAT to be aware of?

Very strong-willed, needs firm, consistent training—not candidates for obedience trials. Often aloof with humans, can be dog aggressive; prone to resource guarding. High prey drive, not trustworthy off-leash, demon escapologist, destructive if bored. Normally quiet, but when feeling emotional lets out the notorious "Shiba scream."

WHAT medical problems?

Generally a robust and healthy breed, but inherited disorders include kneecap dislocation (patellar luxation), hip malformation (dysplasia), and eye cataracts. All breeding stock should be tested for these problems.

Small dogs

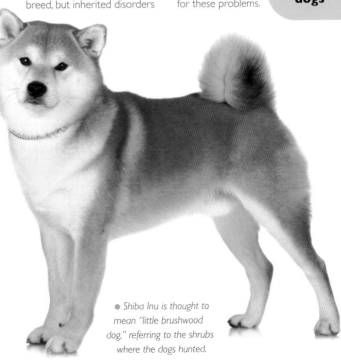

● *Shiba Inu is thought to mean "little brushwood dog," referring to the shrubs where the dogs hunted.*

Cocker Spaniel

From the 1920s, the Cocker Spaniel in America evolved along such different lines from the English type that it become a distinct breed in its own right, achieving separate status in 1946. The Cocker Spaniel is smaller than his English cousin, with a shorter back, more domed head shape with shorter muzzle, and much more profuse coat. He has the same sweet nature and abundant energy as the English Cocker and is, if anything, even more of a companion breed. Despite his glamorous looks, he retains his working intelligence, which should be sensibly channeled to prevent him from becoming bored and destructive.

His crowning glory in the show ring and major drawback as a pet is his voluminous coat, which needs a great deal of care. Prospective owners must recognize that this is a high-maintenance breed and professional assistance with grooming may be needed even when the coat is clipped short.

WHAT colors?

Black, chocolate, red, buff, cream, sable, black and tan, roan and parti-color (white with distinct markings in any accepted color, with or without tan markings).

WHAT grooming does the coat need?

Maximum. Maintaining a full show coat in good condition is a skilled and time-consuming task, and most pet owners will need professional help. Reputable breeders will recommend a good grooming service or may provide this. Many pet owners opt to have the coat clipped short, but remember that this entails a substantial cost every six to eight weeks.

HOW suitable are they as family dogs?

This happy little dog makes a wonderful pet for an active family with plenty of time for exercise, play, and training and whose members are prepared to commit themselves wholeheartedly to his grooming needs. Gentle and playful, he is great fun for sensible children and greatly enjoys participating in family activities.

WHAT type of home?

A country home is ideal for this active breed. However, the Cocker Spaniel will adapt to city and apartment life as long as he has access to a park where he can enjoy a good run every day.

WHAT type of owner?

This breed needs an active, affectionate owner who has plenty of time for energetic walks, enjoys the stimulus of training a responsive dog, and is committed to time-consuming coat care. Cocker Spaniels are happy as part of a family or as companions for the active elderly. They dislike being left alone, however, so are not recommended for owners who are out at work all day.

HOW compatible with other pets?

These friendly little dogs usually get along well with other dogs and with cats in their own household, but they were bred to hunt and have a strong chasing instinct, so strange cats had better watch out. Smaller pets, such as rabbits and hamsters, should be introduced with great care and contact should always be supervised.

Character Trait	Poor	Average	Good	Excellent
Attitude toward other dogs				
Quietness				
Not destructive				
Protective behavior				
Not likely to stray				
Good with children				
Ease of training				

Original purpose: Finding and retrieving game
Male height: 14.5-15.5 in (37-39.5 cm)
Female height: 13.5-14.5 in (34-37 cm)
Weight: 24-28 lb (11-13 kg)
Lifespan: 12-15 years

HOW much exercise?

Regular, energetic walks are essential for these very active little dogs—at least an hour's walk a day and more if possible, together with free exercise at home and active playtime. An underexercised spaniel is likely to be bored, badly behaved, and overweight.

HOW easy to train?

These working dogs are intelligent, enthusiastic, and eager to please. Given a consistently firm but gentle, positive approach, they are highly trainable. They are sensitive and easily put off by harsh treatment, but they can also be willful and easily distracted if their interest is not maintained, so handlers need to keep lessons fun and rewarding.

WHAT good points?

Happy, sweet-natured, loyal, playful, gentle, affectionate, even-tempered, intelligent, responsive, energetic.

WHAT to be aware of?

Demanding in terms of coat care and company. Does not like being left alone. Beware commercially bred pups that may have temperament problems.

WHAT medical problems?

This breed has a number of potential health problems, so only choose pups from healthy stock. Various eye problems including hereditary cataracts (breeding stock should have current eye certificates), hip malformation (dysplasia), prone to ear infections, skin ailments, and allergies.

Small dogs

● *A shorter back, more domed head, shorter muzzle, and more profuse coat distinguish the Cocker Spaniel from his English cousin.*

Tibetan Terrier *Other names: Dhoki Apso*

The Tibetan Terrier is the classic shaggy dog in miniature. Despite his name he has no terrier characteristics, but rather resembles a small-scale Old English Sheepdog. His attractive shaggy appearance and happy temperament make the Tibetan Terrier an appealing companion. Under the glamorous coat, he is a sound, unexaggerated, medium-sized dog capable of fitting into any home environment, with an outgoing,

affectionate nature that makes him an excellent family dog. Tibetans are "people dogs," and what they do need is their owners' time, both in terms of the company they love and the grooming that the flowing coat requires.

The breed evolved as a companion, guard, and herder in the harsh conditions of the Tibetan mountains, where it was greatly prized. It was not introduced to the West until 1926 and was initially overshadowed by its close relative, the Lhasa Apso, but today has achieved a deserved popularity.

WHAT colors?

All colors, including black, gray, smoke, cream, gold, white, parti-colored and tri-colored. Liver and chocolate colors occur but are not accepted in the show ring.

WHAT grooming does the coat need?

The profuse double coat needs a great deal of attention. Daily brushing is essential to prevent knots and tangles. The facial hair needs cleaning after each meal, and on top of that a trip to the groomer every eight to ten weeks is advisable. Some owners prefer to keep the coat clipped short for the dog's comfort and for ease of care.

HOW suitable are they as family dogs?

This breed makes an ideal family dog. He is devoted to his family, likes to be involved in their activities, and has endless energy. Children need to learn to treat him with respect, but he will respond in kind, and he is a sensible size to be managed easily by older children.

WHAT type of home?

Adaptable to most circumstances, the Tibetan Terrier can be just as happy in the city or country. What matters to him is the company of his human family.

WHAT type of owner?

Tibetan puppies can be very exuberant and need a fairly firm hand, so this may not be the ideal first dog. A sensible, experienced owner will bring out the best in them. Their prime need is to be part of the family, receiving plenty of time and attention.

HOW compatible with other pets?

Normally Tibetan Terriers get along well with other dogs. Although usually sensible as adults, they can be very bouncy as youngsters and need to be taught how to behave around cats and other pets.

HOW much exercise?

The Tibetan will adapt to his owner's lifestyle in terms of exercise needs, content to enjoy short walks or long ones. However he is a lively dog with plenty of stamina who will enjoy as much exercise as his owners can offer.

HOW easy to train?

This is a strong-willed little dog, willing to please but needing sensible, consistent, and above all early training. He has a great deal of energy that needs to be directed, and is well suited to

Character Trait	Poor	Average	Good	Excellent
Attitude toward other dogs				
Quietness				
Not destructive				
Protective behavior				
Not likely to stray				
Good with children				
Ease of training				

Original purpose: Companion and guard
Male height: Not above 17 in (43 cm)
Female height: Slightly smaller than males
Weight: 18-30 lb (8-13.6 kg)
Lifespan: 13-14 years upward

advanced training disciplines like agility and competitive obedience.

WHAT good points?

Hardy, family oriented, loyal companion, intelligent, quick learner, alert, lively, not nervous or aggressive, excellent watchdog.

WHAT to be aware of?

These are active dogs who jump and climb. If neglected and left to their own devices, youngsters can easily become hyperactive and noisy. They demand attention.

WHAT medical problems?

Generally a very healthy breed. However, prospective puppy owners should check that breeding stock has been tested for hip dysplasia and for two eye conditions: progressive retinal atrophy (degeneration of light receptor cells) and dislocation of the lens (primary lens luxation). Dislocation of the kneecaps (patellar luxation) and hernias also occur.

Small dogs

Boston Terrier *Other names: Boston Bull*

The smart and stylish Boston is a delightful companion who suits most modern lifestyles. A compact little dog who fits well into apartment living, he has an easy-care coat and low exercise requirements, and his sunny disposition wins him friends everywhere. His only demand is for company. This is not a dog who will be happy on his own. He needs plenty of love and attention (and repays this generously). He is gentle enough to be chosen as a companion for an elderly person, lively enough to flourish as a child's playmate and sociable enough to enjoy family life. Physically, however, he does not cope well with extremes of temperature and needs extra care in hot weather to prevent breathing difficulties.

The Boston is an all-American breed. It is hard to believe, but this gentle and friendly pet descends from early 19th-century fighting dogs, deriving from the same bulldog-terrier crosses that produced the Bull Terrier.

WHAT colors?

Brindle or black with even white markings. Ideally these markings comprise white muzzle, blaze, collar, breast, part or whole of forelegs, and hindlegs below hocks. However, mismarked pups make just as good pets.

WHAT grooming does the coat need?

This is an easy-care coat, needing only occasional (weekly) brushing to remove dead hairs. However, the face should be cleaned daily with a damp cloth, paying particular attention to the area of skin around the eyes. The short coat has the advantage of minimal shedding.

HOW suitable are they as family dogs?

With a considerate family that appreciates his needs, the Boston is a marvelous family dog. If raised with children, they will usually become a child's best friend. As with any breed, children need to be supervised and taught to

● *Alertness, intelligence, and self-confidence radiate from this all-American Boston Terrier.*

respect the dog's individual needs, but they will appreciate the Boston's playful and responsive nature and bold personality.

WHAT type of home?

Created in the city of Boston, this compact little dog was designed for city life and can be quite comfortable in an apartment. However, he is quite prepared to enjoy the delights of the country as well. Wherever he lives, care

must always be taken to protect him from extremes of temperature.

WHAT type of owner?

Any loving, responsible owner who wants a close companion and is not too keen on long walks will suit the Boston. He is an excellent companion for children and the elderly and a great family dog, provided always that care is taken to avoid circumstances where over heating may cause distress.

HOW compatible with other pets?

Bostons are just as friendly with other animals as with people, although some dominant males may display intermale aggression with other dogs. As with all breeds, they benefit from early socialization with their own kind and with any other household pets with which they may be expected to share a home.

HOW much exercise?

Bostons are active dogs who need daily exercise, but they are not great walkers. A short daily walk will

Character Trait	Poor	Average	Good	Excellent
Attitude toward other dogs			■	
Quietness		■		
Not destructive			■	
Protective behavior		■		
Not likely to stray		■		
Good with children			■	
Ease of training			■	

Original purpose: Stable dog
Male height: 15-17 in (38-43 cm)
Female height: 15-17 in (38-43 cm)
Weight: 10-25 lb (4.5-11.5 kg)
Lifespan: 10-14 years

suffice, supplemented by playtime indoors or in the yard. Avoid exercise in hot weather, as this breed overheats very easily. Bostons like to go everywhere with you, but would often prefer to be carried rather than walk.

HOW easy to train?

Bostons are strong-minded, stubborn little dogs who need to be persuaded that training sessions are fun, but they are also highly intelligent and quick to learn if it suits them. They enjoy learning tricks and, with patience, can achieve impressive levels of obedience.

WHAT good points?

Companionable, lively, intelligent, affectionate, sociable, gentle, playful, nonaggressive, entertaining, well-suited to city life.

WHAT to be aware of?

Like all short-faced dogs, Bostons may have breathing difficulties when exposed to heat or overexertion, and are liable in any case to snort, snuffle, wheeze, and snore. They also have a tendency to flatulence.

WHAT medical problems?

Breathing problems are inevitable with short-faced breeds, but should not be a problem if care is taken to avoid overheating or overexertion. Youngsters should be tested for inherited juvenile cataract and lack of thyroid hormone (hypothyroidism). Skin tumors also occur in this breed.

Small dogs

● Like other short-faced breeds, the Boston can develop breathing problems and also overheats quite easily. Strenuous exercise in hot weather should be avoided.

English Cocker Spaniel
Other names: Cocker Spaniel

The nickname of the "Merry Cocker" is well-deserved—he is a happy, friendly, enthusiastic character whose tail never stops wagging. A keen worker, he is just as ready to pour his energy into the role of family pet. This is a lively and loving breed that needs, and revels in, company. He is devoted to his owners, sociable with visitors, and good with children—his kindness and working intelligence make him a great hearing ear dog, support dog for the disabled, and therapy dog. Outgoing yet gentle, he is however highly demanding in terms of attention, exercise, and grooming.

Spaniels developed to assist falconers and later shooters by finding, flushing, and retrieving game. The smallest of the land spaniels, the English Cocker was recognized as a separate breed in 1892. Today show and working strains have diverged, the latter being stockier, less heavily coated and even more energetic.

WHAT colors?
English Cockers come in a wide variety of colors including golden, red, liver, black, blue roan, black and white, orange and white, lemon and white, tri-color, and black and tan.

WHAT grooming does the coat need?
The thick, silky coat needs quite a lot of attention, ideally a daily brush and comb plus a thorough grooming at least once a week. The long ears and ear fringes need particular care. In addition, the coat needs regular stripping or clipping. Professional grooming may be needed. Neutering can cause coat changes, leading to a thicker, softer coat needing extra work.

HOW suitable are they as family dogs?
This is a wonderful breed for an active family: English Cockers thrive on family life. They are generally good with children, but won't tolerate teasing or rough treatment,

● *Friendly and energetic, the English Cocker is happiest with an active family.*

so younger members of the family should be supervised.

WHAT type of home?
A country home is ideal. However, if they have the exercise and attention they need, English Cockers will adapt happily to life in a city and are compact enough to live happily in an apartment.

WHAT type of owner?
This breed is best suited to active, sociable owners who expect a close relationship with their dogs and have time and the inclination for exercise, grooming, and training. Cockers are happy as part of a lively family, but make equally good companions for the active elderly. Not a breed for those who are out at work all day, as they may suffer separation anxiety.

HOW compatible with other pets?
English Cockers are usually as friendly with other animals as with people—but this is a sporting breed, so don't expect them to resist chasing the neighbor's cat until fully trained.

HOW much exercise?
Cockers have boundless energy and need regular walks, free exercise and active playtime. Denied the opportunity for exercise, they are likely to become frustrated, destructive—and overweight.

HOW easy to train?
Intelligent and eager to please, this working breed is highly trainable and needs the mental stimulation of training lessons. Start early to prevent puppy mischief

Character Trait	Poor	Average	Good	Excellent
Attitude toward other dogs				
Quietness				
Not destructive				
Protective behavior				
Not likely to stray				
Good with children				
Ease of training				

Place of origin: **Britain**

Original purpose: Finding and retrieving game
Male height: 15-17 in (38-43 cm)
Female height: 14-16 in (35.5-41 cm)
Weight: 26-34 lb (12-15.5 kg)
Lifespan: 12-15 years

escalating into disregard of your wishes. Training must be gentle but firm. They are sensitive to harsh treatment, but can also be quite independent, headstrong, and easily distracted by scents when outdoors.

WHAT good points?
Happy, sweet-natured, loyal, playful, gentle, affectionate, even-tempered, intelligent, responsive, energetic.

WHAT to be aware of?
Demanding coat care. Does not like being left alone. "Rage syndrome" (sudden outbreaks of unprovoked aggression, possibly an inherited condition) has been an occasional but alarming problem in the breed, mostly in reds and goldens, but is quite rare.

Small dogs

WHAT medical problems?
English Cockers are generally a healthy breed, but hereditary problems include progressive retinal atrophy (degeneration of the light receptor cells in the eyes)—breeding stock should be eye tested—kidney disease, heart problems, and dislocating kneecaps (patellar luxation).

Basenji

A dog who washes his face like a cat, climbs like a monkey, and crows like a rooster, the Basenji is a breed with a difference. Classed as a "primitive" breed, he originated as the hunting dog of Central African tribesmen. As a pet for the modern household, he is endearing but distinctly challenging. Catlike in character, he is fastidiously clean, fond of comfort, affectionate but independent, and not geared toward obedience. He is also an active hunting dog who needs plenty of physical and mental exercise. Company, stimulus, and supervision are essential; a bored Basenji gravitates toward mischief. Famously barkless, he is certainly not mute but yodels, chortle crows, and, if distressed, shrieks like a siren.

First known to the West in the 19th century, the Basenji was not established in Britain until 1936, reaching the U.S. five years later. Since then he has become well-known but not overpopular.

WHAT colors?
Red and white, tan and white, black and white, brindle, black. Feet, chest, and tail tip are white, and white legs, blaze, and collar are also acceptable.

WHAT grooming does the coat need?
The short, fine coat requires very little attention: a weekly rubbing with a hound glove is sufficient. Basenjis are very clean dogs who wash themselves like cats, shed very little, and have no "doggy" smell.

HOW suitable are they as family dogs?
Not recommended for inexperienced families, as these dogs are demanding, challenging, and require a lot of input. They can be very good with older children if raised with them, but are usually too active and impish for households with toddlers.

WHAT type of home?
The Basenji is best suited to a country home, but can cope with

● *Although barkless, the Basenji has a wide range of vocal skills.*

city life, even in an apartment, if he has enough exercise and attention. Homes need to be Basenji proofed, as this breed is highly inquisitive and often destructive. High, secure fencing is a must: Basenjis are escape artists who can burrow under obstacles and scramble up chain-link fences with ease.

WHAT type of owner?
This is one for dedicated owners only, who appreciate the challenge of an independent, willful, catlike charmer with plenty of energy and a sense of mischief. Basenji owners need patience, stamina, and a sense of humor and should be prepared spend time on socializing, training, and daily exercise. Not a dog for obedience enthusiasts, or for anyo who will be seriously upset by damage to household items.

HOW compatible with other pets?
Basenjis are generally fine, even playful with other dogs, provided they are well socialized in puppyhood, although some are aggressive toward dogs of the sam sex. They have strong hunting and chasing instincts, and most should not be trusted with small pets.

HOW much exercise?
Basenjis are active dogs who need a fair amount of daily exercise. Their keen hunting drive and low obedience instinct mean that they should not be trusted off-leash in the vicinity of livestock, and are difficult to recall if they discover ar interesting scent. If there is a local lure chasing or racing society, this i an ideal way of using up a Basenji's abundant energy.

Character Trait	Poor	Average	Good	Excellent
Attitude toward other dogs				
Quietness				
Not destructive				
Protective behavior				
Not likely to stray				
Good with children				
Ease of training				

Original purpose: Hunting
Male height: 16-18 in (41-46 cm)
Female height: 15-17 in (38-43 cm)
Weight: 21-24 lb (9.5-11 kg)
Lifespan: c. 12 years

HOW easy to train?

Difficult. Basenjis are intelligent and quick to learn, but have no innate predisposition toward obedience. They are independent thinkers who need positive, firm, consistent, and reward-based training, and even then will generally obey only when it suits them. It is important to persist, even if only to keep them entertained and out of mischief.

Small dogs

WHAT good points?

Affectionate, gentle, quiet, clean, neat, independent, spirited, curious, self-confident, friendly, lacks "doggy" odor.

WHAT to be aware of?

High energy level, very demanding of time and attention, easily bored, can be very destructive, and can be noisy.

WHAT medical problems?

Generally healthy, but known disorders include hemolitic anemia, eye disorders (cataracts, progressive retinal atrophy), kidney disease, and lack of thyroid hormone (hypothyroidism).

● *Compact and smart, the Basenji is also energetic and willful.*

Medium Dogs

This group contains some of the most popular family dogs, animals that are big enough to play with the children but not too big for the average home. They include a selection to suit all tastes, from the elegant Whippet to the lumbering Basset Hound, and from the live-wire Border Collie to the laidback Bulldog.

Bulldog

A controversial breed, the Bulldog is physically exaggerated to an unusual degree, with his big head, foreshortened face, thickset body, massive chest, and bowed legs. These exaggerations are associated with health problems such as breathing difficulties, impaired activity, and whelping problems, and a poor specimen of Bulldog (of which there are sadly many) often has a reduced quality of life. Having said that, a well-bred, well-raised Bulldog is nothing like as handicapped as some claim and should be happy, healthy, and quite active. They are great characters, amiable, affectionate, strong-minded, and humorous, though probably not the best choice for a novice owner.

The Bulldog's ancestors were fighting dogs, longer-legged and more agile than today's breed, which developed in the 19th century. Modern variations such as the Regency and Victorian are reconstructions of the old type, not recognized by kennel clubs but growing in popularity.

WHAT colors?

Practically any color except black or black and tan; commonly brindle, red and fawn, with or without black mask or muzzle, white and pied (white and another color).

● A great character—but he may have some health problems.

WHAT grooming does the coat need?

Minimal; regular brushing with a hound glove to remove dead hairs is all that is needed. Facial wrinkles should be cleaned daily with cotton to prevent them from becoming damp and sore or from developing eczema.

HOW suitable are they as family dogs?

With his kind temperament and affectionate nature, the Bulldog is a great pet for a considerate family who want a less active dog but are prepared to give him the loving care and company he needs. He is excellent with sensible children, though puppies under two years old can be too exuberant and clumsy for the comfort of toddlers and the frail elderly.

WHAT type of home?

So long as he has his family, the Bulldog can be happy in the country or the city. He enjoys access to a yard, which should provide plenty of shade in summer.

WHAT type of owner?

The Bulldog is ideal for owners who don't want to walk miles but have plenty of time to spend with him, who appreciate a dog who is an individual and are not expecting rigid obedience. Owners also need to be confident and experienced and have plenty of patience with a dog who likes his own way, is physically strong, and as a puppy can be boisterous and mischievous.

HOW compatible with other pets?

This good-natured breed generally gets along very well with other pets. Some males can be rather challenging with other males.

HOW much exercise?

With their short legs, heavy muscles, and potential breathing problems, Bulldogs don't need a great deal of exercise, but they should not be allowed to become couch potatoes. Two half-hour walks a day at a steady pace, avoiding hot or humid weather, will keep them fit and sound.

HOW easy to train?

Difficult. Bulldogs are strong-minded, not to say obstinate, and have no innate tendency to obedience, although they are sensible dogs who are willing to

Character Trait	Poor	Average	Good	Excellent
Attitude toward other dogs				
Quietness				
Not destructive				
Protective behavior				
Not likely to stray				
Good with children				
Ease of training				

Original purpose: Bull baiting and companion
Male height: 12-15 in (30-38 cm)
Female height: 12-15 in (30-38 cm)
Weight: 40-50 lb (18.2-22.7 kg)
Lifespan: 8-12 years

cooperate if it makes sense to them. With firm, loving handling, some individuals have even been trained for competitive obedience and agility. Bullying a Bulldog will get you nowhere: Training needs to be positive and reward-based (most Bulldogs are highly motivated by food rewards).

WHAT good points?
Loyal, affectionate, good-humored, brave, protective, reliable, tenacious, fun-loving, excellent watchdog.

WHAT to be aware of?
Snorting, wheezing, snoring, and flatulence. Many health problems. Essential to choose breeder with care, and locate a vet who knows the breed.

Medium dogs

WHAT medical problems?
Bulldogs have more health problems than most breeds, including eye disorders (inturned eyelids, out-turned eyelids, cataracts, and faulty tear ducts), breathing difficulties, dental and skin problems, heart defects, elbow and kneecap dislocation (luxation), hip malformation (dysplasia), and vertebral deformities. They are prone to overheating and to bloat. Some have malformed (screw) tails so tight that the dog has difficulty defecating. Buying a puppy from anyone but a reputable breeder is asking for trouble.

Basset Hound

The Basset Hound is a gentleman—peaceful, mild, and naturally well-behaved—and also a dog of great character. Good-humored and affectionate, he fits well into family life. He is first and foremost a hound, so he needs more exercise than those short legs might suggest and is hard to recall once he starts following a scent. He also needs the company of his human "pack." A lonely Basset will make his feelings known loud and clear across the neighborhood. However, his equable temperament and engaging personality make him a delightful family member.

The Basset is an ancient breed developed in France as a pack hound to be followed on foot, and introduced into the U.K. and the U.S. in the late 19th century. Show standards have led to exaggeration of type. Today, working Bassets are longer-legged and less deep in the chest than the average pet or show dog.

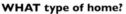

WHAT colors?

Any recognized hound color; typically tri-color (black, white, and tan) or bi-color (lemon and white).

WHAT grooming does the coat need?

The short, easy-care coat only needs brushing about twice weekly with a stiff bristle brush. However, the pendulous ears need frequent checking and cleaning, and folds of loose skin and wrinkles also need regular checks to ensure they are dry and not developing sores.

HOW suitable are they as family dogs?

Bassets make great family dogs. They are peaceful, sensible, and nonaggressive, gentle with children, and devoted to their family and friends. However, they may be too powerful and too stubborn for children to take them for walks without parental supervision, and time must be made for their exercise requirements.

WHAT type of home?

The Basset is a fairly big dog, and he needs space. He is happiest as a country dweller, but will adapt to apartment life and is quiet and sensible indoors, as long as he has several long walks a day. He does need company, or neighbors are likely to complain about his deep, musical voice.

WHAT type of owner?

Bassets are not for those who want a super clean home. They molt, drool, have quite a strong doggy smell, and, being low to the ground, pick up a lot of dirt. They need patient owners who appreciate a dog of independent character, enjoy long walks in all weather, and can provide plenty of company—Bassets hate being left alone.

HOW compatible with other pets?

The Basset's friendly nature means that he will usually get along well with other dogs. However, his innate hunting drive means that small household pets like cats and rabbits should be introduced with care.

HOW much exercise?

Bassets need a great deal of exercise—two good walks a day, including the opportunity to run free off-leash. Allowing a Basset to become overweight and unfit is likely to lead to back problems. However, growing puppies should not be overexercised while young. Build up walks gradually from six months onward.

HOW easy to train?

The Basset's reputation for being stubborn and self-willed is well earned. This is not a suitable breed

Character Trait	Poor	Average	Good	Excellent
Attitude toward other dogs				
Quietness				
Not destructive				
Protective behavior				
Not likely to stray				
Good with children				
Ease of training				

Original purpose: Hunting as pack hound
Male height: 13-15 in (33-38 cm)
Female height: 11-14 in (28-36 cm)
Weight: 40-60 lb (18-27 kg)
Lifespan: 10-12 years

for obedience enthusiasts. It is important to work on training the recall, or your Basset will follow his nose whenever he is off leash, happily deaf to your calls.

WHAT good points?

Good-natured, cheerful, companionable, gentle, peaceful, friendly, reliable, affectionate, sensible, great with children, oodles of personality.

WHAT to be aware of?

Physical exaggeration means potential health problems. Stubborn nature means that sensible discipline is essential—males can be quite dominant if not adequately trained from puppyhood.

Medium dogs

WHAT medical problems?

The long back means a risk of back problems, especially if a dog is allowed to become overweight. Elbow deformity (dysplasia) occurs in the breed, as do eye problems, and skin wrinkles may develop dermatitis. The breed is prone to gastric torsion (bloat), so avoid taking a Basset out for a strenuous walk immediately after mealtime.

● *A dog of great character, the Basset is good-humored but more stubborn than his sweet expression may suggest.*

Staffordshire Bull Terrier

The Staffordshire Bull Terrier is impressive and imposing— he has well-defined musculature, strong jaws and large teeth, a broad chest, and loose shoulders allied to a low-slung body. It should come as no surprise to know that his ancestors were bred for fighting and bull baiting. They were prized for their courage and tenacity, of course, but also for their levelheaded and obedient nature—this dog was not a hot-headed brawler, but a cool, calculating, and big-hearted opponent who would not flinch from taking on a larger animal and then hanging on for grim death.

The breed derives from the crossing of an Old English Bulldog with a type of terrier, possibly the extinct Black and Tan. The resulting dog combined the strength and tenacity of a bulldog with the agility and quick-wittedness of a terrier. When bull baiting and dog fighting were banned, the Staffy was developed as a reliable companion breed. It was recognized by the Kennel Club in 1935 and by the AKC in 1974.

WHAT colors?
Red, fawn, white, black, blue, or brindle, or any one of these colors with white.

WHAT grooming does the coat need?
The coat is smooth, short, and close. A daily five-minute grooming session with a bristle brush or a hound glove will remove dead hair and encourage the coat to shine. Most Staffies like water and enjoy the occasional bath.

HOW suitable are they as family dogs?
A marvelous family pet, Staffordshire Bull Terriers are devoted and loyal companions. They dote on their owners and are remarkably fond of children—they nicknamed "the nanny dog." They have a tremendous sense of fun and love playing games like chase and fetch. They are also very protective of their family circle and so are an excellent choice of companion for women who live alone.

WHAT type of home?
These are highly adaptable dogs— despite their pronounced musculature and very powerful, athletic outline, they do not have to be kept in acres of open country- side. Staffies are happy living in an urban environment, even in an apartment without a yard, provided that they get regular exercise every day and can have access to open spaces for uninhibited play and recreation.

WHAT type of owner?
For the right owner, this breed is an absolute prince among dogs, offering unswerving loyalty and constant devotion. But prospective owners must be aware that they have to make an equal commitment to the dog; this is not the right breed for a "hands off" owner. They are athletic and vigorous animals that seek companionship and entertain- ment; the ideal owner should also be an active individual who will enjoy energetic bouts of exercise with their four-legged friend— certainly not the right choice for the infirm or housebound.

HOW compatible with other pets?
Staffordshire Bull Terriers are not afraid to fight, and so care should exercised when introducing them other pets or when out walking when you are likely to come acro other dogs. Provided that puppies have been properly socialized dur their formative weeks of growth, they should respond positively to other animals and members of the family circle. If you are unsure of your dog's likely reactions to othe dogs, it makes sense to walk him a leash while you assess his reactions to the outside world.

Character Trait	Poor	Average	Good	Excellent
Attitude toward other dogs				
Quietness				
Not destructive				
Protective behavior				
Not likely to stray				
Good with children				
Ease of training				

Place of origin: **Britain**

Original purpose: Fighting dog and companion
Male height: 14-16 in (35.5-41 cm)
Female height: 14-16 in (35.5-41 cm)
Weight: 24-38 lb (11-17 kg)
Lifespan: 12-14 years

HOW much exercise?

Staffies need more exercise than many other breeds. Regular walks and play sessions are a must, and they will thrive on an even more energetic regime. Staffies need to be well-exercised both to maintain their physical condition and to keep them mentally stimulated.

HOW easy to train?

This breed is highly intelligent and responds well to training. Owners, however, have to be firm (not harsh) and consistent in their training exercises, as Staffies can display a stubborn streak. They respond best to praise and encouragement; reprimands and anger will dampen their spirits.

WHAT good points?

Tenacious, strong, fun-loving, devoted, fearless, reliable, and even-tempered, easy to groom.

WHAT to be aware of?

While this is a friendly and companionable breed, his history means that he has a combative and fearless character that can lead to confrontations with other dogs if you are not in control of the situation. This dog demands a lot of attention; don't consider a Staffordshire if you are not 100 percent committed to the breed.

WHAT medical problems?

These terriers are strong and robust dogs that do not suffer from many congenital illnesses. Tumors can be a problem, as can cataracts and kidney stones.

Medium dogs

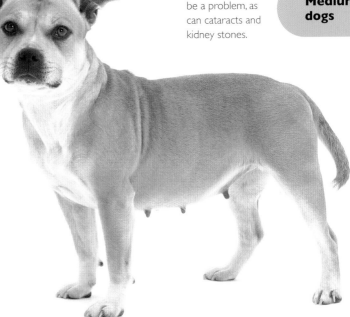

American Staffordshire Terrier *Other names: American Pit Bull Terrier*

19th century dog-fighting men combined Bulldog and terrier blood to produce the ideal dog for their savage sport. Their "bull-and-terrier" creation developed in different directions in different continents. In Britain, it became the foundation of the Staffordshire Bull Terrier, while stock exported to the U.S. around 1870 developed into a larger, heavier breed, recognized by the AKC in 1936 as the American Staffordshire Terrier.

The American Staffordshire Terrier (AmStaff) is a wonderful dog in the right hands, intelligent, good humored, and eager to please. He makes a devoted companion, a versatile worker, and an outstanding protection dog. However, his fighting ancestry, strong will, powerful build, and potential for aggression make good socialization and expert training essential. This i not a suitable choice for novices or for anyone who cannot earn his respect.

WHAT colors?

Any color, solid, parti-colored, or patched is permissible; but all white, more than 80 percent white, black and tan, and liver are not encouraged.

WHAT grooming does the coat need?

The short coat requires minimal care. Weekly brushing with a firm bristle brush to remove dead hairs will keep it in perfect condition.

HOW suitable are they as family dogs?

A well-bred, well socialized AmStaff is a great family dog and trustworthy with children. However, only breeders who place a high priority on good temperament should be considered, and only owners who are already experienced with this breed should consider an AmStaff when looking for a family dog.

WHAT type of home?

This active breed is best suited to a country home, but will adapt to city life as long as he has enough exercise. Secure fencing is a must.

WHAT type of owner?

Only confident, strong-minded, and experienced owners who are thoroughly committed to a proper regime of socialization, training, and exercise should consider this breed. Potential owners should also consider the serious impact of breed-specific legislation. AmStaffs are banned in some countries and subject to draconian controls in others.

HOW compatible with other pets?

Be very careful. Thorough socializatio is essential to ensure that an AmStaff does not become aggressive toward other dogs. He should be supervised with other animals at all times—if another dog provokes him, he will no take it lying down. In ideal circumstances, he will be trustworthy with cats in his own household. In general, he is not recommended for home with other pets.

HOW much exercise?

This powerful and active breed need plenty of regular exercise. However, he should be kept leashed in public t avoid any risk of a fight, to reassure passersby in view of the breed's poo public image, and in many areas this i a legal requirement.

HOW easy to train?

Experienced handlers will find the AmStaff a joy to work with, eager to perform whatever task is set him. However, he needs firm, confident leadership, as he is strong-willed and has a mind of his own. It is a mistake

Character Trait	Poor	Average	Good	Excellent
Attitude toward other dogs				
Quietness				
Not destructive				
Protective behavior				
Not likely to stray				
Good with children				
Ease of training				

Original purpose: Fighting
Male height: 18-19 in (46-48 cm)
Female height: 17-18 in (43-46 cm)
Weight: 57-67 lb (26-30 kg)
Lifespan: 12-14 years

imagine that tough dogs need tough treatment. The AmStaff responds to praise and motivational training far better than to a domineering approach.

WHAT good points?

In the right hands, the AmStaff is a dog of many virtues, brave, loyal, affectionate, intelligent, responsive, and good-natured.

WHAT to be aware of?

In the wrong hands, the AmStaff is potentially a dangerous dog. Be aware of breed-specific legislation and its implications, including poor public image and refusal of many insurers to consider this breed.

WHAT medical problems?

Generally a healthy breed, the AmStaff may suffer from hip malformation (dysplasia), hereditary cataracts, heart problems, skin disorders, and ataxia (an inherited disorder of the nervous system).

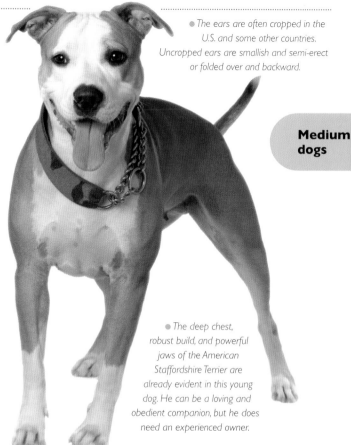

● The ears are often cropped in the U.S. and some other countries. Uncropped ears are smallish and semi-erect or folded over and backward.

Medium dogs

● The deep chest, robust build, and powerful jaws of the American Staffordshire Terrier are already evident in this young dog. He can be a loving and obedient companion, but he does need an experienced owner.

Australian Cattle Dog

This compact, powerful, and workmanlike herder was developed in the 19th century by Australian cattlemen specifically for the harsh conditions of the outback. Crossing imported drovers' dogs with native dingoes, they produced a tough and tireless dog to drive cattle across the wild country of the outback, a job that required brains and stubbornness as well as high energy and stamina. Consequently, he makes a great companio for an active owner with plenty of work for him t do, but he is likely to prove too challenging for th average family.

Given enough physical and mental occupation the ACD is a devoted and stimulating companion, ready to go anywhere and tackle any challenge. Intelligent and quick to learn, he is nonetheless a dog with a mind of his own who doesn't do slavis obedience — if he thinks you are wrong, he will d things his way.

WHAT colors?
Red speckled, sometimes with red markings; blue, blue speckled, or blue mottled. Blues may have tan markings on the face, chest, legs, and underside.

WHAT grooming does the coat need?
The short, weather-resistant coat benefits from a weekly brushing with a firm bristle brush, with extra attention when it molts once or twice a year.

HOW suitable are they as family dogs?
For an active family with older, sensible children—over the age of ten—the ACD makes a loving and protective companion who wants to be closely involved in all family activities. He will guard the children with his life; he will probably also nip them if he thinks they are misbehaving. He is not recommended for small children, who are likely to bring out his urge to herd by biting their heels.

WHAT type of home?
The only suitable home for an ACD is one that can provide work to occupy him. With an owner committed to canine activities such as working trials or agility, he may cope with life in a city, provided he has a securely fenced yard. However, he is much better suited to life in the country. Trying to accommodate such an active breed in an apartment would almost certainly be a recipe for disaster

WHAT type of owner?
Not one for the novice, the ACI needs an active and confident owner whose way of life include commitment to canine activities. Potential owners should be able provide firm, fair leadership—th a strong-willed dog who will ride roughshod over wimps—and be content to spend most of their t with their dog. ACDs don't thriv solitude. A bored, lonely ACD is potential wrecking machine, and noisy to boot.

HOW compatible with other pets?
Small furries are there to be cha And eaten. ACDs will live with c they are brought up together, bu will still count neighboring cats a game. If sensibly socialized, they generally fine with other dogs, b can be same-sex aggressive.

HOW much exercise?
Lots. This dog needs long daily w

Character Trait	Poor	Average	Good	Excellent
Attitude toward other dogs	■			
Quietness	■			
Not destructive	■			
Protective behavior				■
Not likely to stray			■	
Good with children		■		
Ease of training			■	

Original purpose: Cattle herder
Male height: 18-20 in (46-51 cm)
Female height: 17-19 in (43-48 cm)
Weight: 31-51 lb (14-23 kg)
Lifespan: 12-15 years

(at least two hours), but he also needs mental work, so activities should include training exercises and stimulating games such as Frisbee chasing or hide-and-seek. He is an ideal hiking or running companion, and will enjoy agility, flyball, tracking, etc.

HOW easy to train?
Clever and a quick learner, the ACD is also strong-willed and dominant. Handlers need to be just as strong-minded and able to establish leadership without bullying tactics. Persistence and consistency are essential. You will need to earn this dog's respect before he is prepared to listen; once that is achieved, his capacity for learning is endless.

WHAT good points?
Loyal, intelligent, quick learner, protective, dedicated to his family, eager to work, fast, and agile.

WHAT to be aware of?
Hardheaded and stubborn. Strong drive for herding and heeling (biting ankles), for chasing, and for guarding—likely to nip anyone he thinks suspicious. Prone to biting, he needs to learn restraint in puppyhood. Highly destructive if left alone; very vocal. Short hairs molt everywhere.

WHAT medical problems?
Inherited disorders include eye problems (progressive retinal atrophy, primary lens luxation), deafness, and hip and elbow malformation (dysplasia). All breeding stock should be hip and elbow tested and have current eye certificates; and all pups should be hearing tested.

Medium dogs

● *ACDs come in striking colors, but puppies are born white (apart from any solid patches on face or body). Red or black hairs grow through the white coat later to produce the ticked effect.*

Soft Coated Wheaten Terrier
Other names: Irish Soft Coated Wheaten T...

Combining a perennial shaggy-dog appeal with the game terrier spirit, the Wheaten is a merry, active, medium-sized dog who makes an excellent pet. His ancestors were Irish farm dogs, so he is somewhat steadier and less aggressive than some terrier breeds though as energetic, enthusiastic, and self-opinionated as any. Bouncy and sociable, he enjoys a close involvement in family life and needs time, attention, and exercise for mind and body to keep him out of mischief. The silky coat, which adds so much to his appeal, does take considerable, regular maintenance, so this is not a breed for busy owners.

Wheatens were part of Irish family life for many years before the breed achieved recognition—in 1937 in its native land, nine years later in the UK, and not until 1973 in the U.S. Still not a breed that everyone recognizes in the street, they are deservedly growing in popularity, both as family companions and as show dogs.

WHAT colors?

Clear light wheaten—the shade of ripening wheat. Dark shading on ears not uncommon. Puppies are born dark, lightening gradually, and may not clear to the correct color until 18-24 months old.

WHAT grooming does the coat need?

The coat is soft, silky, and abundant; loosely waved or curly, and does not shed. If neglected, it mats and tangles. Regular (ideally daily) grooming down to the skin is essential, using a pin brush followed by a metal comb to ensure that no tangles are left. Show dogs are trimmed to create a neat outline; pet owners often clip some of the hair covering the eyes to improve the dog's vision.

HOW suitable are they as family dogs?

This is a great dog for a lively family willing to include him in all their activities. Wheatens are very good with sensible children. Their sense of fun and abundant energy makes them great playmates, although like most terriers they can be too excitable to be recommended for households in which very young children are living.

WHAT type of home?

Wheatens are just as happy in the city as in the country as long as they have reasonable exercise and plenty to do. They will appreciate a yard, which needs to be securely fenced—otherwise they are very likely to disappear over or under inadequate barriers in pursuit of trespassing cats.

WHAT type of owner?

This is a breed for an active, strong willed owner who appreciates an exuberant and extroverted dog and has plenty of time for socialization, exercise, play, training, and grooming. Wheatens are not part-time dogs; they require a lot of commitment—which they will repay in full.

HOW compatible with other pets?

Early socialization is essential to ensure that terrier bossiness does not become aggression, but if accustomed to other dogs in puppyhood, the Wheaten will be friendly and playful—though if he meets with aggression, he won't back down. He is fine with cats in own household if raised with them, but generally not to be trusted with strange cats or small pets.

Character Trait	Poor	Average	Good	Excellent
Attitude toward other dogs	▪	▪		
Quietness		▪		
Not destructive			▪	
Protective behavior			▪	
Not likely to stray	▪			
Good with children			▪	
Ease of training	▪			

Original purpose: Vermin hunter and farm dog
Male height: 18-19 in (46-49.5 cm)
Female height: 17-18 in (44-46 cm)
Weight: 35-45 lb (16-20.5 kg)
Lifespan: 13-14 years

HOW much exercise?

Plenty. This active breed will take all the exercise he can get, at the least two half-hour walks a day plus playtime. Be careful when he is off-leash, as he has a strong chase instinct like many terriers, and will disappear over the horizon after rabbits, squirrels, or any other four-legged temptation that may cross his path. That beautiful coat will need considerable attention after a muddy country walk.

HOW easy to train?

Difficult. He is a terrier, a bossy dog who needs to be persuaded kindly but firmly that he is not the pack leader. He can be trained, but it takes time and dedication, and he is never likely to excel at formal obedience. Keep training sessions short, reward-based, and fun to get his attention and maintain his focus.

WHAT good points?

Happy, good-tempered, confident, spirited, bold, exuberant, affectionate, lively, inquisitive, good watchdog.

WHAT to be aware of?

Highly boisterous and bouncy. Early socialization needed to prevent aggression toward strange dogs. A heavy commitment to regular coat care. is required.

Medium dogs

WHAT medical problems?

The main problem is a tendency toward kidney disorders (renal dysplasia), with some occurrence of hip deformity (dysplasia), and sensitivity to anesthesia.

Chinese Shar-Pei _Other names: Chinese Fighting Dog_

A striking-looking breed, the Chinese Shar-Pei has a hippo's head, dramatically wrinkled skin, and the bristly fur that gave him his name (literally "sandpaper skin"). Despite his scowling expression, he is a calm, good-natured dog who makes a great companion. Though, like other Oriental breeds, he is quite independent and needs to establish a relationship of mutual respect with his owner. Excessive skin folds cause skin and eye disorders, so look for responsibl breeders producing unexaggerated stock.

From near extinction in the 1960s to fashion icon today, the dog with a skin several sizes too large has come a long way. Dating back to at least the 13th century, the Shar-Pei was the all-purpose dog of Chinese peasant farmers, used for hunting, guarding, herding, and dog-fighting contests. The breed nearly died out under Communist rule in China, but was revived by dedicated breeders in Hong Kong, reaching the West in the 1970s.

WHAT colors?
Black, red, fawn, cream, chocolate, blue, apricot; may have dark mask and often has darker shading down back and ears with lighter shading on underparts. Parti-color ("flowered") dogs are unacceptable by AKC standards, but some breeders consider them an authentic breed color.

WHAT grooming does the coat need?
Low-maintenance. Groom once a week with a hound glove or bristle brush to maintain healthy skin. The tiny ears need regular cleaning with cotton swabs.

HOW suitable are they as family dogs?
Very. This is a breed that is happiest as a family dog and is particularly good with children. Early socialization is important to ensure that his natural aloofness with strangers does not develop into suspicion, and new owners should research the breed to familiarize themselves with his health needs.

WHAT type of home?
The Shar-Pei is happy in the city or country as long as he is part of the family. He can adapt to apartment living if he has enough daily exercise. He does appreciate a large yard where he can play and space to run.

WHAT type of owner?
This is a dog for owners looking for calm companionship; capable of firm, sensitive leadership and who have time for training, exercise, mental stimulation, and affection. Shar-Peis need company and are not suitable for owner who are out all day, leaving them alone. They may tur out to be too strong-min for novices.

HOW compatible with other pets?
Early socialization is importan it is with all guard breeds. A properly socialized Shar-Pei v be good with other dogs, although there is always the possibility of intermale aggression being expressed. He is okay with l own cats but has strong chase instincts and should not be trustec with strange cats or with farm livestock.

HOW much exercise?
This is an adaptable breed that wi happy with as much or as little exercise as is offered. Given a larg yard, they will exercise themselves quite well with active play. Howeve regular walks are enjoyed and goo for their health. Aim for two brisk daily walks, but avoid exercise in h weather as this breed overheats e

Character Trait	Poor	Average	Good	Excellent
Attitude toward other dogs	▓			
Quietness			▓	
Not destructive		▓		
Protective behavior				▓
Not likely to stray		▓		
Good with children		▓		
Ease of training			▓	

Original purpose: Guarding, hunting
Male height: 18-20 in (46-51 cm)
Female height: 18-20 in (46-51 cm)
Weight: 45-60 lb (20.4-27.2 kg)
Lifespan: 8-10 years

HOW easy to train?

Given confident leadership and firm but gentle training, this intelligent breed can be trained to a high standard. Strong-minded and independent, they will only obey when a mutual respect has developed. They are quick to learn but easily bored with constant repetition. Keep training sessions varied to maintain interest.

WHAT good points?

Calm, independent, good-natured, affectionate, devoted to owners, playful, intelligent, excellent watchdog.

WHAT to be aware of?

Fashionable breeds attract commercial breeders producing unhealthy stock. Avoid puppies whose parents have excessive wrinkles and skin folds. Bristly coat can cause a rash in some people. Loud snoring. May need special care with diet.

WHAT medical problems?

A range of skin disorders, inward-turning eyelids (entropion) and drooping lower lids (ectropion), lens dislocation, blocked tear ducts, lack of thyroid hormone (hypothyroidism), kidney problems, "swollen hock syndrome" or "familial Shar-Pei fever" (inherited condition leading to bouts of joint swelling and fever), gastric torsion (bloat), some hip deformity (dysplasia).

Medium dogs

Whippet

A small but workmanlike sighthound, the Whippet was developed as "the poor man's greyhound," providing rabbits for the pot and entertainment in the form of coursing and racing. Although he retains his hunting and running instincts, he makes an ideal pet, quiet and very affectionate. His convenient size, easy-care coat, and gentle disposition make him an undemanding companion. All he needs is love, exercise, and a cozy bed. This racing dog can reach 35 mph (56 km/h) in 15 seconds and loves to run, but he is a sprinter, not marathon runner, and needs only moderate exercise —at home, he is a regular couch potato who loves hi comfort.

Whippet-type dogs have been known since ancient times, but the modern Whippet was probably the creation of 19th century miners in the north of England. AKC recognition in 1890, gave him social acceptability as show dog and smart companion.

WHAT colors?
Any color or mixture of colors, including black, blue, brindle, cream, red, fawn, white, and parti-color.

WHAT grooming does the coat need?
The fine, short coat is very low maintenance. A weekly brushing with a rubber hound glove, followed by a swift polish with a scrap of silk or chamois leather, will keep his coat in perfect condition.

HOW suitable are they as family dogs?
Highly suitable. This is one of the best family dogs. He is gentle, affectionate, responsive, and has a natural affinity for children. He fits into most lifestyles and is very adaptable in terms of exercise. Families should be prepared for the fact that, before growing up into sensible dogs, Whippet puppies are likely to be mischievous whirlwinds who need lots of attention.

● Graceful and elegant, the Whippet is nonetheless a highly functional worker who retains his hunting instincts.

WHAT type of home?
Happy to live wherever his owners choose, the Whippet makes a great sporting dog in the country or in the city. Provided he has his regular walks, he will live happily in an apartment. He appreciates a yard and should have access to a park or other area where he can safely enjoy running off-leash.

WHAT type of owner?
The Whippet is a great choice for a gentle, easygoing, and reasonably active owner who wants loving companionship and has access to a secure park or area where this little sighthound can run safely. His calmness and quietness at home make him suitable for a single elderly owner, but he is just as well suited to family life with children for playmates.

HOW compatible with other pets?
Whippets are generally friendly with other dogs and with cats in the same household. They are bred to chase, so they should not be trusted with small pets such as rabbits or guinea pigs, and nextdoor's cat is likely to be viewed as fair game.

HOW much exercise?
Medium—think in terms of 2 miles (3 km) a day plus 20 minutes' free

Character Trait	Poor	Average	Good	Excellent
Attitude toward other dogs				
Quietness				
Not destructive				
Protective behavior				
Not likely to stray				
Good with children				
Ease of training				

Original purpose: Rabbiting, racing
Male height: 19-22 in (48-56 cm)
Female height: 18-21 in (46-53 cm)
Weight: 27-30 lb (12.5-13.5 kg)
Lifespan: 12-15 years

running in a secure place, although your Whippet will enjoy a great deal more exercise if that suits your lifestyle. As a sighthound, he must be kept on a leash near traffic or livestock. This breed thoroughly enjoys organized activities such as lure coursing, whippet racing, agility, and flyball.

HOW easy to train?

Fairly easy. Whippets are not as geared toward obedience as some breeds, but more trainable than most sight-hounds. Alert, intelligent, and eager to please, they respond to positive training methods with plenty of encouragement and rewards. A heavy-handed approach will only upset this sensitive breed. Because of the Whippet's strong chase instinct, a lot of work needs to be put in on the recall.

WHAT good points?

Gentle, affectionate, adaptable, good-natured, loyal, clean, quiet, very good with children, low maintenance.

WHAT to be aware of?

Strong chasing instinct. Feels the cold. No sense of heights—beware open windows. Puppies are real live wires (and take two to four years to grow up and mature).

WHAT medical problems?

Medium dogs

This very healthy breed is largely free from genetic problems, although progressive retinal atrophy (degeneration of the light receptor cells in the eyes) occurs in some blood-lines. Thin skin prone to damage from brambles, barbed wire, and so on.

● *Typical of sighthounds, the Whippet loves to run but also revels in a couch potato lifestyle between bouts of exercise.*

Border Collie

Often considered the canine Einstein, the Border Collie is highly intelligent and highly trainable, excelling not only at sheepdog trials but at competitive obedience, agility, flyball, search and rescue, and as a sniffer dog. This is a dog that could be described as a workaholic. He lives for work in one form or another, and becomes highly frustrated if not kept occupied. Suited to highly dog-oriented homes only, he needs early socialization, sensitive handling, and a major commitment of time and attention. Given plenty of stimulation, exercise, and employment, he is a loyal, affectionate, highly responsive and rewarding companion—but not a dog to take on lightly.

Developed in the hills of the English, Scottish, and Welsh borders, the breed was famous worldwide as a worker long before receiving belated AKC recognition in the 1990s. Today it has added success in the show ring to its many achievements.

WHAT colors?

Black and white is the most common variety, but other accepted colors include tri-color, brown and white, and red or blue merle (a sort of marbled effect distinguished by the presence of irregular dark blotches against a lighter background of the same basic pigment).

WHAT grooming does the coat need?

Two coat types are recognized, smooth and rough. Smooth coats need only a weekly grooming with a stiff bristle or slicker brush to remove dead hairs. Rough coats should be groomed daily, paying particular attention to the areas behind the ears and under the tail.

HOW suitable are they as family dogs?

The question should be: How suitable is a particular family for a Border Collie? For those with the time and inclination to keep him happy and occupied, the Border can be a great family member. Many families cannot commit enough time and effort, and a frustrated Border is a major liability. Not recommended with young children: Borders can be hyperactive and overexcitable, and their innate herding instincts can lead to nipping.

WHAT type of home?

This highly active breed really needs a country home, and certainly a fair-sized yard with a very secure fence.

WHAT type of owner?

Only energetic people who can provide companionship and have a keen interest in training should consider this breed. He needs to be kept busy, and is emphatically not a dog for couch potatoes. He is not an ideal first dog.

HOW compatible with other pets?

Generally good with other animals, but they do need sensible early socialization to prevent nervous aggression. The strong herding instinct may be a problem with other pets.

HOW much exercise?

Probably the most active breed of dog, the Border Collie needs a great deal of exercise and is absolutely tireless. However, physical exercise alone will simply keep him on his toes, and must be balanced by mental stimulation to avoid frustration and hyperactivity. Activities such as agility and flyball are a great way to combine exercise for body and mind.

HOW easy to train?

Highly intelligent, exceptionally sensitive, and a quick learner, the Border is very trainable in the right

Character Trait	Poor	Average	Good	Excellent
Attitude toward other dogs		■		
Quietness		■		
Not destructive	■			
Protective behavior			■	
Not likely to stray		■		
Good with children			■	
Ease of training				■

Original purpose: Sheepdog
Male height: 20-23 in (51-58.5 cm)
Female height: 18-21 in (46-53 cm)
Weight: 30-49 lb (14-22 kg)
Lifespan: 10-14 years

...ands. With unfocused or inconsistent handling, he will learn bad habits just as easily. His incredibly quick responses mean that his handler needs to be equally quick to keep one step ahead. Lessons need to be challenging and stimulating to keep his interest.

WHAT good points?

Keen, alert, responsive, highly intelligent, sensitive, loyal, faithful, energetic, good watchdog.

WHAT to be aware of?

One of the most demanding breeds, he needs work or can be destructive, often developing stereotypic behavior (repeated meaningless actions such as tail chasing) if frustrated. Good socialization essential.

WHAT medical problems?

This is generally a hardy breed, but it can suffer from inherited eye disorders (Collie eye anomaly, progressive retinal atrophy) and joint problems. Breeding stock should be eye tested and hip scored, and puppies should be hearing tested.

Medium dogs

● *Always alert, this working dog has unlimited resources of energy.*

Bull Terrier *Other names: English Bull Terrier*

A powerful dog with a uniquely egg-shaped head, the Bull Terrier originated as a 19th-century fighting breed combining Bulldog and terrier blood, but by the 1860s a more elegant show strain had developed. Despite his ancestry, the modern Bully is first and foremost a cheerful companion, enthusiastic, fun-loving and has a great sense of humor. He loves human company and is generally good-tempered, although early socialization is vital to ensure that he is safe with strange dogs.

The Bully is a lovable clown who can be gentle and reliable, but he is not a dog for the novice owner. Strong-willed and physically powerful, he needs firm, patient handling. He can be hard to live with, being boisterous, destructive if bored, and often more into playing the fool than working on obedience. Potential owners should also think about public perception of bull breeds and breed-specific legislation.

WHAT colors?

Pure white, white with colored patches on head, brindle, black, red, and tri-color. Colored dogs may have white markings on chest, under-belly, tail tip, socks, and facial blaze.

WHAT grooming does the coat need?

Mimimal. Daily to weekly brushing with a hound glove or hard-bristled brush will keep the coat healthy.

HOW suitable are they as family dogs?

In the right hands the Bully is an outstanding family dog, affectionate, stable, and gentle with sensible children. He is not recommended for households with very young children, as he does not tolerate teasing very well, can be possessive with food, and as a youngster (up to approximately three years old) can be too rough and rowdy for the safety of little ones.

WHAT type of home?

This people-oriented breed can thrive in a city or country, but city dogs need a secure yard with strong fencing—Bullies can and will barge through flimsy barriers. Owners should have access to areas where a Bully can be exercised safely off-leash to burn off energy.

WHAT type of owner?

This energetic, stubborn, powerful breed needs an active, experienced owner, assertive enough to cope with a dominant breed but kind and affectionate, ready to appreciate a dog with personality plus, and possessed of a strong sense of humor. Owners must also have plenty of time for training, exercise, play, and company—Bullies are miserable if left alone.

HOW compatible with other pets?

Given plenty of early socialization and training, many Bullies live happily and lovingly with cats and other dogs; others are best as sole pets. A great deal of planning and care is important when introducing a Bull Terrier to other animals. His ancestors were bred to kill animals and he often still has a strong prey drive. Males can be dominant with other males and, although not naturally quarrelsome, this breed will never back down from a challenge.

HOW much exercise?

This active breed needs plenty of exercise, although not all Bullies will agree with you on this point. They are often quite content to be couch potatoes, and have to be persuaded of the importance of

Character Trait	Poor	Average	Good	Excellent
Attitude toward other dogs				
Quietness				
Not destructive				
Protective behavior				
Not likely to stray				
Good with children				
Ease of training				

Original purpose: Fighting and ratting
Male height: 18-24 in (46-61cm)
Female height: 18-24 in (46-61cm)
Weight: 52-62 lb (24-28 kg)
Lifespan: 11-13 years

keeping fit. Be careful where you let a Bull Terrier off leash. If he meets a badly behaved dog, there could be trouble.

HOW easy to train?

Moderate to difficult. Bullies are not naturals for the obedience ring, although it is essential that they be trained to an acceptable standard of behavior. A firm, patient approach with plenty of positive reinforcement in the form of food rewards or toys will achieve the best results.

WHAT good points?

Cheerful, affectionate, friendly, active, courageous, protective, entertaining, extroverted, stable, and reliable in the right hands, great sense of humor.

WHAT to be aware of?

Not for owners who work full-time. Not the easiest breed to train. Enjoys chewing and has powerful jaws: provide tough chew toys to deflect his interest away from furniture. Tends to believe that, given enough determination, anything from shoes to trash cans is edible.

Medium dogs

WHAT medical problems?

Some Bull Terriers suffer from kidney disease (familial nephropathy), heart defects, kneecap dislocation (patellar luxation), skin problems, and (especially whites) inherited deafness. Behavioral problems such as compulsive tail chasing do also occur.

● *Once known as the "Gladiator," the Bully is no longer required to be aggressive—but he still needs watching with other dogs.*

Brittany *Other names: Brittany Spaniel*

France's favorite pointing dog, the Brittany is the smallest and perhaps most enthusiastic of the Continental all-around gundogs bred to hunt, point, and retrieve game. He is enthusiastic, energetic, and tireless, very much a working dog who needs plenty of exercise for body and mind. He is also sweet-natured and affectionate, and makes a wonderful companion and family dog—provided he has suitable outlets for his abundant energy such as fieldwork, obedience, or agility.

The Brittany resulted from a happy combination of French and English breeds. Workmanlike Breton spaniels, dating back to at least the 1700s and known as Fougeres ("high-spirited"), were crossed in the 19th century with setters and pointers brought over by British sportsmen, resulting in a superb gundog that achieved breed recognition in the early 1900s. Having reached the U.S. in the 1920s and the U.K. not until the 1970s, the Brittany is now deservedly popular worldwide.

WHAT colors?

Brittanys come in a rainbow spectrum of orange and white, liver and white, black and white, roan, or tricolor (liver, white, and orange or black, white, and orange), with spots, ticking or flecking—no two dogs are identically colored.

WHAT grooming does the coat need?

The flat, medium-length coat is moderately low maintenance, needing little more than 10 minutes brushing and combing twice a week. Some individuals have more feathering on ears and legs, which will need extra attention. Check the ears and any feathering for burrs and twigs after country walks.

HOW suitable are they as family dogs?

If he has plenty of stimulation, exercise, and employment, the Brittany is a wonderful family dog who loves attention. He is excellent with children—owners often comment that he will cooperate with the children of the family better than with his master! However, if he has no job to do, he may be too hyperactive to make a good family pet, and as a youngster is often too exuberant for the comfort of small children.

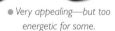

● *Very appealing—but too energetic for some.*

WHAT type of home?

Better suited to country than city life, the Brittany needs access to land where he can enjoy long, interesting walks and off-leash gallops. He is very active indoors and needs a fair-sized, securely fenced yard where he can burn off some energy.

WHAT type of owner?

The Brittany is not for couch potatoes. Only active people who enjoy long country walks in all weather and have time for training and stimulating canine activities should consider this high-energy breed. This is a dog that does not respond well to insensitive handling and needs a gentle owner who can be firm and consistent without being tough.

HOW compatible with other pets?

If properly socialized in puppyhood, the Brittany is generally friendly with other dogs and good with cats in his own household—though strange cats had better be careful. This is a hunting breed with an innate chase instinct, so small pets such as rabbits are best kept safely out of harm's way.

Character Trait	Poor	Average	Good	Excellent
Attitude toward other dogs				
Quietness				
Not destructive				
Protective behavior				
Not likely to stray				
Good with children				
Ease of training				

Original purpose: Hunting, pointing, and retrieving game
Male height: 19-20 in (48-51 cm)
Female height: 18-19 in (46-48 cm)
Weight: 30-40 lb (13.5-18 kg)
Lifespan: 13-15 years

HOW much exercise?

This very active dog needs long, interesting walks plus one or two hours' free running every day. Mental exercise is just as important, so if he is not working as a gundog owners should consider agility, competitive obedience, or working trials to keep him happy and occupied. He is not suited to unemployment!

HOW easy to train?

Eager to please and a quick learner, the Brittany is highly trainable, although some individuals can be stubborn and need gentle but firm direction. Stick to a calm, consistent, reward-based approach. This is a very sensitive dog that reacts badly to rough handling, but responds well to encouragement.

WHAT good points?

Affectionate, sensitive, responsive, eager to please, intelligent, enthusiastic, energetic, good-natured, gentle.

WHAT to be aware of?

High working drive and energy, frustrated if unemployed. Needs a lot of attention and may suffer from separation anxiety.

WHAT medical problems?

Some hip malformation (dysplasia) reported; also occasional progressive retinal atrophy (degeneration of the light receptor cells in the eyes), epilepsy, hemophilia, and some skin disorders.

Medium dogs

 A great gundog, and a wonderful companion in the right hands.

English Springer Spaniel

One of the larger spaniels, the handsome and versatile English Springer is popular as a working gundog, a family pet, and as a sniffer dog, detecting anything from drugs to illegal immigrants. Extroverted and enthusiastic, he has endless vitality and stamina and really loves to work—and to play. This is not a dog for anyone seeking a placid companion, as he is strong-willed, active, and excitable. His good humor, sociable nature, and willingness to learn make him a wonderful companion for active owners who can provide the mental and physical exercise he needs.

Spaniels developed to assist falconers and later shooters by finding, flushing, and retrieving game. The tallest of the land spaniels, the Springer was recognized as a separate breed in 1910 by the AKC. Today, show and working strains have diverged, the latter, which are smaller and stockier, being unsuited for pet life because of their strong working drive.

WHAT colors?
Liver and white, black and white, or either of these with tan markings.

WHAT grooming does the coat need?
The Springer's coat is easy to keep in good condition with a brisk daily brushing and combing. Ears need particular attention, after meals and after foraging in the yard. On country walks the coat will pick up an astonishing amount of mud and foliage, which need to be cleaned out promptly before mats and tangles can form.

HOW suitable are they as family dogs?
An ideal family dog who loves children and is always ready for play but patient and tolerant with the very young. As a puppy (and there are those who would say he never really leaves puppyhood behind), the Springer can be a whirlwind of energy needing a lot of time and attention from all family members—he is not an ideal choice for busy families with a hectic lifestyle.

WHAT type of home?
Essentially a country dog, the Springer is too active and energetic to be happy cooped up in an apartment. A yard is a must—along with tolerant owners who can cope with the Springer's passion for digging holes.

WHAT type of owner?
This ebullient breed needs an owner who enjoys long walks—Springers are great companions for joggers, though generally too lively for the elderly. Patience and gentleness are also needed when training this sensitive character—and a sense of humor is vital, especially during the puppy stage when Springers can be quite wild.

HOW compatible with other pets?
Like most spaniels, this is a friendly breed and good with other dogs if sensibly socialized when young. Springers are generally good with other pets in the home, but exercise caution with regard to strange cats—chasing is such a temptation to Springers.

HOW much exercise?
Regular long walks and free-running exercise are essential for such an active breed. Fair-weather walkers should not consider a Springer—he needs his walks every day, rain or shine.

Character Trait	Poor	Average	Good	Excellent
Attitude toward other dogs			X	
Quietness		X		
Not destructive		X		
Protective behavior	X			
Not likely to stray		X		
Good with children				X
Ease of training				X

Original purpose: Finding and retrieving game
Male height: 19-21 in (48-53 cm)
Female height: 18-20 in (46-51 cm)
Weight: 49-53 lb (22-24 kg)
Lifespan: 10-14 years

HOW easy to train?

Intelligent, quick to learn, and eager to please, the Springer is a rewarding dog to train, but it is vital to start his education early. Puppies left to their own devices become pests. Springers need to be motivated and respond well to praise; harsh training methods are counterproductive.

WHAT good points?

Friendly, happy disposition, obedient, nonaggressive, active, devoted to his owner, willing, intelligent, tireless.

WHAT to be aware of?

A demanding breed in terms of exercise and attention. Not for the house proud. They love muddy walks, and their coats carry in astonishing amounts of mud and vegetation.

WHAT medical problems?

Springers are generally a healthy breed. However, all breeding stock should be eye tested for defects such as progressive retinal atrophy (degeneration of the light receptors in the eyes). This is one of the few breeds affected by fucosidosis, a disease of the nervous system, but this is rare and affected stock can be identified by blood tests. As with all drop-eared breeds, ear infections are not uncommon.

Medium dogs

● *Working Springers don't have the heavy ear fringes that are required in the show ring—they leave them behind on brambles.*

Portuguese Water Dog

Handsome and hardworking, this is a dog with an extravagant amount of energy, intelligence, enthusiasm, and coat. A couch potato's nightmare, he is nonetheless a wonderful companion for equally active and enthusiastic owners. Given enough outdoor exercise, he is content to be quietly companionable within the home. He is very people oriented, and doesn't thrive if left alone for long periods.

The PWD developed as the sea-going assistant of Portuguese fishermen, a powerful swimmer able to position and retrieve nets and tackle, carry items and messages out to boats, and even drive fish into the nets—tasks that required endless stamina and high trainability. In the early 20th century, modern fishing techniques made water dogs redundant, and by the 1970s the PWD was rated the rarest dog breed in the world. Enthusiasts have since revived the breed, and it is steadily gaining popularity in the U.S.

WHAT colors?

Black or brown, with or without white markings (commonly chest spots, paws, chin). Parti-colors are becoming more common in the U.S., although the Portuguese frown upon more than 30 percent white coloration. All-white dogs occur, but they are not common.

WHAT grooming does the coat need?

Quite a lot. The dense, curly or wavy coat needs grooming at least every other day, using a slicker brush and comb to remove tangles. Most owners opt for a professional trim every four to six weeks. For ease of care, pet owners often favor a retriever clip, with the coat cut back to about an inch long all over, rather than the traditional lion clip. Even cut short, weekly brushing is needed to prevent mats.

HOW suitable are they as family dogs?

The PWD is a great dog for an active family with time for walks,

● *The retriever clip has become popular with PWD owners in recent years.*

play, grooming, and company. He is usually good with older children, but is likely to be too bouncy and too mouthy for the comfort and safety of little ones or frail elderly relatives. He loves to jump up in exuberant greeting, and has a natural inclination to grab hands and clothing.

WHAT type of home?

A dog this active really needs a home with a fenced yard where he can burn off energy. As an apartment dog, he will need an inordinate amount of outdoor exercise. His ideal home will have access to long country walks, and most PWDs would also ask for a nearby river, lake, or seashore where they can indulge their innate passion for swimming.

WHAT type of owner?

The PWD demands active owners who have time and the inclination for long walks, play, training sessions grooming, and general companionship. His intelligence and strong will require a confident owner with good understanding of the canine mind. He may be too much of a challenge for the inexperienced to take on.

HOW compatible with other pets?

On the whole, PWDs get along well with pets in their own homes especially if raised with them, though smaller furries such as rabbits and guinea pigs could be

Character Trait	Poor	Average	Good	Excellent
Attitude toward other dogs			■	
Quietness		■		
Not destructive		■		
Protective behavior			■	
Not likely to stray			■	
Good with children				■
Ease of training			■	

Original purpose: Fishermen's working companion
Male height: 20-23 in (50.8-58.4 cm)
Female height: 17-21 in (43.2-53.3 cm)
Weight: 35-60 lb (15.9-27.2 kg)
Lifespan: 12-15 years

...injured by overenthusiastic play and should be kept safe from possible harm. Most PWDs are friendly with other dogs, but, as with any breed, puppyhood socialization is important.

HOW much exercise?

Lots. At the very least, an hour of vigorous exercise each day is essential, and more is better. The Portuguese Water Dog makes a great jogging or hiking companion; he loves ball games and mental challenges. He also loves to swim, which is excellent exercise for him. He can be a star at canine activities such as agility, tracking, or obedience work, and, of course, water work trials.

HOW easy to train?

These are intelligent dogs who love learning. Training needs to be fun and stimulating, as a PWD is bright enough to become bored with dull repetitions. He also tends to have a mind of his own, and can be stubborn if he doesn't see the point of a particular exercise—inexperienced owners may encounter problems here.

WHAT good points?

Friendly, sociable, loving, loyal, intelligent, eager to learn, fun-loving, tireless, athletic, minimal molting.

WHAT to be aware of?

Super energetic; strong-willed; demanding coat care; prone to jumping up; very mouthy; destructive chewers if bored and lonely; tendency toward separation anxiety.

Medium dogs

WHAT medical problems?

Inherited problems include hip malformation (dysplasia), progressive retinal atrophy, juvenile dilated cardiomyopathy (a heart defect causing sudden death of puppies), GM1 storage disease (a fatal liver condition), Addison's disease (a hormonal disorder), and hemangiosarcoma (a form of cancer). It is vital to seek out a breeder who carries out full health tests, including hip scores and current eye certificates.

Samoyed

With his sparkling white coat and characteristic smiling face, the Samoyed is an eye-catching beauty, and in temperament he is friendliness personified. This is a dog who really wants to be part of the family. Happy, sweet-natured, and affectionate, he makes a great companion. However, keep in mind that this is a working breed, and consequently needs to keep busy. He wants plenty of exercise and play, but also benefits from activities such as agility, tracking, mushing, or therapy work. Denied a proper outlet for his energy, he can be noisy and destructive. He also needs a lot of coat care—so don't consider a Samoyed unless you are prepared to make the commitment.

In his native Siberia, the Samoyed served the Samoyede tribes as reindeer herder, draught animal, and bed warmer. Introduced to the West in 1889, he is now employed largely as a companion—a role at which he excels.

WHAT colors?

Typically thought of as white, but cream and biscuit shaded also acceptable. The breed originally included a wide range of colors including black, brown, spotted, but after its introduction to the West, white came to predominate.

WHAT grooming does the coat need?

This is a dense coat requiring daily brushing plus a weekly thorough combing down to the skin. If neglected, it mats and tangles into an unmanageable mass. Extra work is needed during the heavy molt once or twice a year, when mounds of fur are shed—many owners collect bags of combings, which can be spun into a high-quality soft wool.

HOW suitable are they as family dogs?

Samoyeds make wonderful family pets as long as they can be in the heart of the family—they don't cope well with being ignored, and they demand attention. They love human company and are generally good with children. A busy family without time for exercising, grooming, and cuddling would not find a Samoyed a suitable choice.

WHAT type of home?

The Samoyed needs space and a well-fenced yard—many of this breed are escape artists. Essentially a country breed, he will adapt to city life only if sufficient exercise can be provided.

WHAT type of owner?

Samoyeds thrive with affectionate, energetic owners who enjoy long walks and grooming sessions, are prepared to spend plenty of time with their dogs, and are laid-back about dog hair on furniture. This breed wants to be the center of attention and may be too demanding for some. Not recommended for the frail, as Samoyeds are strong dogs who tend to pull on the leash.

HOW compatible with other pets?

This friendly dog usually gets along well with pets in his own home. However, he has a strong chase instinct; most will chase small animals like rabbits when on walks and should not be expected to ignore the cat nextdoor. Most are good with other dogs, although some males may be rather dominant.

HOW much exercise?

The Samoyed needs plenty of vigorous outdoor exercise, including free running in a safe open space. It is almost impossible to tire him out. Joggers and hikers will find him a great companion. Alternatively, sports such as sledding, carting, or agility are a great way to satisfy his need for lots of action.

Character Trait	Poor	Average	Good	Excellent
Attitude toward other dogs		▓	▓	
Quietness	▓			
Not destructive	▓	▓		
Protective behavior	▓			
Not likely to stray	▓	▓		
Good with children			▓	▓
Ease of training		▓		

Original purpose: Reindeer herd and sled dog
Male height: 21-23.5 in (53-60 cm)
Female height: 19-21 in (48-53 cm)
Weight: 50-66 lb (23-30 kg)
Lifespan: 10-12 years

HOW easy to train?

Not the easiest breed to train, although individuals vary considerably. This is a strong-willed breed with a sense of humor and little natural tendency toward obedience, so training has to be patient, persistent, and consistent.

Medium dogs

WHAT good points?

Friendly, happy, intelligent, gentle, active, sensitive, affectionate, full of fun, energetic, good-natured.

WHAT to be aware of?

Needs lots of attention. Heavy molt once or twice a year. Can be very destructive if bored, and generally very vocal.

WHAT medical problems?

Generally healthy. Occasional hip deformity (dysplasia) and some tendency toward diabetes. Other problems include kidney failure, glaucoma (increased pressure in the eyeball), abnormal development of the retina (retinal dysplasia), and heart conditions.

● The characteristic Samoyed smile reflects a happy nature.

Australian Shepherd

Confusingly, the Australian Shepherd is an American creation. His ancestors arrived in the U.S. in the 1900s, the herding dogs of emigrant Spanish Basque shepherds accompanying imported Australian sheep. It was in the U.S. that these "little blue dogs" established themselves as a proficient working breed. They achieved AKC recognition as recently as 1993 and since then have become widely known and appreciated.

At a casual glance, the Aussie resembles a burlier Border Collie, often strikingly colored in marbled and pastel shades. He has the sheepdog virtues of intelligence, tenacity, and versatility, with strong herding and guarding instincts and abundant energy. Very much a working dog, he needs a job to do and excels at activities such as agility, flyball, and obedience. This is a demanding breed, strong-minded, protective, and often territorial—not the ideal choice for a novice, but a rewarding and devoted companion when properly socialized and trained.

WHAT colors?

A spectacular range of blue merle (a kind of marbled effect), black, red merle, and red, with or without white markings and/or tan to copper points. Eyes may be blue, brown, or bi-colored.

WHAT grooming does the coat need?

The dense coat needs brushing down to the skin with a stiff bristle brush two or three times a week to remove dead hair.

HOW suitable are they as family dogs?

Provided he has enough physical and mental exercise to keep him happy, the Aussie makes a great family dog, devoted and protective. However, busy families with demanding jobs and young children are unlikely to have enough time to keep him appropriately occupied. He is not recommended for homes with small children, as he may be tempted to play too roughly for their comfort.

WHAT type of home?

This is a dog with high energy levels, better suited for a country home with a fair-sized yard and access to suitable land for exercise. City life is unlikely to provide enough activity for him.

WHAT type of owner?

The Aussie needs an active, experienced owner with plenty of time, who can provide socialization and appropriate employment, whether this be herding sheep or racing around an agility ring. He is not suitable for owners who go out to work and expect to leave him alone in the house. A bored Aussie is likely to express his unhappiness through destructive behavior.

HOW compatible with other pets?

Good early socialization is important to ensure that the Aussie gets along with other animals.

Character Trait	Poor	Average	Good	Excellent
Attitude toward other dogs		■		
Quietness		■		
Not destructive		■		
Protective behavior			■	
Not likely to stray		■		
Good with children			■	
Ease of training				■

Original purpose: Sheepdog
Male height: 20-23 in (51-58 cm)
Female height: 18-21 in (46-53 cm)
Weight: 40-65 lb (18.2-29.5 kg)
Lifespan: 12-15 years

does have strong chasing instincts, so watch out for small pets and neighbors' cats. Some individuals are very dominant with other dogs and need careful supervision.

HOW much exercise?

A great deal. This is a very active breed and virtually tireless—a great companion for joggers. He needs at least an hour's vigorous walking a day plus active play and mental stimulation.

HOW easy to train?

This intelligent breed can be trained to a very high standard but needs a slow and steady approach. Aussies are slow to mature, and a lot of patience is required. They are willing to please but need to understand fully what they are doing and why, rather than learning by rote. They need encouragement rather than pressure.

WHAT good points?

Intelligent, loyal, affectionate, responsive, attentive, enthusiastic, energetic, protective, versatile, highly trainable.

WHAT to be aware of?

Challenging breed that needs something to do. Different bloodlines very different in temperament (some highly reactive and energetic, some calmer). To ensure the right choice, meet the family before choosing a pup.

WHAT medical problems?

Most Aussies are sound, but hereditary problems include hip deformity (dysplasia), dislocating kneecaps (patellar luxation), skin disorders, and eye defects (juvenile cataracts, collie eye anomaly, progressive retinal atrophy, glaucoma, lens dislocation). Breeding stock should be hip scored and eye tested. Merles should not be mated together, as this can produce white puppies that are often deaf and/or blind.

Medium dogs

● *This handsome dog is strikingly colored in various merle shades.*

Siberian Husky

The Siberian Husky was born to run. Beautiful and stylish enough to grace a catwalk, he is an athletic working dog who needs mental and physical stimuli. He loves to race, to pull sleds or carts, or to go backpacking. Because he also loves people, in between these activities he makes an affectionate, gentle, and playful companion who enjoys being part of the family. Don't consider this active and intelligent breed unless you can provide the exercise and company he needs. A bored Siberian is destructive indoors and a great escapologist outside. He is also strong-willed, with an intense hunting drive—not an ideal choice for the novice.

Developed by the Chukchi people of Siberia as a sled dog, the breed was introduced to the U.S. in the 1900s for sled racing. It achieved AKC recognition in 1930 and was taken up by U.K. breeders in the early 1970s, becoming increasingly popular.

WHAT colors?

All colors, including black, white, tan, gray, red brown, and sable, often with striking head markings and beautiful coat patterns. Coat color and pattern change over time, so puppies may look quite different as adults. Eyes may be a gleaming ice blue, brown, parti-color, or even one blue and one brown.

WHAT grooming does the coat need?

The weatherproof coat is relatively easy care. A weekly thorough brushing with a pin-wire brush to remove dead hair will keep it healthy. This breed molts heavily twice a year, when more vigorous grooming is required.

HOW suitable are they as family dogs?

Provided he has appropriate occupation, the Siberian's friendly nature makes him a good family pet—though youngsters (up to two years) are likely to be too rough for small children. In any case, most families with young children will not have sufficient time to keep him suitably occupied.

WHAT type of home?

Huskies are not city dogs. They need space. They should have a large yard or paddock with room to run and very secure fencing—this breed can jump, chew through, or dig under most fences—and with access to countryside where they can burn off energy. Their intense hunting drive means they are unlikely to be popular in areas where they may encounter livestock.

WHAT type of owner?

The Siberian Husky is a dog for active outdoor types who can provide firm, competent leadership and who will enjoy canine activities. He is not suited to anyone who wants a dog that can run free in the park and will return on command. However, he is a great companion for hikers and backpackers, and for those who live in areas where there are sled-racing clubs and the like.

HOW compatible with other pets?

Huskies get along well with other well-adjusted dogs but will take up challenge if one is offered. In regard to other species, they have a very strong hunting drive and will chase anything that moves. They will usually accept cats in the same household if brought up with them but should never be regarded as safe with livestock.

Character Trait	Poor	Average	Good	Excellent
Attitude toward other dogs			▓	
Quietness	▓			
Not destructive		▓		
Protective behavior	▓			
Not likely to stray	▓			
Good with children			▓	
Ease of training		▓		

Original purpose: Hauling sleds, carrying packs, hunting
Male height: 21-23.5 in (53-60 cm)
Female height: 20-22 in (51-56 cm)
Weight: 35-60 lb (16-27 kg)
Lifespan: 12-15 years

HOW much exercise?

An adult Husky needs a 4 mile (6-7 km) brisk walk every day at the minimum, with no maximum. It is impossible to tire him out. Most Siberians must be exercised on a leash because of their natural urges to roam and to hunt. Puppies should have limited exercise to prevent damage to growing bones. Build up gradually from about six months until 18 months, when they are fully grown.

HOW easy to train?

Moderately difficult. Siberians are intelligent but independent and not programmed for obedience. They need and will respond to training, but patience is essential—and don't expect too much. Early socialization is a must, and training needs to start early and to be very patient.

WHAT good points?

Affectionate, playful, active, gentle, friendly, alert, outgoing, intelligent, clean, tireless, minimal "doggy" smell.

WHAT to be aware of?

For experienced owners only. Strong instinctual urge to run and may never be trustworthy off leash; champion escapologist; strong hunting drive and unsafe with livestock. Can be destructive and noisy if left alone. Sheds hair heavily.

WHAT medical problems?

Generally a healthy breed, but some occurrence of eye problems (juvenile cataracts, corneal defects, and progressive retinal atrophy) and occasional hip deformity (dysplasia)—breeding stock should be hip scored and eye tested. Huskies are sensitive to some drugs, particularly anesthetics and sedatives.

Medium dogs

● *Despite the languid pose, he is almost inexhaustible!*

Large Dogs

Big dogs often suffer the misfortune of being purchased as image builders. They deserve better. There are some wonderful breeds in this group, but think before you buy. Their upkeep needs a major commitment of time, space, and money, and training is essential when you own a dog of this size.

Golden Retriever

This handsome and kindly gundog is an all-around dog, a great working dog, and family pet but also widely used as guide dog for the blind, service dog for the disabled, therapy dog, and sniffer dog. Intelligent, friendly, and cheerful, he is ideal for anyone who enjoys long walks and wants a loving companion to share in activities. He needs plenty of regular exercise and mental stimulation.

Owners should be prepared for an exuberant dog with a sense of humor who loves retrieving, can't resist splashing about in water, and carpets the house with mud and golden hairs.

The Golden originated in the 1860s from yellow pups that cropped up accidentally in black retriever strains, receiving a breed standard in 1931. Since then he has become hugely popular—too much so, as puppy farmers churn out stock with uncharacteristically aggressive temperaments, so it is essential to buy from responsible breeders.

WHAT colors?
Any shade of gold or cream. Early dogs in the U.S. were mostly darker shades of golden. In 1920, the standard was altered to include lighter shades.

WHAT grooming does the coat need?
Coats vary in length and thickness, but all need at least a weekly brushing down to the skin with a hard brush and combing through the feathers. A quick daily combing will remove dead hairs and reduce the amount of hair shed in the house. The coat will also need cleaning and tidying after muddy walks—and if there is mud anywhere, a Golden will find it.

HOW suitable are they as family dogs?
The Golden's kind, affectionate temperament and love of children make him an ideal family dog provided he has enough exercise. He needs to be part of the family and fully involved in their activities.

Time must be spent on his training, as he is a big, heavy, energetic dog who can bowl children over if he has not been taught good manners.

WHAT type of home?
The Golden would prefer a country home but can be just as happy with city life provided he has enough exercise and mental stimulation. He needs a well-fenced yard and access to a park where he can burn off energy. He is generally too active to be confined to an apartment.

WHAT type of owner?
This is a great dog for active, affectionate owners who enjoy long daily walks and seek a kind, easygoing companion that is reliable with children. Owners should enjoy training to channel a dog's intelligence and physical energy in acceptable directions—and be prepared to cope with a mischievous, high-energy puppy who turns into an exuberant adolescent. They also need a relaxed attitude to dog hairs and mud on carpets and clothes.

HOW compatible with other pets?
The Golden's friendly nature extends to other pets as well as people. As a youngster he can be too bouncy for the safety of small pets, and he may have a tendency to carry them around—his soft mouth won't hurt them, but they may not care for the experience. He is fine with cats in his own household, but may chase strange cats just for the fun of it.

HOW much exercise?
Gundogs like the Golden were

Character Trait	Poor	Average	Good	Excellent
Attitude toward other dogs				
Quietness				
Not destructive				
Protective behavior				
Not likely to stray				
Good with children				
Ease of training				

Original purpose: Retrieving shot game
Male height: 22-24 in (56-61 cm)
Female height: 20-22 in (51-56 cm)
Weight: 55-75 lb (24.9-34 kg)
Lifespan: 10-13 years

bred to work all day in the field and have endless energy and stamina, so they need a lot of outdoor exercise daily, in all weather. Puppies under nine months need limited exercise to prevent damage to growing bones but have endless energy for play—and mischief.

HOW easy to train?

Goldens are intelligent, quick to learn, eager to please, and highly trainable, though handlers need patience with exuberant youngsters and need to allow for a tendency toward stubbornness and a sense of humor. Start training early and keep training sessions fun and reward based to maintain their interest.

WHAT good points?

Friendly, outgoing, loyal, stable, affectionate, intelligent, obedient, kindly, confident, active, sensitive, full of fun.

WHAT to be aware of?

Only buy from responsible breeders to be sure of good temperament. Not a part-time dog—he needs a lot of commitment and can be clingy.

Large dogs

WHAT medical problems?

Hip malformation (dysplasia) and cataracts are serious problems in this breed. All breeding stock must have hips and eyes screened. Some epilepsy and a tendency to aquire skin problems (eczema, allergies).

● *A pair of high-energy Goldens take a break.*

Collie

The attractive and intelligent Collie of northern Britain first came into the limelight in the 19th century, when it took the fancy of Queen Victoria. The breed was smartened up for the show ring, and the modern "Lassie" is a glamourized version of his tough herding ancestors, taller, more elegant, and with a glorious, richly colored coat. Today, the Collie has lost much of his intense working drive, while retaining the intelligence and loyalty of his ancestors. This is a very handsome dog, loving, sweet-natured, and a wonderful family pet—when he is in the right hands.

This is not, however, a breed suitable for everyone. Collies are very demanding dogs in terms of time and attention. They need company, extensive socialization, and mental stimulation. They are highly sensitive and can become neurotic in a stressful environment. The coat, which is the breed's crowning glory, requires hours of work.

WHAT colors?

Three recognized colors: sable and white (any shade from gold through to mahogany); tri-color (black with white collar and tan markings over eyes, inside legs, and under tail); and blue merle (a sort of marbled effect distinguished by the presence of irregular dark blotches against a lighter background of the same basic pigment), with or without white and/or tan markings. In the U.S. white is also an accepted color variety.

WHAT grooming does the coat need?

This is a maximum maintenance coat that needs frequent, regular brushing—at least every other day—to prevent mats and tangles. It is essential to brush right down to the skin to work through the dense undercoat. A de-matting rake is a useful grooming tool to reduce the undercoat to manageable levels.

HOW suitable are they as family dogs?

For the family that has time for him, the Collie takes some beating as a companion. Given a well-balanced family life, he is a loyal, devoted, and well-mannered pet, particularly fond of and good with children. However, his high sensitivity makes him react badly to stress and family tensions, so he is not the best choice for a home with a hectic and unpredictable lifestyle.

WHAT type of home?

This breed is essentially a country dog needing access to the outdoors, although he will adapt to city life given sympathetic owners. He needs company and involvement in family activities. If left alone, he may become noisy and destructive through boredom. Not the ideal dog for the house proud, as he molts heavily and his coat carries in mud and muck.

WHAT type of owner?

A calm and patient personality is required to get the best out of this breed—a sensitive dog needs a sensitive owner. This is emphatically not a breed that can be left alone at home all day while his owner goes out to work. Collie owners should also be prepared to commit time to socializing, grooming, and training.

HOW compatible with other pets?

His kind, tolerant nature makes the Collie generally excellent with other household pets. Some Collies retain a strong herding instinct that they may attempt to employ upon other pets, circling and nipping in a manner that is unlikely to be appreciated. Providing other

Place of origin: **Scotland**

Character Trait	Poor	Average	Good	Excellent
Attitude toward other dogs				
Quietness				
Not destructive				
Protective behavior				
Not likely to stray				
Good with children				
Ease of training				

Original purpose: Herder
Male height: 22-24 in (56-61 cm)
Female height: 20-22 in (51-56 cm)
Weight: 51-75 lb (23-34 kg)
Lifespan: 12-15 years

activities should keep this instinct under control.

HOW much exercise?
The Collie's exercise needs are surprisingly moderate for his size. He will keep fit with a daily walk of an hour or so, ensuring that he has time for free running off leash—and taking care to ensure that his herding instinct does not lead him to chase other dogs, joggers, children, and bicycles.

HOW easy to train?
Intelligent, eager to please, and quick to learn, this breed is easy to train provided his sensitive nature is recognized. Gentle, consistent, reward-based training is required. Harsh scolding or physical punishment will only make the dog nervous and uncooperative. This is a breed that needs the mental stimulation and reassurance of training sessions to build confidence.

WHAT good points?
Friendly, intelligent, loyal, affectionate, protective, sensitive, sweet-natured, nonaggressive, polite with strangers and other pets.

WHAT to be aware of?
Tendency to develop separation anxiety when left alone. Highly reactive to loud noises. Some strains may be very high-strung and neurotic.

WHAT medical problems?
Generally a healthy breed with few problems. However, all puppies should be screened for eye problems (Collie eye anomaly). Epilepsy, inward-turning eyelids (entropion), and Collie nose (nasal solar dermatitis) characterized by skin lesions around the nose also occur, and the breed is susceptible to skin complaints.

Large dogs

Labrador Retriever

This versatile gundog stars not only in the shooting field but as guide dog for the blind, sniffer dog detecting anything from drugs to gas leaks, life-saving search and rescue dog, service dog for the disabled—and one of the most popular family dogs. However, these achievements don't happen by magic. They depend on good breeding and excellent training. Reputable breeders aim to produce a good temperament as well as a good physique, but even the best-bred Labs can be real hooligans if left to their own devices. These are powerful, energetic dogs whose intelligence needs channeling. Given sensible owners, Labs are great companions and reliable family dogs, eminently trainable and adaptable

The breed originated in Canada as a water dog, but it was in 19th-century Britain that its retrieving skills made it the sportsman's favorite. Today, show and working strains have diverged, the latter being lighter in build.

WHAT colors?

Black, yellow (ranging from cream to fox red, but never termed golden in this breed), or chocolate.

WHAT grooming does the coat need?

This is an easy-care coat but does benefit from weekly grooming with slicker or stiff bristle brush to remove dead hair and massage the skin. Tends to molt year-round—get the vacuum cleaner ready.

HOW suitable are they as family dogs?

This good-natured dog is ideal for an active family prepared to spend plenty of time on exercise and training and with someone at home most of the time. These very sociable dogs need company and can be destructive and noisy if left alone too long. Labs are generally very good with children, but may be too big and boisterous for the comfort of little ones. They also tend to mouth hands in play—gently, but sometimes too much for youngsters.

● Dark or light in color, the versatile Lab is a tireless worker in the field as well as a loving companion in the home.

WHAT type of home?

A country home is best, but a Lab will be just as happy with city life provided they have enough exercise and mental stimulation. He does need a well-fenced yard and access to a park where he can burn off energy. Not an ideal apartment dog because of his size and bounciness —nor suited to homes with low coffee tables and fragile ornaments for the same reason.

WHAT type of owner?

Labradors need owners who enjoy long walks every day, regardless of the weather, who are prepared for a mischievous puppy that grows into an exuberant adult, and who enjoy training a responsive dog. They are not the best choice for the house proud. Labradors mean mess, with muddy footprints, slobber, tail marks on the walls, and a fair amount of chewing.

HOW compatible with other pets?

Friendly and kindly, Labradors are generally good with other dogs and household pets, although, as with all breeds, early socialization is important. Their innate retrieving instinct means that small pets like rabbits and guinea pigs may find themselves being carried around, unharmed but soggy, and some males may be rather dominant with other male dogs they encounter.

Character Trait	Poor	Average	Good	Excellent
Attitude toward other dogs				■
Quietness			■	
Not destructive		■		
Protective behavior	■			
Not likely to stray		■		
Good with children				■
Ease of training				■

Original purpose: Retrieving game
Male height: 22-24.5 in (56-62 cm)
Female height: 21-23.5 in (54-60 cm)
Weight: 55-75 lb (25-34 kg)
Lifespan: c. 12 years

HOW much exercise?

Lots. Think in terms of at least two hours' walking a day—more will be appreciated. This breed has a tendency to be lazy and greedy, so it is easy to turn a Labrador into an obese couch potato who will trudge round the block once a day —but a dreadful waste of all that Labrador delight in life.

HOW easy to train?

Labradors are eminently trainable. They like to please, and they enjoy the mental and physical exercise of training sessions. Young Labradors do enjoy playing the fool, and it takes patience and persistence to get through this stage. Keep training sessions fun and reward based to maintain their interest.

WHAT good points?

Cheerful, loving, energetic, trust-worthy, good with children, patient, eager to please, nonaggressive, intelligent, highly trainable.

WHAT to be aware of?

High exercise needs. Watch out for commercial breeders producing puppies with poor temperament and health problems.

WHAT medical problems?

Labs are generally healthy, but hip and elbow malformation (dysplasia), weakness of the muscle that propels food down the gullet (megaosophagus), degeneration of receptor cells in the eye (progressive retinal atrophy), muscle weakness (myopathy), and lack of thyroid hormone occur. All breeding stock should have hips and eyes screened.

Large dogs

Boxer

The Boxer is a loving clown, bursting with energy and retaining a puppyish playfulness often well into old age. He is a fun dog, but one who requires a major commitment. He needs a lot of exercise, a lot of training, a lot of affection—and a lot of patience. For those who want a high-energy dog, this most exuberant of breeds makes a wonderful companion, but he is usually too boisterous for anyone who prefers peace and quiet. Very much a people dog, he adores his family and needs them to adore him—Boxers don't thrive without plenty of human companionship.

The Boxer developed in the 1880s from the German Bullenbeisser ("bull-biter," originally a hunting mastiff) and English Bulldog. Early Boxers served nobly in World War I as scouts, messengers, and guards. Today the breed is a popular companion—and one whose undoubted intelligence and ability are often underused.

WHAT colors?

Dark red to fawn, or brindle, with or without white markings not exceeding one third of ground color. White boxers occur quite frequently, but are not accepted by the AKC because a high percentage are born deaf.

WHAT grooming does the coat need?

The Boxer's short, dense coat is very low maintenance, needing only a quick brushing from time to time to remove dead hairs.

HOW suitable are they as family dogs?

Loving, playful, and protective, the Boxer is a wonderful dog for an energetic, experienced family with older children—and a sense of humor. He is a great playmate for children who are used to dogs and too big to be bowled over by a hurtling Boxer, but is too boisterous for toddlers or the frail elderly. He needs a sensible, orderly home where he can learn good manners. In a rowdy, chaotic household his natural exuberance will often make him unmanageable.

WHAT type of home?

A Boxer can be a city dog or a country dog as long as he has plenty of exercise, but this energetic dog needs space and is not suited to life in an apartment. He should have access to a yard, as large as possible and with a well-maintained high fence—Boxers are great escapologists.

WHAT type of owner?

Boxers do best with experienced, active, affectionate owners who appreciate their sense of fun and have time, energy, and a sense of humor. Although powerful and strong-willed, they are sensitive dogs who need kindness. They are not recommended for novices, the physically frail, or anyone whose lifestyle cannot accommodate a whirlwind of energy.

HOW compatible with other pets?

Most Boxers are good-natured and friendly with other animals, although some can be dominant with other dogs of the same sex. They can be too boisterous for the comfort of smaller animals—a playful pounce from a Boxer can hurt a little dog and won't do much for the health of a hamster.

Character Trait	Poor	Average	Good	Excellent
Attitude toward other dogs		▧		
Quietness			▧	
Not destructive		▧		
Protective behavior				▧
Not likely to stray			▧	
Good with children			▧	
Ease of training		▧		

Original purpose: Guard and companion
Male height: 22.5-25 in (57-63.5 cm)
Female height: 21-23 in (53-59 cm)
Weight: 50-80 lb (22.6-36.2 kg)
Lifespan: 8-10 years

HOW much exercise?

As much as possible, as often as possible! Think in terms of a minimum of one to two hours' walking a day, but remember that Boxers are poorly suited to extremes of temperature. Like other short-faced breeds, they can overheat easily, and they also feel the cold. Active sports like agility and flyball provide mental stimulation as well as exercise.

HOW easy to train?

Boxers are a challenging breed to train, strong-minded, stubborn but also sensitive. In the right hands they are very capable dogs, but they need an owner they can respect as well as love.
Training should

start early and be firm but kind, consistent, and patient. This breed is slow to mature and would rather play the fool than work unless persuaded that lessons are fun, too.

WHAT good points?

Cheerful, lively, strong, loyal to owner, affectionate, equable, fearless, self-assured, playful, brave, intelligent, outgoing, energetic.

WHAT to be aware of?

Large dogs

A demanding breed. Boxers bounce. They also snore, slobber, and break wind. Some Boxers have a strong guard instinct; others don't.

WHAT medical problems?

Boxers have a high incidence of heart defects and also of cancer. They are also prone to bloat (gastric torsion); hip malformation (dysplasia) and lack of thyroid hormone (hypothyroidism) also occur. Progressive axonopathy (affecting the nervous system and leading to paralysis) was a major problem, now largely under control.

● *Boxers have lots of "bounce," and need a firm hand in training.*

Vizsla

The Vizsla is a working multi-purpose gundog bred to hunt, point, and retrieve game. His roots go back to the Middle Ages, when he was developed as the favorite sporting dog of the Hungarian nobility. Today he is still very much a working dog, but his beauty and people-oriented nature have made him increasingly popular as a companion breed. Affectionate, outgoing, and friendly, he makes a delightful family member for those who can satisfy his needs for loa of exercise, stimulation, and social life. He wants to with his family the whole time and is not a dog whe can be content when left alone. His working talents suit him for activities such as competitive obedienc agility, tracking, and so on.

His cousin the Wirehaired Vizsla is classed as a separate breed, and was created in the 1930s by introducing German Wirehai Pointer blood to give a more protective coat.

WHAT colors?

Russet gold. Small white marks on chest and feet are acceptable though not desirable.

WHAT grooming does the coat need?

Minimal. The short, smooth coat needs little more than a weekly brushing with a firm bristle brush to remove dead hairs.

HOW suitable are they as family dogs?

A poor choice for a family wanting a placid, undemanding pet, the Vizsla is a wonderful dog for families who recognize the needs of a working dog. He is devoted to his owners, eager to please, protective without being aggressive, and reliable with children. Denied exercise and attention, he will become frustrated and may turn mischievous.

WHAT type of home?

A country home with plenty of space for exercise is the ideal home

● *The short, smooth coat of the Vizsla requires only minimal upkeep.*

for a Vizsla. But his people come first with him, and he will adapt to city life as long as he has plenty of regular activity and is allowed to participate fully in family life. He needs a secure yard—if bored, he can easily clear a 6-foot (2-m) fence in his quest for something to do.

WHAT type of owner?

Vizslas need active owners, preferably with an interest in canine activities whether sporting or obedience oriented ar a sensitive approach to training. Th is not a part-time pet but one whe needs to be part of the family. Don't consider a Vizsla unless you appreciate an affectionate, demanding, tactile, and talkative relationship with your dog.

HOW compatible with other pets?

If appropriately socialized in puppyhood, Vizslas get along well with other animals. However, remember that they are hunting dogs with an innate chasing instinc so don't expose small pets such as rabbits to their attentions or expe them to ignore the neighbor's cat without proper training.

HOW much exercise?

A great deal, every day, including plenty of free galloping. This is not a breed for the sedentary owner! Puppies under nine months should be limited to short walks and yard play to prevent damage to growing bones.

Character Trait	Poor	Average	Good	Excellent
Attitude toward other dogs				
Quietness				
Not destructive				
Protective behavior				
Not likely to stray				
Good with children				
Ease of training				

Original purpose: Hunting, pointing, and retrieving game
Male height: 22.5-25 in (57-63.5 cm)
Female height: 21-23.5 in (53-60 cm)
Weight: 44-66 lb (20-30 kg)
Lifespan: 12 years or more

HOW easy to train?

This breed is eager to please and responds well to firm, patient training but it may take time, as Vizslas can be late developers. They are highly sensitive dogs, sometimes willful and easily distracted, and do not take well to rough handling.

Although a working dog, the Vizsla is a gentle and sensitive animal. As a companion, he demands lots of attention and plenty of exercise.

WHAT good points?

Lively, intelligent, obedient, sensitive, affectionate, loyal, responsive, gentle-mannered, versatile, protective, easy-care coat, and little "doggy" smell.

WHAT to be aware of?

A delightful but demanding breed that may be too clingy for some. His habits include a tendency to mouth hands or arms, which may be off-putting to the unprepared, but this is a gesture of friendship, not an attempt to bite! Vizslas are also a highly vocal breed prone to "talking."

WHAT medical problems?

Generally a healthy breed. Conditions known to occur include hip malformation (dysplasia), blood disorders including von Willebrand's disease and hemophilia, epilepsy, tail defects, and sensitivity to anesthesia. Recent concerns about osteochondritis dissecans (OCD), which affects cartilage in the joints of the limbs.

Large dogs

Airedale Terrier

The "King of the Terriers" deserves his title not just for his size (he is the biggest of all terrier breeds) but for his versatility. Airedales have shone as police dogs, search and rescue dogs, therapy dogs, and hunters of anything from rats to grizzly bears, as well as serving heroically in World War I as sentry, messenger, and ambulance dogs. Above all, this handsome dog excels as a loyal companion and watchdog. Affectionate but independent, he is a strong-willed character who needs occupation for mind and body, otherwise he can be a bit too much of a live wire for the average family.

The Airedale developed in northern England as hunting dog and, despite his classic terrier appearance probably has otterhound ancestry. Officially recognized by the AKC in 1888, by the 192? he was one of the most popular breeds in both the U.K. and the U.S.

WHAT colors?

Black and tan or grizzle and tan. The body saddle, top of the neck, and top surface of tail are black or grizzle, and the rest of the dog tan. Pups are born black, gradually developing the tan coloring from about ten weeks old.

WHAT grooming does the coat need?

The dense, wiry coat benefits from daily combing, and also needs hand stripping at least twice a year—a skilled task that many owners prefer to leave to a professional. Clipping achieves the same effect of tidying the outline, but spoils the texture and color. Left to its own devices, the nonshedding coat grows into a thick, unruly fleece that is hard work to comb.

HOW suitable are they as family dogs?

The Airedale is a great companion and protector for an active family who have time to satisfy his needs for mental and physical exercise. Properly trained and exercised, he is great with children. However, Airedale puppies (up to at least two years old) may be too boisterous for the very young. Busy families should be aware that a young Airedale is a full-time job.

WHAT type of home?

Airedales have endless energy and need space for exercise and play. They are ideal dogs for country dwellers, but will adapt to city life with a sufficiently committed owner. A well-fenced yard is a must, but don't imagine you can just leave your Airedale there to exercise himself—while happy to play in the yard, he will also require full participation from his owner.

WHAT type of owner?

Airedales are powerful as well as energetic, and owners need to be physically strong and active, with a taste for long walks. He needs considerable time and attention from his owner, as well as firm, patient training and mental stimulation. A sense of humor is also a must. Many Airedales have a strong streak of mischief and can be rowdy and disruptive.

HOW compatible with other pets?

Good if brought up with them— early socialization, as always, is the key to success. However, this is a boisterous breed that may be too rough for the health of small pets and that also has strong chasing instincts. Some males can be aggressive with other dogs.

Character Trait	Poor	Average	Good	Excellent
Attitude toward other dogs				
Quietness				
Not destructive				
Protective behavior				
Not likely to stray				
Good with children				
Ease of training				

Original purpose: Hunting
Male height: 23-24 in (58-61 cm)
Female height: 22-23 in (56-58 cm)
Weight: 44-50 lb (20-23 kg)
Lifespan: 12-13 years

HOW much exercise?

Plenty. The Airedale has boundless energy to burn off. He needs space to play at home and regular long walks. A great dog for joggers, backpackers, and hikers (but remember that puppies should not be encouraged to walk too far until they are physically mature).

HOW easy to train?

Moderate. Much depends on the trainer. In the right hands, the Airedale can achieve a great deal, but he has no predisposition to slavish obedience. Training must be fun and stimulating to capture his interest, as he is easily bored with repetitive exercises. Owners need to be patient and flexible—and to retain a sense of humor.

WHAT good points?

Loyal, affectionate, protective, intelligent, sensitive, humorous, adventurous, fun-loving. His nonmolting coat suits many allergy sufferers.

WHAT to be aware of?

High maintenance in terms of grooming, exercise, and attention. Very active, sometimes to the point of rowdiness. Strong-willed and stubborn. Can be noisy and destructive. Early socialization essential to control protective and chasing instincts.

WHAT medical problems?

Generally a hardy and healthy breed. Problems that occur include hip deformity (dysplasia)—(parents should have hip certificates)—and skin problems.

Large dogs

● *Largest of the terriers, the Airedale has lots of energy and makes a great companion for an active owner.*

Dalmatian

Instantly recognizable with his distinctive spotted coat, the Dalmatian is a dog for the energetic owner. In the 18th century he was employed as a fashionable carriage dog, escorting horse-drawn carriages for 20 miles (30 km) or more. Today his outgoing, friendly character and striking good looks have made him popular as a family companion, but he still retains his love of exercise and his affinity with horses.

The *101 Dalmatians* films have inspired many to acquire Dalmatian puppies without considering whether a dog bred to run marathons will fit into their lifestyle—don't make this mistake! This is a great dog for the right home—loving, intelligent, good-natured, and playful—but quite unsuitable for couch potatoes.

The Dalmatian's origins are obscure. There is no evidence to connect the breed with Dalmatia (part of former Yugoslavia), and it is probable that its present type was actually established in 18th-century England.

WHAT colors?

Best known is the classic white with black spots, but liver (brown) spots are also acceptable. Show dogs require well rounded, evenly distributed spots; mismarked dogs cannot be shown but make just as good pets. Puppies are born pure white, developing their spots from about ten days old.

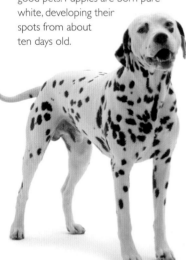

WHAT grooming does the coat need?

The short sleek coat is low maintenance, needing only regular brushing to remove loose hair. Prospective owners should be aware that this breed does shed, and white hairs show up obviously on clothes and furniture.

HOW suitable are they as family dogs?

For an active family, the Dalmatian makes a great family dog. He is good with children and loves to play. However, he is probably not a good choice for households with children under the age of ten, as he is boisterous and powerful and can be very hard work before he matures.

WHAT type of home?

The Dalmatian needs a home with access to suitable exercise areas, but this doesn't mean he has to live in the country. He is an adaptable dog who will readily adapt to city life as long as he has enough company and enough exercise. Ideally he should have a large, securely fenced yard where he can work off some of his energy by running around.

WHAT type of owner?

These energetic dogs need energetic owners who like long walks and have time for lively ball games. Dalmatians also need company and tend to express loneliness loudly and destructively. While a well-reared adult Dalmatian is a delightful companion, adolescent Dallies are often boisterous hooligans who are likely to be too much for young children or the frail elderly.

HOW compatible with other pets?

Dalmatians have an innate affinity with horses and are usually good with other pets in general. They are, however, big bouncy dogs who may play too enthusiastically for smaller breeds and other family pets to enjoy their company.

HOW much exercise?

The Dalmatian was bred to run marathons, and adults need plenty of exercise—at least an hour's brisk walk a day. (Pups under a year old should have exercise limited to

Character Trait	Poor	Average	Good	Excellent
Attitude toward other dogs			■	
Quietness		■		
Not destructive		■		
Protective behavior			■	
Not likely to stray		■		
Good with children			■	
Ease of training			■	

Original purpose: Carriage dog
Male height: 23-24 in (58.5-61 cm)
Female height: 22-23 in (56-58.5 cm)
Weight: 40-60 lb (18.1-27.2 kg)
Lifespan: 12-14 years

prevent damage to growing bones.) If deprived of exercise, he will have to work off his surplus energy somehow, probably at the cost of household furnishings.

HOW easy to train?

This intelligent breed learns easily and can be trained to a high standard, but training can be an uphill struggle. They are strong-minded dogs who can be very stubborn, and it takes patience, persistence, and absolute consistency to get them into the habit of obedience.

WHAT good points?

Loyal, intelligent, easygoing, friendly, tireless, protective, outgoing, a great companion for long walks.

WHAT to be aware of?

Exercise and training essential to prevent hooligan behavior. A heavy

shedder. Choose your breeder with care, as some commercial breeders have produced strains with atypically poor temperament.

WHAT medical problems?

Inherited deafness (responsible breeders test puppies' hearing at six weeks—

ask for a certificate). Predisposition to form dangerous bladder stones, especially on high protein diet. Some skin problems.

● *These Dalmatian puppies will grow up to be big, boisterous, and bouncy dogs.*

Large dogs

German Shorthaired Pointer

This is a working multipurpose gundog bred to hunt, point, and retrieve game. He was developed between the 17th and 19th centuries by crossing slow, heavy German pointers with other breeds for improved performance and a more stylish appearance. The result is a versatile gundog who has also achieved renown as search and rescue dog, sniffer dog, therapy dog, and even sled dog. Affectionate,

sociable, and good-tempered, he makes a great family companion as long as his needs for physical and mental exercise are satisfied.

Introduced to the U.S. in 1925, the GSP was recognized by the AKC in 1930. British sportsmen were slower to adopt the breed and KC recognition was not granted until 1954. Today the GSP is recognized worldwide. His cousin, the German Wirehaired Pointer, is a bigger, more workmanlike breed, with a rugged individualism better suited to a working lifestyle and an experienced owner.

WHAT colors?

Solid liver, liver and white (spotted, ticked, or both).

WHAT grooming does the coat need?

The short dense coat is easy care, needing only weekly brushing (twice a week during the molt) to remove dead hair.

HOW suitable are they as family dogs?

The GSP is a wonderful dog for

families who can provide employment for this intelligent and energetic breed. He is devoted to his owners, eager to please, and generally good with children. However, he is a disastrous choice for a family who cannot keep him busy, and as a youngster he is normally too exuberant and demanding to suit a household with very young children.

WHAT type of home?

More suited to country than city life, the GSP needs to live within easy reach of the countryside or a large park where he can enjoy a gallop. He needs a secure yard, although keen gardeners may not need him—he is a great digger and no respecter of plants. He can spend a lot of time outdoors as long as he has enough time with his family but prefers indoor life.

WHAT type of owner?

These active dogs need active owners who enjoy walking in all weather and can provide them with a job to do—if not as gundogs then in activities such as agility or working trials. They are not part-time pets. They need to be part of the family. Not recommended for the elderly or for homes with young children because of their high energy level.

HOW compatible with other pets?

If properly socialized in puppyhood the GSP is generally friendly with other dogs and good with cats in his own household. Some males can be aggressive with strange dogs, and some are enthusiastic cat chasers. This is a hunting breed with an innate chase instinct, so small pets such as rabbits and guinea pigs are best kept out of harm's way.

HOW much exercise?

A great deal—at least two hours' free running a day. The GSP was bred to work all day and he needs

Character Trait	Poor	Average	Good	Excellent
Attitude toward other dogs				
Quietness				
Not destructive				
Protective behavior				
Not likely to stray				
Good with children				
Ease of training				

Original purpose: Hunting, pointing, and retrieving game
Male height: 23-25 in (58.5-63.5 cm)
Female height: 21-23 in (53-58.5 cm)
Weight: 45-70 lb (20.4-31.7 kg)
Lifespan: 12-14 years

● GSPs need minimal grooming, but must be given plenty to do.

plenty of varied exercise and occupation, including the opportunity for off-leash galloping. Agility, competitive obedience, or working trials will provide appropriate mental stimulation. Puppies under nine months should not be overexercised to prevent damage to growing bones.

HOW easy to train?

Intelligent and eager to please, the GSP is highly trainable. Training is a must for this active dog, who will channel his energy into misbehavior if not properly directed. Youngsters can be easily distracted and slow to mature, but persistence pays off. Stick to a calm, consistent, reward-based approach. This is a sensitive dog that reacts badly to rough handling.

Large dogs

WHAT good points?

Gentle, affectionate, even-tempered, alert, intelligent, obedient, very loyal, sociable, tireless, easy-care coat.

WHAT to be aware of?

High maintenance in terms of exercise and training. Needs a lot of input from owners. Tendency to suffer from separation anxiety.

WHAT medical problems?

Generally healthy , but hip and elbow malformation (dysplasia) and cataracts have been reported.

Chesapeake Bay Retriever

This powerfully built retriever is an individualist. Physically and mentally adapted for the tough work of retrieving shot wildfowl from icy water, he has a dense, water-repellent coat, webbed feet, and a great deal of natural determination. A superb hunting dog, he also excels as guard, sniffer dog, service dog for the handicapped, and even livestock dog, and makes a great companion as long as his working drive is satisfied. He is more serious and strong-willed than most retrievers and tends to be a one-man dog, devoted to his owner and his owner's family but aloof with strangers. Socialization is essential to prevent this from becoming shyness or aggression.

Said to originate from two Newfoundland dogs shipwrecked off Chesapeake Bay on the east coast of America in 1807, the Chesapeake was first registered with the AKC in 1878 and was declared the official state dog of Maryland in 1964.

WHAT colors?

Various shades of brown including the attractively named dead grass (straw to bracken) and sedge (red gold to strawberry blond). White spots on chest, toes, and belly are permitted.

WHAT grooming does the coat need?

The dense, springy, oily coat needs minimal maintenance. Weekly grooming with a rubber brush will remove dead hairs and help to distribute the natural oil evenly through the coat. Overgrooming can damage the coat, however, making it less waterproof.

HOW suitable are they as family dogs?

Provided his working drive is satisfied, the Chesapeake is a great family dog, intensely loyal to his people and usually very tolerant and protective of children.

● *A working dog, the Chesapeake is happiest in a country home.*

As a youngster he is likely to be too bouncy for the comfort of small children, and like most retrievers has a tendency to mouth hands. So, he is better suited to families with older children.

WHAT type of home?

As an energetic working breed, the Chesapeake is best suited to a country home. He can cope with city life if he has plenty of exercise and attention, and a securely fenced yard, but is not suitable for an apartment.

WHAT type of owner?

A strong-willed dog with a powerful working drive, the Chesapeake is not recommended for novices or couch potatoes. He needs an active owner who can keep him employed, who enjoys outdoor exercise in all weather, and who has some experience of socializing and training an assertive breed. This is not a part-time breed but one that needs plenty of companionship. He should not be left alone at home for long periods.

HOW compatible with other pets?

Socialization is essential if a Chesapeake is to get along well with other animals. They tend to be dominant, and males in particular may be intolerant of other dogs

Character Trait	Poor	Average	Good	Excellent
Attitude toward other dogs			●	
Quietness	●			
Not destructive		●		
Protective behavior			●	
Not likely to stray		●		
Good with children			●	
Ease of training			●	

Original purpose: Retrieving waterfowl
Male height: 23-26 in (58.5-66 cm)
Female height: 21-24 in (53-61 cm)
Weight: 55-80 lb (25-36 kg)
Lifespan: 10-13 years

of the same sex and may display territorial aggression toward other animals. They have a strong hunting drive and tend to see small animals —sometimes including cats—as prey to be chased.

HOW much exercise?

This breed needs a great deal of vigorous, athletic exercise, preferably including swimming. Walking is not enough. Mental exercise is also important. Deprived of exercise, the Chesapeake is likely to turn his energy toward mischief. Puppies under a year old should not be overexercised, as this may damage growing bones.

HOW easy to train?

Chesapeakes are intelligent and attentive, and respond well to firm, fair, consistent training. Rules need to be established in puppyhood. If this is neglected, this strong-minded and independent dog is likely to take over. Training sessions

need to be made fun—boring repetition and a heavy-handed approach are likely to make the Chesapeake "switch off."

● *Chesapeakes need both mental and physical stimulation.*

WHAT good points?

Loyal, protective, hardworking, calm, confident, devoted, intelligent, sensitive, serious.

WHAT to be aware of?

A working breed that needs employment. Can be prone to dominance problems if not properly socialized and trained.

WHAT medical problems?

Generally a healthy breed; some incidence of hip and elbow malformation (dysplasia), progressive retinal atrophy (degeneration of the light receptor cells in the eyes), and cataracts.

Large dogs

Standard Poodle

There is a great deal more to the Standard Poodle than a fancy haircut. Although today he is usually regarded as a companion breed, he was originally a functional water retriever and still makes a highly efficient gundog—he excels at a range of tasks, from service dog for the disabled to sledding, and is a popular choice for competitive obedience and agility. As a companion, he is good-tempered, responsive, and sensitive to his owner's moods—and also a fun dog with abundant energy and a notable sense of humor. He is one of the few larger breeds suitable for novice owners, although he does need quite a bit of regular exercise and a great deal of coat care.

Poodles date back to at least the 15th century, achieving AKC recognition in 1887. The oldest and largest of the three Poodle breeds, the Standard was bred down to produce Miniatures and Toys.

WHAT colors?

Any solid color, including white, cream, brown, apricot, black, silver, and blue. Parti-colors occur but are not recognized by the AKC.

WHAT grooming does the coat need?

The thick curly coat does not molt and keeps growing if not clipped. Daily grooming with a slicker brush and wide toothed comb is essential to prevent the coat from matting, and it needs clipping every six to eight weeks. Show dogs are presented in an elaborate lion clip that requires a great deal of maintenance; pets are usually more comfortable with a practical short trim (sporting or puppy clip).

HOW suitable are they as family dogs?

The Standard Poodle makes a great family dog as long as he is treated as a member of the family and not denied attention. Most Standards love children, make great playmates,

● *Standard Poodles need lots of grooming, whatever the clip.*

and are often very protective. They are, however, demanding dogs who need company and stimulating activities, and they do not do well in stressful surroundings.

WHAT type of home?

This is an adaptable breed, equally well suited to city or country. For his size, the Standard Poodle takes up surprisingly little space and can even thrive in an apartment provided he has enough attention and exercise. In the country, he can happily walk his owners off their feet.

WHAT type of owner?

Poodles need loving owners who can give them loads of attention. They are ideal for anyone who wants an entertaining and responsive companion, has a lively sense of humor, and is committed to grooming. The Standard Poodle is a good choice for people who enjoy long, energetic walks and for those who enjoy canine activities such as agility, which exercise both mind and body.

HOW compatible with other pets?

This friendly dog is generally excellent with other animals, although he will find it amusing to chase strange cats, squirrels, or anything else that can run unless he is taught not to do so.

HOW much exercise?

Standard Poodles need a fair amount of exercise, at least two brisk walks a day plus active playtime—and at most as much as their owners can take. A team

Character Trait	Poor	Average	Good	Excellent
Attitude toward other dogs				
Quietness				
Not destructive				
Protective behavior				
Not likely to stray				
Good with children				
Ease of training				

Original purpose: Water retriever, companion
Male height: 23-26 in (58-66 cm)
Female height: 21-24 in (53-61 cm)
Weight: 45-70 lb (20-32 kg)
Lifespan: 11-13 years

of Standards has completed the gruelling 1,158-mile (1,865-km) Iditarod sled race in Alaska! Mental exercise is equally important, whether in the form of games or formal obedience training.

HOW easy to train?
The intelligent Poodle is one of the most trainable of breeds. He is eager to learn, quick to respond, and very capable. He needs sensible and sensitive handling and a handler with a sense of humor. Poodles are easily bored by repetition and often have a creative approach to obedience training.

WHAT good points?
Intelligent, good-tempered, obedient, eager to learn, affectionate, reliable, lively, sensitive, adaptable, fun-loving, nonaggressive.

WHAT to be aware of?
High coat care and exercise requirements. Can be noisy; some lines oversensitive, needing gentle handling. Youngsters often rowdy and mischievous.

● *As a companion, the Poodle is generally most comfortable with his coat in the practical short trim seen here.*

WHAT medical problems?
Inherited disorders include hip malformation (dysplasia), eye problems (cataracts and progressive retinal atrophy), and von Willebrand's disease (an hereditary bleeding disorder). Standard Poodles are also vulnerable to bloat (gastric torsion) and ear infections.

Large dogs

Saluki
Other names: Persian Greyhound, Gazelle Hound

This beautiful eastern sighthound is a dog with a mind of his own—a companion rather than a pet. Graceful and aristocratic, he is nonetheless essentially a working dog, bred for speed, endurance, and a powerful hunting drive. He was developed by nomadic Arab tribes to course hare and gazelle in harsh desert conditions, and his working instincts remain intact. He was born to run, he will chase anything that moves, and he is not programmed for obedience. He has a catlike self-sufficiency and independence—and, like a cat, he tends to choose where he will give his affection.

Given enough exercise and an owner who appreciates sighthound nature, he is a sweet-natured, gentle, undemanding, and faithful companion. However, too many Salukis end up in rescue because they have been bought by people attracted to their beauty but unable to cope with their needs. A neglected Saluki becomes a liability!

WHAT colors?
Any color except brindle is acceptable. Colors include white, cream, fawn, golden red, grizzle, tri-color (white, black, and tan), black and tan.

WHAT grooming does the coat need?
This is an easy-care coat, requiring weekly brushing. There are two coat varieties, smooth and feathered, the latter having fringes on ears, tail, and legs, which need combing. Ear fringes may become fouled if they dangle in the Saluki's dinner. Either hold them back in a headband at mealtimes or clean after every meal.

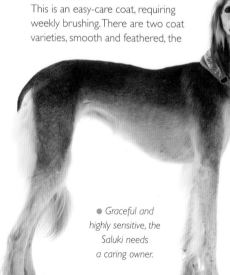

● *Graceful and highly sensitive, the Saluki needs a caring owner.*

HOW suitable are they as family dogs?
The Saluki is not the ideal pet for the average family because of his high exercise needs, strong hunting instinct, and high-strung, sensitive nature. He is good with sensible children if raised with them, but he does not enjoy roughhousing or conventional canine games such as chasing sticks or retrieving toys.

WHAT type of home?
A Saluki needs space, so a home with a large secure yard is best. He can cope with city life if enough exercise is provided, although he is unsuited to apartment living. He does need access to areas where he can run free without danger to himself (i.e. no dashes across busy roads) or to local livestock. Farmers will not welcome unleashed Salukis near their animals.

WHAT type of owner?
This is a breed for an active person with access to land where a Saluki can run free, who will respond sympathetically to this sensitive dog, and is not looking for formal obedience but is prepared to spend time and effort on training.

HOW compatible with other pets?
Salukis are generally friendly with other dogs, especially other sighthounds. They can be good with cats within their own household if raised with them. However, their natural instinct is to chase and kill anything that looks

Character Trait	Poor	Average	Good	Excellent
Attitude toward other dogs				
Quietness				
Not destructive				
Protective behavior				
Not likely to stray				
Good with children				
Ease of training				

Original purpose: Hunting
Male height: 23-28 in (58.5-71 cm)
Female height: 23-28 in (58.5-71 cm)
Weight: 45-60 lb (18.1-27.2 kg)
Lifespan: 12-14 years

like prey, so they should not be trusted with small pets or livestock.

HOW much exercise?

A great deal. Salukis need at least an hour's walk every day, plus free running. However, their strong hunting drive and deafness to the recall mean that areas where they can be trusted off-leash are hard to find. Many owners find that the answer is to join a lure coursing club, where hounds like the Saluki pursue an artificial hare.

HOW easy to train?

Difficult. The Saluki is wayward, independent, and not remotely obedient—not a dog for obedience enthusiasts. Nonetheless, careful socialization and training are essential to make him

● *The Saluki's coat needs only weekly grooming, but more frequent care must be taken of the ear fringes.*

a pleasant companion. Training must be gentle, patient, reward based, and consistent: Salukis are slow to mature, sensitive, and respond badly to harsh treatment.

WHAT good points?

Dignified, intelligent, independent, affectionate, good-natured, faithful, gentle, fun-loving, and an excellent watchdog.

WHAT to be aware of?

Large dogs

Strong hunting drive; hard to recall when off leash. High-strung and does not react well to stress. Early socialization vital to prevent shyness.

WHAT medical problems?

Salukis are generally a healthy breed, although congenital heart problems, autoimmune diseases, and thyroid problems have been reported. Sensitive to anesthesia. Some occurrence of "sudden death syndrome," unexplained deaths of dogs usually while they are under five years of age.

Dogue de Bordeaux

This burly French mastiff is the descendant of medieval war dogs and hunting dogs, developing over the centuries into an all-purpose working dog used for herding, guarding, hunting, hauling carts —and for the bloody sports of bull baiting and dog fighting. Sometimes described as France's answer to England's Bullmastiff, the breed was little known outside France until 1988, when the comedy film *Turner and Hooch*

brought it into the limelight.

Since then, this magnificent dog with his strikin red color and quizzically wrinkled face has won many fans—perhaps too many for his own good, fo this is not a breed for the novice. Dignified, gentle and loyal with his own family, he is a powerful and strong-willed dog who takes his guard role serious and needs early socialization and training to preve the display of aggression toward strangers. This is loveable dog in the right hands—but a liability the wrong ones.

WHAT colors?

All shades of red and fawn; may have white patches on chest and toes, and red or black facial mask.

WHAT grooming does the coat need?

The short coat is easily maintained by weekly brushing with a slicker brush. However, the facial wrinkles may need wiping daily to avoid soreness, especially in heavily wrinkled specimens.

HOW suitable are they as family dogs?

For a family experienced with giant breeds, and who have older children, the Dogue de Bordeaux can be an excellent family dog. As an adult, he is calm and gentle with children. His size and strength make him unsuitable for a home with small children—a half-grown puppy can knock over an adult with one bounce, and young Dogues (under three years old) are great bouncers. They are also very loving and like to sit on people, not realizing their own weight.

● *The massive and powerful Dogue de Bordeaux needs a strong and confident owner whose will and determination matches his own.*

WHAT type of home?

A large country house with a securely fenced yard is best. These big dogs need space and are not suitable for a confined apartment. Playful and clumsy, they can send furniture flying, so small or cluttered rooms are not a safe environment. The short muzzle means that they are prone to overheating, so they need somewhere cool to relax in hot weather.

WHAT type of owner?

The Dogue needs a strong, confident, and experienced owne who has time to train and sociali. him and to provide the company he craves. If left alone too much, he will be miserable and probably destructive. I a breed for the fastidious— snoring, snorting, drooling, and flatulence are part of t package.

HOW compatible with other pets?

Be careful. With training, he will accept other pets in the househo though smaller animals run the ri of being trampled. Early socializati with other dogs is essential, as th breed tends to be dominant and can be dog aggressive, especially with dogs of the same sex. Some have strong chasing instincts, so watch out for neighbor's cat.

HOW much exercise?

Moderate. An adult Dogue needs daily walks to build up and maint. good muscle but should not be

Character Trait	Poor	Average	Good	Excellent
Attitude toward other dogs				
Quietness				
Not destructive				
Protective behavior				
Not likely to stray				
Good with children				
Ease of training				

Place of origin: **France**

Original purpose: Guarding, hunting
Male height: 23.5-26.5 in (60-68 cm)
Female height: 22.5-26 in (58-66 cm)
Weight: 99-110 lb (45-50 kg or over)
Lifespan: 8-9 years

allowed to overheat. Puppies under two years must not be over-exercised, which is likely to damage growing bones.

HOW easy to train?

Moderately difficult. Early, firm, and consistent training is essential. Dogues are stubborn, strong-willed, and often dominant. However, a dog of this size absolutely must be under control. This is an intelligent breed that responds well to training once persuaded that it wishes to do so. Praise and food rewards are more motivating than force, which is usually counterproductive.

WHAT good points?

Loyal, affectionate, vigilant, courageous, even-tempered, protective, a devoted family dog.

WHAT to be aware of?

Needs socialization and training to control his protective and territorial instincts. Puppies are powerful and boisterous. Not a dog to take on lightly.

Large dogs

WHAT medical problems?

Hip and elbow malformation (dysplasia), some heart murmurs, cancer. Loose skin on face can lead to eyelid problems (entropion and ectropion).

Spinone Italiano

He looks like a shaggy hound, but the Spinone is a versatile gundog bred to hunt, point, and retrieve game. Like most gundogs, he also makes a great family dog provided his needs for exercise and company are met. Intelligent, playful, and easygoing, he is nonetheless not a dog who will suit everyone. He is certainly not a part-time commitment, but needs to be fully involved in family life. Neither is he the best choice for the house proud. He tends to drool, while that attractively scruffy coat carries in a lot of dirt, and often betrays a distinct doggy smell. Highly sensitive, he needs early socialization and sympathetic training. In the right environment, however, he will blossom into a devoted and very individual member of the household.

The Spinone is said to be one of the oldest gundog breeds, but has only recently become popular outside his native Italy.

WHAT colors?

White, white with orange or brown markings, or brown roan (white flecked with brown, with or without large brown markings).

WHAT grooming does the coat need?

A thorough weekly or twice-weekly brushing with a wire slicker brush will keep the oily weatherproof coat in good condition, with some stripping of dead hair during the molt. The beard and pendulous ears collect food and mud. They need washing daily to prevent a buildup of dirt, which could lead to infections.

HOW suitable are they as family dogs?

Gentle, laid back, and affectionate, the Spinone is an excellent dog for an active country-dwelling family who can meet his needs for exercise and attention. He has a great affinity with children, with whom he is patient, playful, and dependable—although in puppy-

● *This Spinone appears to have had all the exercise he craves!*

hood he may be too boisterous for the comfort of toddlers.

WHAT type of home?

A country home with plenty of space for exercise is the ideal home for a Spinone. But his people come first with him, and he will adapt to city life as long as he has plenty of regular activity and is allowed to participate fully in family life. Not recommended for apartment life.

WHAT type of owner?

A patient, gentle owner who wants a dog as a constant companion, enjoys country walks and other canine activities, and who is not excessively house proud will find the Spinone a rewarding choice. This dog needs good deal of company, physical activity, and mental stimulation. He is not suitable for treating as a part-time pet—he has to be fully involved in all aspects of his owner's life.

HOW compatible with other pets?

The sociable Spinone gets along well with other animals and enjoys the company of other dogs, although, as with all breeds, early socialization is important. However, this is a hunting dog with an innate chasing instinct, so introduce other pets with care and don't expect him to ignore the neighbor's cat without proper training.

HOW much exercise?

A great deal. The adult Spinone needs at least 60–90 minutes of walking every day, including plenty

Character Trait	Poor	Average	Good	Excellent
Attitude toward other dogs				
Quietness				
Not destructive				
Protective behavior				
Not likely to stray				
Good with children				
Ease of training				

Original purpose: Pointing and retrieving game
Male height: 23.5-27.5 in (60-70 cm)
Female height: 23-25.5 in (58-65 cm)
Weight: 64-86 lb (29-39 kg)
Lifespan: 12-14 years

of free galloping. This is not a breed for the sedentary owner! Puppies under nine months should be limited to short walks and yard play to prevent damage to growing bones.

HOW easy to train?

This highly intelligent breed responds well to training provided the approach is patient, gentle, and consistent. The Spinone is highly sensitive, usually quite submissive, and does not take well to rough handling. He is also a slow maturing breed, so training takes time based on a "little and often" principle.

WHAT good points?

Faithful, intelligent, patient, affectionate, docile (as an adult!), nonaggressive, easygoing, playful.

WHAT to be aware of?

A demanding breed that can be destructive when bored. Timid if not socialized. Definitely not for the house proud. Highly vocal breed, prone to "talking." Most are confirmed scavengers and food stealers.

WHAT medical problems?

Usually a healthy breed; occasional hip malformation (dysplasia) (breeding stock should be hip scored), ectropion and entropion (malformed eyelids). Some lines carry cerebellar ataxia, a hereditary condition in which affected puppies lose control of their limbs and rarely survive their first year.

Large dogs

● *The oily coat of the Spinone does not need much grooming, but the beard and ears require daily attention.*

German Shepherd Dog *Other names: Alsatian*

One of the world's most popular dogs, the German Shepherd's virtues are numerous. Intelligent and adaptable, he makes an ideal working companion, helping to rescue people in distress, assisting people with disabilities, working alongside the police and military, and proving to be a vigilant guard dog. Beneath the proud, courageous exterior lies an even-tempered character that makes the German Shepherd an alert, loyal, and devoted family dog. Athletic and tireless, he needs plenty of exercise and stimulation to flourish—owners must have sufficient time and vitality to devote to the needs of this splendid dog.

The German Shepherd derives from an old breed of herding and working dog that flourished in Germany many centuries ago. First exhibited at a show in Hanover in 1882, it was introduced into the U.K. and the U.S. after World War I. Also known for a time as the Alsatian, the breed gained official AKC recognition in 1908 as the German Shepherd Dog.

WHAT colors?

All black, bi-color (mostly black with some gold on legs), black and gold, gray, gold, sable. Whites, albinos, blues, and livers are not accepted in the breed standard, and do not make show dogs.

WHAT grooming does the coat need?

Weatherproof, straight harsh outer coat with thick undercoat. Though attractive, a long coat is not accepted in the show ring. Short-coated German Shepherds only need one good brushing a week; long-coated dogs need vigorous grooming daily.

HOW suitable are they as family dogs?

When properly trained German Shepherds are ideal family dogs, loyal, obedient, and protective of family members. They are vigorous and strong animals that need plenty of exercise, so are not suitable for the elderly or sick who might have trouble exercising and controlling such an athletic companion.

WHAT type of home?

These are essentially working dogs, so they need a home environment that will allow

ample opportunity for exercise, activity, and tasks to perform. Ideal dogs for country dwellers; city owners should really have a reasonably sized yard and/or convenient access to a park for long walks. Not a dog to coop up behind four walls all day long.

WHAT type of owner?

An owner of this intelligent breed must be prepared to devote considerable time and attention to the dog every day. He needs physical activity and mental stimulation; if you cannot spend quality time daily with your dog, do not consider a German Shepherd—is unfair to subject the breed to a life of boredom and solitude if you are out at work all day.

HOW compatible with other pets?

Normally gets along well with other dogs and cats in the home, but be careful about the introductions—a boisterous new puppy can overwhelm and irritate existing pets, which can cause friction.

HOW much exercise?

An adult dog needs at least one good walk a day lasting around an

Character Trait	Poor	Average	Good	Excellent
Attitude toward other dogs				
Quietness				
Not destructive				
Protective behavior				
Not likely to stray				
Good with children				
Ease of training				

Original purpose: Herder and guard
Male height: 24-26 in (61-66 cm)
Female height: 22-24 in (56-61 cm)
Weight: not to exceed 75-95 lb (34-43 kg)
Lifespan: 12-13 years

hour, ideally with time spent running safely off the leash. The German Shepherd thrives on exercise.

HOW easy to train?

This breed is highly intelligent, has excellent working ability, and loves a challenge. GSDs are generally very responsive to training and highly suitable for advanced training disciplines, like agility and competitive obedience.

WHAT good points?

Reliable, self-confident, athletic, bold, obedient, loyal, even-tempered, immensely willing, good guard dog.

WHAT to be aware of?

Shy or nervous GSDs should be avoided because they may exhibit aggressive tendencies when unsettled. GSDs left alone for long periods or that lack mental stimulation may become destructive or start to bark excessively.

WHAT medical problems?

This breed can suffer from allergies, epilepsy, malformation of the hip joint (dysplasia), inflammation of the cornea, lameness (panosteitis), chronic degenerative radiculomyelopathy (gradual loss of use of hind legs), anal furunculosis (ulcerated anal tissue), and skin problems.

Large dogs

● *Intelligent and loyal—rightfully one of the world's favorites.*

Old English Sheepdog *Other names: Bobtail*

The ultimate shaggy dog, the Old English Sheepdog is big, boisterous, and very hairy. He is often born tailless (and sometimes docked), hence his popular nickname "Bobtail." He is a good-natured, happy, playful dog who likes to have something to do. He is also a very high-maintenance breed, needing a lot of physical and mental exercise, company, attention, and hours of grooming—hard work, but a great companion in the right hands. Old English Sheepdogs are sociable creatures who need to be involved in family activities, and, like most working breeds, can be destructive if bored.

The OES originated as a tough shepherd's and drover's dog, but today has become a glamorous show dog and loveable companion. In recent years, media exposure has made the breed too popular for its own good—many end up in rescue, as impulse buyers discover cute puppies become demanding and labor-intensive dogs.

WHAT colors?

Body and hindquarters any shade of gray, grizzle, or blue, with or without white socks; head, neck, forequarters, and underbelly white.

WHAT grooming does the coat need?

A lot… and then some more. A big coat on a big dog, it needs three or four hours a week with brush and comb (for a pet)—up to 15 hours for a show dog. If dead hair is not combed out frequently, it mats into lumps. Expect a massive cleanup job after walks in the rain, and regular cleaning of the rear and legs— an unpleasant task if the dog has an upset stomach. Professional grooming recommended; pet owners often prefer to have the coat clipped down to a puppy trim for ease of care.

HOW suitable are they as family dogs?

The OES thrives as a family dog and is a great playmate for older children, gentle by nature though physically heavy and rather clumsy. However, they are too big and bouncy to be recommended to households with toddlers or frail elderly people.

WHAT type of home?

This is a country dog who needs space. He is not suitable for an apartment, nor for a home without a yard. He is not recommended for homes where everything is kept immaculate. Big hairy dogs can make a great deal of mess, especially after a rainy and muddy walk.

WHAT type of owner?

These dogs need active owners who enjoy long walks, have plenty of time for exercise and training, and are committed to grooming or to frequent trips to a professional groomer. This is not a dog for people who are out all day, as he needs company, and is definitely not one for the house proud.

HOW compatible with other pets?

The OES is generally good with other dogs if well socialized in puppyhood, though he can be suspicious of strange dogs. He will be friendly with cats in his own household, but is likely to chase others. Small pets are at risk of being squashed.

HOW much exercise?

Adults will enjoy as much exercise as you can give, and should have at least two hours' daily exercise plus playtime in the yard. Avoid walks in hot weather, as the heavy coat easily leads to overheating. Puppies should not be overwalked, to

Character Trait	Poor	Average	Good	Excellent
Attitude toward other dogs			●	
Quietness		●		
Not destructive		●		
Protective behavior			●	
Not likely to stray			●	
Good with children				●
Ease of training			●	

Original purpose: Droving and herding
Male height: 24-26 in (61-66 cm)
Female height: 22-24 in (56-61 cm)
Weight: 60-90 lb (27.2-40.8 kg)
Lifespan: 10-12 years

prevent damage to growing bones, but they have endless energy that needs to be burned off in several concentrated sessions of play.

● *The OES needs an owner prepared to make considerable commitments to both grooming and daily exercise.*

HOW easy to train?

Moderate. They are intelligent and quick learners who are always interested in something new to do. They are also strong-willed and stubborn, and can be very uncooperative if their interest is not captured, so make training sessions fun for best results. This breed needs mental stimulus, and is capable of a range of activities from agility to herding.

WHAT good points?

Even-tempered, bold, faithful, trustworthy, nonaggressive, intelligent, playful, loyal, affectionate, outgoing, people oriented.

Large dogs

WHAT to be aware of?

Massive grooming commitment. Can be overterritorial and possessive of toys or food.

WHAT medical problems?

Hip and elbow malformation (dysplasia), osteochondritis (joint disease), eye disorders including cataracts and progressive retinal atrophy (degeneration of the light receptor cells in the eyes), thyroid disorders, hemophilia (a blood disorder), heart problems. Breeding stock should have hips and eyes checked.

Weimaraner *Other names: Weimar Pointer*

The "Gray Ghost" is one of the most striking gundog breeds, with his metallic gray coat and light eyes. A superb and versatile working dog, he is intelligent, eager, and devoted to his owner. He is also a high-powered dog with abundant energy and a dominant character who needs extensive socialization, training, attention, and affection from an experienced and equally strong-willed handler. In the right hands, he is a marvelous dog; but he must have employment. A bored, underexercised Weimaraner can be a nightmare—possessive, over-protective, restless, noisy, and destructive.

German hunters employed dogs of Weimaraner type as early as the 17th century, but by the 19th century the Weimaraner was kept exclusively at the German court of Weimar. Introduced to the U.S. in 1929 and to the U.K. in 1952, the breed is now renowned worldwide as a working gundog.

WHAT grooming does the coat need?

This is an easy-care coat. Brush about twice a week to remove dead hairs and daily during the molt. Long-haired Weimaraners need the feathering behind ears and legs and on the tail to be combed through regularly.

HOW suitable are they as family dogs?

As long as he has the opportunity to employ his working abilities to the fullest, the Weimaraner is an admirable family dog, generally gentle and reliable with children. However, he is a powerful, boisterous dog, not recommended for families with small children or frail elderly people, and generally too head-strong for the average household.

WHAT type of home?

This is a country dog who needs a well-fenced yard and access to suitable land for serious amounts of exercise. He is not suited for confined small spaces such as apartments or homes with tiny yards.

WHAT colors?

Ideally silver gray, but mouse gray or roe gray acceptable, with a metallic sheen. May have a dark eel stripe down their back, and small white mark is permissible on the chest. Eye color amber or blue gray, never dark. Puppies are born with stripes, which disappear before they leave the nest.

WHAT type of owner?

Weimaraner owners need to be physically strong and mentally tough, capable of the firm but kind leadership that this breed needs. Ideally they should be looking for a working companion, and will need plenty of time for training and exercising. This is a breed for outdoor types who enjoy a great deal of exercise—not a dog for novices nor for couch potatoes or the frail.

HOW compatible with other pets?

If well-socialized in puppyhood the Weimaraner is generally good with other dogs but tends to be dominant and will not back down challenged. He is fine with cats in his own household if raised with them, but he is a hunting dog with an innate chasing instinct who should not be trusted with small pets such as rabbits—or the neighbor's cat.

HOW much exercise?

Adults need a great deal of exercise every day, including the opportunity for off-leash galloping. Puppies und

Character Trait	Poor	Average	Good	Excellent
Attitude toward other dogs				
Quietness				
Not destructive				
Protective behavior				
Not likely to stray				
Good with children				
Ease of training				

Original purpose: Hunting, pointing, and retrieving game
Male height: 24-27 in (61-68.5 cm)
Female height: 22-25 in (56-63.5 cm)
Weight: 65-75 lb (29.4-34 kg)
Lifespan: 10-13 years

nine months should be limited to short walks and yard play to prevent damage to growing bones.

HOW easy to train?

Depends on the owner. This is a challenging breed, willful and easily bored. He can be trained to a very high standard by an owner who can establish firm but kind leadership right at the start, but may be too much of a handful for most novices. Training should be firm, patient, and gentle, keeping lessons short and interesting.

WHAT good points?

Intelligent, friendly, outgoing, fearless, devoted, protective, sensitive, powerful, versatile.

WHAT to be aware of?

A very strong-willed dominant dog who needs work to do. Potential aggression toward other dogs can be a problem if not properly socialized as a puppy.

Large dogs

WHAT medical problems?

Generally a healthy breed; some problems with entropion (inverted eyelids), cataracts, hip malformation (dysplasia), bloat (gastric torsion), and heart defects. Over-rapid growth in puppies is also a problem in the breed.

● Although bred for hunting, Weimaraners want to be part of the household and so can be quite demanding dogs to keep.

● The beautiful gray color and luster of the coat is obvious in this fine male Weimaraner. The short coat is very low maintenance.

Bullmastiff

This impressively powerful dog was developed in 19th century England, using a blend of Mastiff and Bulldog to create the "Gamekeeper's Night Dog" to tackle violent poaching gangs. Today his career in protection work has been taken over by more versatile and trainable breeds, and his main role is as companion and watchdog. Dignified, loyal, and affectionate, he is gentle with his own family but retains all the guarding instincts of his ancestors. With proper socialization and training to ensure that his protective drive does not veer toward aggression, he is a lovable family companion, but this strong and stubborn dog is not a suitable choice for the inexperienced. He needs space and supervision, and his sheer size can be a problem, especially because he often thinks he's a lapdog.

Modern Bullmastiffs vary in type. Beware of stock with overheavy bone and foreshortened faces, which may have health problems.

WHAT colors?

Any shade of brindle, fawn or red, with black muzzle, dark markings around the eyes, and dark ears. A little white on the chest is acceptable, but white markings elsewhere are undesirable.

WHAT grooming does the coat need?

This is a low-maintenance coat, needing only regular brushing (say ten minutes twice a week) with a firm bristle brush. Grooming should include checking the feet, because they carry a lot of weight.

HOW suitable are they as family dogs?

In the right home and with the right upbringing, the Bullmastiff can be an excellent family dog. However, his size and strong guarding instincts make him unsuitable for most families with small children. He may be over-protective, putting visiting children at risk if he misinterprets rough play, and as a youngster (up to about three years old) he tends to be quite rowdy and liable to knock over small people.

WHAT type of home?

Big dogs take up a lot of space, so this is not the ideal breed for a small house. A large country house with a strongly fenced yard (Bullmastiffs can simply walk through lightweight fences if they feel the need) is more suitable. This breed does not tolerate extremes of temperature, so they need somewhere cool and shaded to relax in hot weather.

WHAT type of owner?

This is a dog for a strong, easygoing, confident and experienced owner who has the time to train and socialize him and to provide the company this breed craves. Bullmastiff owners should also be prepared to put up with snoring, snorting, slobbering, and flatulence.

HOW compatible with other pets?

Be careful. Adult Bullmastiffs can be aggressive with other dogs of the same sex, and early socialization is important. They are usually good with the family cat if raised together, but should not be trusted with strange animals. Smaller pets may be at risk of being trodden on.

HOW much exercise?

The Bullmastiff's exercise needs are moderate, but he does need daily walks. This breed tends to be lazy and should be encouraged to exercise, as they tend to put on weight. Puppies under two years

Character Trait	Poor	Average	Good	Excellent
Attitude toward other dogs		▩		
Quietness			▩	
Not destructive			▩	
Protective behavior				▩
Not likely to stray			▩	
Good with children			▩	
Ease of training	▩			

Original purpose: Protection
Male height: 25-27 in (63.5-69 cm)
Female height: 24-26 in (61-66 cm)
Weight: 100-133 lb (45-60 kg)
Lifespan: 8-10 years

must not be overexercised, which is likely to cause damage to growing bones.

HOW easy to train?

Moderately difficult. Strong and stubborn, the Bullmastiff needs to be persuaded that he is not the leader of the family. Training should start early, and be firm, patient, and consistent, keeping sessions short and interesting. Bullying tactics will get you nowhere with this breed. Praise and food rewards are more effective.

WHAT good points?

Fearless, loyal, protective, alert yet calm, high-spirited, active, reliable, tolerant, stoical, courageous, powerful.

WHAT to be aware of?

Not a dog for the novice. Although adults are generally calm and sensible, puppies are hard work. Guard instincts mean this breed can be a real liability if not properly trained and socialized.

Large dogs

WHAT medical problems?

This breed has a short lifespan and serious problems with bone and joint problems such as hip malformation (dysplasia); eyelid problems (entropion) may also occur. Bullmastiffs are also prone to cancer and susceptible to bloat.

● This is a guard breed, and puppy socialization is vital to ensure that your pet accepts visitors to the home. Training is essential for such a large dog.

Rhodesian Ridgeback

Originally developed to track lions and hold them at bay until the hunters arrived, the Rhodesian Ridgeback nowadays employs his courage, loyalty, and protective instincts in the role of companion and watchdog. He is a handsome dog who is built to combine speed, agility, and stamina with muscular power and who owes his name to the distinctive ridge of hair down his spine. He is also a strong-willed dog who needs an equally strong-minded owner who can provide early socialization, appropriate training, and a heavy investment of time. In the right hands, he is an excellent companion, very much a "people dog" with strong but discriminating guard instincts.

The Ridgeback was developed in South Africa from a mixture of ridge-backed Hottentot dogs and European settlers' sporting breeds, achieving formal recognition in Africa in 1922 and reaching the U.K. shortly thereafter. The breed was recognized by the AKC in 1955.

WHAT colors?

Light wheaten to red wheaten; may have dark muzzle and ears, and a little white on chest and toes is permissible.

WHAT grooming does the coat need?

The short sleek coat requires little maintenance. A weekly brushing with a hound glove will keep it in good condition.

HOW suitable are they as family dogs?

With careful early socialization and in the right hands, the Ridgeback can be a great family dog. He is an excellent and good-tempered companion for older children who treat him with respect, although, as with all powerful guard breeds, supervision is advisable. Not a good choice for households with pre-school children, particularly as puppies (under two years) are very exuberant and quite likely to send toddlers flying.

WHAT type of home?

The Ridgeback is best suited to a country home with a well-fenced yard—this very athletic dog can clear quite high fences and will be tempted to do so if bored. He can cope with apartment living only if provided with plenty of exercise and attention, and should only be considered as a city dog if there is easy access to suitable exercise areas for free running.

WHAT type of owner?

This rewarding but demanding breed needs a strong, confident, and experienced owner who is able to establish leadership and who has plenty of time and energy for training, exercise, and companionship. Ridgebacks are not suited to homes where they will be left alone for long periods, as they can be very destructive if neglected. Not one for dedicated gardeners. They dig with enthusiasm and are likely to regard treasured shrubs as delicious chew toys.

HOW compatible with other pets?

Be careful. If properly socialized, Ridgebacks are not quarrelsome with other dogs, but they are very dominant and some may display aggression toward dogs of the same sex. Cats in the same household will usually be accepted but strange cats are just asking to be chased. This hunting breed has a very high prey drive, and small pets are at serious risk from them.

Character Trait	Poor	Average	Good	Excellent
Attitude toward other dogs				
Quietness				
Not destructive				
Protective behavior				
Not likely to stray				
Good with children				
Ease of training				

Original purpose: Big game hunting
Male height: 25-27 in (63.5-68.5 cm)
Female height: 24-26 in (61-66 cm)
Weight: 70-85 lb (31.7-38.5 kg)
Lifespan: 10-12 years

HOW much exercise?

Above average—several brisk daily walks (at least 2 miles/3 km a day) and the opportunity for free running. Ridgebacks are natural chasers and need training not to pursue joggers, other dogs, or livestock when off leash. Activities such as lure coursing and agility are a great way for them to burn off excess energy. Puppies under six months should not be overexercised.

HOW easy to train?

These strong-willed, independent dogs can be extremely stubborn and novices are likely to find them difficult. Training needs to start early, while a puppy is young enough to be manageable, and to be firm, fair, and consistent. Reward-based methods (especially food rewards) work best. A heavy-handed approach is usually counterproductive.

WHAT good points?

Dignified, intelligent, affectionate, loyal, powerful, active, protective, nonaggressive, independent.

WHAT to be aware of?

Early socialization essential to avoid dominance aggression. Puppies (and adults) can be very destructive. Can be dog aggressive and overprotective.

WHAT medical problems?

Generally a healthy breed, but inherited defects include hip and elbow malformation (dysplasia), thyroid problems, and cataracts. All puppies should be screened for dermoid sinus (abnormal tissue on back or neck.)

Large dogs

● *Once known as the "African lion dog," the Ridgeback was employed in his native land to hunt, retrieve, take care of children, and guard property, tasks he can still perform.*

Rottweiler

Rottweilers have suffered from bad press over the years, largely because these powerful, imposing dogs have too often attracted unsuitable owners. Like any natural guard breed, Rotties need proper socialization and expert training. They are only suited to strong-minded, experienced handlers who can provide firm leadership. Essentially working dogs, they have brains as well as brawn and in the right hands can be trained to a very high standard. They have served as police and military dogs, guide dogs for the blind, search and rescue dogs, and therapy dogs. This is not a breed to take on lightly, but with sensible discipline, and plenty of love and attention, the Rottie is an admirable companion and reliable family dog.

The Rottweiler takes its name from Rottweil in southern Germany, where it was renowned as a drovers' dog and guard. Today it is one of the world best-known protection dog breeds.

WHAT colors?

Black with rich tan markings on chest, legs, under tail, and face; facial markings to include cheeks, muzzle, and spots above eyes.

WHAT grooming does the coat need?

This is an easy-care coat, needing little more than a good brushing twice a week to remove dead hairs and keep a good shine.

HOW suitable are they as family dogs?

This is a superb family dog for experienced owners who can provide suitable training. A family environment suits the Rottie, who needs human contact if he is to be happy and well balanced. Not recommended with young children because, although generally reliable, there is always an element of risk with powerful guard breeds. Older, sensible children will find the Rottie a good friend but should not be allowed to take him out unsupervised.

WHAT type of home?

This is a big dog who needs plenty of space. Given enough exercise, he can be equally happy in the city or country, but is not suited to apartment living. He needs a securely fenced yard.

WHAT type of owner?

Rottweiler owners should be calm but assertive, able to provide confident leadership and also plenty of affection, as well as having time for training, exercise, and play. This is not a breed for novices or couch potatoes. The Rottie is a working dog who needs a great deal of physical and mental exercise to keep him happy.

HOW compatible with other pets?

Be careful. A properly socialized Rottweiler will accept other animals in the same household as members of his family. However, Rotties are highly dominant and can often be intolerant of dogs of the same sex, and some have a strong chasing instinct that may put cats and other small pets at risk.

HOW much exercise?

The Rottweiler's forebears were expected to drive herds of cattle perhaps 40 miles (65 km) a day and, while few modern owners can offer this level of activity, the breed

Character Trait	Poor	Average	Good	Excellent
Attitude toward other dogs				
Quietness				
Not destructive				
Protective behavior				
Not likely to stray				
Good with children				
Ease of training				

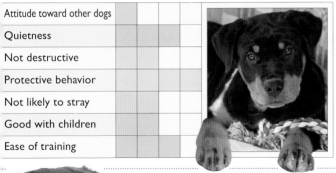

Original purpose: Guarding and herding
Male height: 24-27 in (61-68.5 cm)
Female height: 22-25 in (56-63.5 cm)
Weight: 80-135 lb (36.4-61.4 kg)
Lifespan: 8-11 years

does need plenty of exercise. Puppies under a year old must have their exercise limited to prevent damage to growing bones.

HOW easy to train?

Highly trainable, but need calm, confident handling. Early socialization and training are essential for this powerful and strong-willed breed. The Rottie is quick to learn—and will learn bad behavior unless corrected kindly but consistently.

● *Rottweiler puppies are as appealing as any breed, but remember that they grow up to be big, powerful dogs and need sensible training.*

A confrontational approach will lead to problems. Owners need to earn respect with a firm but sympathetic approach, using reward-based training to motivate the dog to want to learn.

WHAT good points?

Courageous, intelligent, loyal, versatile, confident, affectionate, protective, self-assured, good-natured.

WHAT to be aware of?

Can be very dominant, especially adolescent males, and also territorial. Youngsters should never be allowed to develop bad habits that are difficult to break in maturity. Only buy from responsible breeders who make good temperament a priority.

WHAT medical problems?

Hip malformation (dysplasia), cruciate ligament problems can affect the knees, cancer, heart disease, eye disease.

Large dogs

Bloodhound

Bred for centuries for an incredible sense of smell, the Bloodhound is renowned as the greatest tracker dog of them all, tracing criminals and finding lost people. His name signifies noble breeding (as in "bloodstock") rather than savagery, and he is generally good-natured and affectionate. However, he will not suit most pet homes. This is a powerful dog with minimal predisposition to obedience who eats hugely, can be destructive, bays like the Hound of the Baskervilles, and slobbers profusely. He needs a lot of exercise, but a big dog who is ruled by his nose is not easy to walk. It takes considerable strength to haul him off the trail, and off-leash he is deaf to the recall once he has picked up an interesting scent.

Today famous worldwide, the Bloodhound is said to have originated in Belgium and to have been introduced to Britain by William the Conqueror in 1066.

WHAT colors?

Black and tan, liver and tan (red and tan), and red. A small amount of white on chest, feet or tip of tail is permissible.

WHAT grooming does the coat need?

The short coat is easy care, needing only a weekly rubbing with a hound glove to remove dead hairs. However, the heavy, hanging ears regularly pick up muck and slobber and frequent cleaning is needed to prevent ear infections.

HOW suitable are they as family dogs?

Despite his gentle nature and affection for children, the Bloodhound is not the ideal family dog. He is big and clumsy, and may well bowl over or trample small children or the frail elderly. He can also be food possessive, and children too young to understand this could be at risk. By nature he is often more suited to be a one-person dog rather than a family member.

WHAT type of home?

This is definitely not a city dog. Bloodhounds need a lot of space, so require a home with a large yard or extensive grounds. Secure fencing is a must, or they will disappear after a scent. Though hound aficionados describe the Bloodhound's baying as melodious, a home with deaf or highly tolerant neighbors is recommended.

WHAT type of owner?

This breed is best suited to an owner who has an interest in tracking. Owners also need to be physically fit and strong enough to handle a powerful dog. Bloodhounds are certainly not the breed for anyone who wants to enjoy relaxing country walks. They need a major commitment of time, plenty of company (they dislike being left alone), and firm but sensitive handling.

HOW compatible with other pets?

The good-natured Bloodhound is generally good with other animals, although he is clumsy, and small pets run the risk of being squashed accidentally. Some bloodlines may show aggression to other dogs of the same sex.

HOW much exercise?

A great deal. Puppies should have limited exercise to prevent damage to growing bones, but adults need long walks daily. Bloodhounds will not ignore a scent, so they are

Character Trait	Poor	Average	Good	Excellent
Attitude toward other dogs			■	
Quietness	■			
Not destructive		■		
Protective behavior	■			
Not likely to stray	■			
Good with children			■	
Ease of training	■			

Original purpose: Tracking
Male height: 25-27 in (63.5-68.5 cm)
Female height: 23-25 in (58.5-63.5 cm)
Weight: 80-110 lb (36-50 kg)
Lifespan: 7-10 years

normally walked on a long leash to prevent them from disappearing over the horizon. Off-leash exercise is only safe in totally secure areas.

HOW easy to train?

Difficult. Bloodhounds are stubborn, independent, and willful, but they are also highly sensitive and can be ruined by harsh treatment. Training needs to be firm but gentle, endlessly patient, and realistic—don't expect Collie-style obedience. Adolescent males can be a real handful and need sensible, consistent leadership before they settle down.

WHAT good points?

Affectionate, sensitive, not quarrelsome, dignified, gentle, good-natured, loyal, a superb tracker.

WHAT to be aware of?

Excessive drooling—a shake of the head can send slobber flying 20 feet (6 m). Strong "doggy" smell. Food thief. Highly vocal. Avoid specimens with excessive skin wrinkles and obscured or discharging eyes.

WHAT medical problems?

Bloodhounds are prone to ear infections, inward-turning eyelids (entropion), hip malformation (dysplasia), and skin allergies and are highly vulnerable to gastric torsion (bloat).

Large dogs

● This is a high-maintenance breed that demands serious commitment from an owner.

Bernese Mountain Dog *Other names: Berner Sennenhund*

Striking good looks and a calm, friendly, people-oriented nature give the Bernese considerable appeal as a family dog. He developed in the Swiss mountains as an all-purpose farm dog, herding, guarding, and hauling carts, and remains a versatile worker who enjoys obedience, agility, tracking, herding, and carting. Given the attention he requires, he is a lovable companion, gentle and tolerant. However, this is a demanding breed and not for the inexperienced. He is big, powerful, and strong-willed. He needs occupation for his working intelligence, and he is a highly sociable creature who needs human company. He does not cope well with boredom or loneliness. He also needs a fair amount of exercise and grooming.

The Bernese is the most popular of the four Swiss Mountain breeds developed for work on Alpine farms. The breed was rescued from near extinction in the late 19th century and has now achieved worldwide popularity.

WHAT colors?

Jet black with rich tan on all four legs, cheeks, chest, and over eyes, and white facial blaze and chest marking. White paws and white tail tip are desirable but not essential.

WHAT grooming does the coat need?

The long, thick coat needs regular (twice weekly) brushing and combing, with extra attention during the molt. It is important to groom right down to the skin. Combing the topcoat only will look good on the surface but will leave dead hair clogging the undercoat and eventually matting. This breed sheds heavily—you will need a good vacuum cleaner.

HOW suitable are they as family dogs?

The Bernese is an ideal family dog for an experienced family with plenty of time for him. He likes to be involved in family activities and to be the center of attention. He is generally good with children, although as a youngster he may be too rough and boisterous for young children and needs sensible supervision.

WHAT type of home?

As a large working breed, the Bernese is not ideally suited to city life and certainly not a dog to keep in an apartment. He needs human company. He will not be comfortable in a very warm house or in an unshaded yard in hot weather as his heavy coat makes him highly susceptible to overheating.

WHAT type of owner?

Best for experienced owners who have the time and patience to train a strong-minded, powerful dog and enjoy activities such as carting or agility. Owners should also expect to give and receive a great deal of affectionate attention and appreciate a dog who needs to be a full-time family member.

HOW compatible with other pets?

Most Bernese are good with other animals if raised with them and sensibly socialized. They are big dogs and boisterous in puppyhood, so care needs to be taken to protect smaller pets from accidental injury.

Character Trait	Poor	Average	Good	Excellent
Attitude toward other dogs				
Quietness				
Not destructive				
Protective behavior				
Not likely to stray				
Good with children				
Ease of training				

*Place of origin: **Switzerland***

Original purpose: Herding, guarding, carting
Male height: 25-27.5 in (63.5-70 cm)
Female height: 23-26 in (58.5-66 cm)
Weight: 87-90 lb (40-41 kg)
Lifespan: 6-9 years

HOW much exercise?

This breed has only moderate exercise requirements for its size. Adults are quite adaptable and will thrive on a minimum of half an hour's walk a day, or alternatively will enjoy a great deal more, depending on your lifestyle and their level of fitness. Puppies under twelve months should not be overexercised, which is likely to cause damage to growing bones.

HOW easy to train?

Moderate. Bernese are generally willing to please, but they do have a mind of their own and a sense of humor, so training needs to be firm, patient, and consistent, keeping sessions short and interesting. Some males can be dominant and require an experienced handler. Training should start early. Left to his own devices, boisterous youngsters can become uncontrollable.

WHAT good points?

Good-natured, friendly, confident, protective, intelligent, versatile, affectionate, loyal, active, nonaggressive.

WHAT to be aware of?

A demanding breed, highly rewarding in the right hands but needing a lot of commitment. Sadly, this breed tends to have a very short lifespan.

WHAT medical problems?

Hip and elbow malformation (dysplasia), osteochondritis (a disease affecting developing bone causing foreleg lameness), and a high incidence of cancer. This breed has a notably short average life expectancy, although individuals do reach their teens.

Large dogs

Alaskan Malamute

This magnificent Arctic sled dog was not designed to be a pet. He has a friendly nature, impressive personality, and great natural dignity, but he is essentially a working dog. The "cart horse of the North" was bred to pull heavy loads long distances and is among the most powerful of dog breeds. He needs the stimulus of activities such as backpacking, draft work (pulling a sled or, lacking snow, a wheeled rig), or weight pulling. Given this activity, he can make a great companion, though not for novices as he is powerf[ul], stubborn, and has a strong hunting drive.

Originally developed by the Mahlemiut Inuit of Alaska to haul sleds and carry packs, the breed nea[rly] died out in the 1920s. Preserve[d] a few dedicated breeders, it achie[ved] AKC recognition in 1935, was introduced into the U.K. in 1959 and is now a star of the show [ring].

WHAT colors?

Any shade of gray through to black, or shades of red through to liver, always with white markings on underbody, legs, feet, and face. Characteristic facial markings are present in the form of dark cap or mask. The only solid color allowed is white.

WHAT grooming does the coat need?

The dense coat needs regular deep combing to remove dead hair, about three or four times a week. This breed molts hugely once a year, when hair comes out in clumps and extra grooming is required.

HOW suitable are they as family dogs?

Provided he has appropriate occupation, the Malamute's love of people makes him a great family pet. Although he is generally patient with children, he is not recommended for homes with small children simply because he is so powerful and can cause accidental injury to little ones.

WHAT type of home?

Malamutes are totally unsuited to city life. They need space. An ideal home would have plenty of acreage and opportunities for this dog to enjoy the work at which he excels. A home without near neighbors may be best as, although Malamutes don't bark much, they enjoy a good howl sometimes.

WHAT type of owner?

Malamute owners need to be energetic outdoor types who enjoy being out in all weather. They should be strong-willed and dedicated to working their dogs, as well as having time for grooming and enjoying their dogs' company. This breed is a great companion for hikers and backpackers, and f[or] those who live in areas where the[re] are sled-racing clubs and the like.

HOW compatible with other pets?

Individuals vary, but be cautious! Malamutes have a very strong pr[ey] drive and will chase anything that moves. They will usually accept ca[ts] in the same household if brought up with them, but should never b[e] regarded as safe with livestock. T[hey] can be aggressive toward dogs o[f] the same sex, and early socializat[ion] is essential to prevent problems.

HOW much exercise?

An adult Malamute needs a brisk 4-mile (6-km) walk a day at the minimum, with no maximum. It is impossible to tire him out. Care must be taken when walking in t[he] vicinity of livestock—don't trust him! Puppies should have limited exercise to prevent damage to growing bones. Build up gradually from about six months until 18 months, when they are full grow[n].

Character Trait	Poor	Average	Good	Excellent
Attitude toward other dogs				
Quietness				
Not destructive				
Protective behavior				
Not likely to stray				
Good with children				
Ease of training				

Original purpose: Hauling sleds, carrying packs, hunting
Male height: 25-28 in (63.5-71 cm)
Female height: 23-26 in (58.5-66 cm)
Weight: up to 85 lb (38.5 kg)
Lifespan: 10-12 years

HOW easy to train?

Difficult. Malamutes are intelligent, but not programmed for obedience. They learn quickly, but are equally quick to grow bored with training sessions and are quite likely to ignore commands. Training needs to start early and to be very, very patient. This is a strong-willed breed that needs an equally strong-willed (but never aggressive) owner.

WHAT good points?

Intelligent, hardworking, tireless, affectionate, good with children, loyal, dignified, people friendly, clean, little "doggy" smell.

WHAT to be aware of?

A demanding, dominant dog, not for novices. Large, powerful, and stubborn, needing a great deal of exercise. Strong chase instinct and can be aggressive toward other dogs. Very heavy molt.

WHAT medical problems?

Known problems include hip malformation (dysplasia), cataracts, thyroid problems, bloat, and skin irritations. Responsible breeders will have their stock hip scored and eye tested.

Large dogs

● Brawn, brains, and beauty in one dog—but not an easy pet.

English Setter *Other names: Llewellin Setter (working type)*

The beauty and friendly temperament of this most elegant of gundogs have made him more popular today as a show dog and companion than as a worker. Gentler than the other setter breeds, he makes a wonderful companion dog, provided he has plenty of exercise (including free galloping) and plenty of company. He is a sociable creature who is devoted to his family and does not like being left alone for long periods. He is also highly energetic and fun-loving, and can be quite demanding, especially as a youngster—not a dog for the inactive, nor for house-proud owners who cann[ot] cope with mud, molt, and mischief.

Setters developed in the age of falconry to find and mark the position of gamebirds, perform[ing] the same task later as gundogs. Today the[y] are popular companions, but avoid pup[s] from working bloodlines, which are usu[ally] too active for pet homes.

WHAT colors?

The white coat is ticked with color to create a marbled effect known as belton. Color varieties are blue belton (black and white), orange belton (orange and white), lemon belton (lemon and white), and tri-color (blue or liver belton with tan). Puppies are born white, gradually developing color after the first week.

WHAT grooming does the coat need?

The long, silky, slightly wavy coat needs regular brushing and combing to remove dead hair and prevent tangles, and it is important to comb out mud, grass seeds, and other debris after country walks. Show dogs are also trimmed to achieve a neater effect. Neutering can cause coat changes, leading to a thicker, woollier coat that needs more grooming.

HOW suitable are they as family dogs?

English Setters enjoy the company of children and want to share fully in family life. They make wonderful family pets for the right family, provided they have enough space and plenty of exercise. Young children could be a problem, as this is a big, bouncy breed, especially in youth, which can all too easily knock toddlers over.

WHAT type of home?

This is essentially an outdoor dog, that needs plenty of space and is best suited to a country home. H[e] will adapt to city life if enough exercise is provided, but is not recommended for an apartment. He needs a secure yard with a hig[h] fence to prevent escapes.

WHAT type of owner?

Only those who enjoy regular lon[g] walks in all weather need apply! T[he] English Setter needs a patient owner who will persist with training and can provide plenty of company for this sociable breed. A large, active family with time for exercise, play, and training will suit this dog best.

HOW compatible with other pets?

Generally the English Setter is ver[y] good with other pets, although he needs to learn in puppyhood that cats are not for chasing. He may also be too bouncy and eager for the safety and comfort of smaller animals.

Character Trait	Poor	Average	Good	Excellent
Attitude toward other dogs				
Quietness				
Not destructive				
Protective behavior				
Not likely to stray				
Good with children				
Ease of training				

Original purpose: Gundog (bird dog)
Male height: 25.5-27 in (65-69 cm)
Female height: 24-25.5 in (61-65 cm)
Weight: 55-66 lb (25-30 kg)
Lifespan: c. 12 years

HOW much exercise?

Setters were bred to run for miles and still need plenty of free running exercise. Puppies must not be overexercised, as this will damage young joints. Build up the length of walks gradually from six months onward. This period is the time to teach the recall, as without proper training English Setters tend to suffer from selective deafness when running free.

HOW easy to train?

Individuals vary considerably in trainability: some learn easily, while others can be very stubborn. As a breed, they were not designed for formal obedience, and the best results will be achieved with reward-based training and plenty of patience and repetition. Bullying doesn't achieve good results.

WHAT good points?

Affectionate, gentle, sweet disposition, sociable, adaptable, trustworthy with children, energetic, excellent house companion.

WHAT to be aware of?

Despite his elegant appearance, remember that this is a big, boisterous dog who can be quite clumsy around the house and tends to drool heavily. As a youngster he is very demanding, and slow to mature. Without enough exercise and attention he can be destructive and reckless.

Large dogs

WHAT medical problems?

Hip malformation (dysplasia) and lack of thyroid hormone (hypothyroidism) occur in the breed, and a small percentage of puppies are born deaf. This breed has very sensitive skin, and skin allergies are not uncommon.

● *That beautiful plumed tail wags constantly—any ornaments placed at tail height are at risk!*

Greater Swiss Mountain Dog

For centuries, the farmers of the Swiss Alps used all-purpose farm dogs to drive cattle, draw carts, and act as guards. These gave rise to four recognized breeds of Swiss Mountain dogs: the Appenzeller, the Entlebucher, the Bernese and, largest of the four, the Greater Swiss Mountain Dog. Today the GSMD remains true to his origins. This is a big, powerful working breed with a strong will, a protective nature, and a need for employment, which nowadays may include tracking, agility, weight-pulling, or obedience trials, in addition to his traditional tasks.

With an owner prepared and able to provide plenty of socialization and training, the GSMD makes an excellent household companion, sweet-natured and affectionate. As an adult, he is sociable and sensible, provided owners have put in a lot of work during his rowdy puppyhood, which means the first two or three years.

WHAT colors?

This breed is always tri-color: a black dog with symmetrical tan and white markings. These include tan eye spots, cheeks, sides of chest and legs, and white chest, feet, tail tip and facial blaze.

WHAT grooming does the coat need?

The double coat requires regular grooming with a bristle brush to remove dead hairs, with extra attention being required during the twice-yearly molt.

HOW suitable are they as family dogs?

GSMDs make great family pets as long as the family is prepared to put in the necessary work into training and socializing. They thrive on company and need to be involved in family life. They can be loving and gentle companions to older, sensible and well-supervised children, but their size, strength, and strong herding instinct make them less well-suited to living alongside toddlers.

● These gentle giants can be rowdy puppies and take a long time to grow up, not reaching maturity until they are four or five years old.

WHAT type of home?

A farm dog is a poor choice for a city home. The GSMD is best suited to a country, or at least suburban, home. However, he doesn't need a huge estate to roam. An average (well-fenced) backyard will suffice. He wants to be with his family, indoors or out, and is not a dog to be kept outside on his own.

WHAT type of owner?

Only experienced owners prepared for a lot of commitment should consider this breed. Given dedication to socialization and training, the GSMD is a great dog; without them, given his size, strong will, and extended puppyhood, he is likely to become a liability. Potential owners need to be patient, firm, loving, and at least reasonably active.

HOW compatible with other pets?

Some GSMDs have a high prey drive and may never be wholly trustworthy with small animals; and some tend to be naturally dog aggressive. Again, proper early socialization is the key. If brought up with cats and other household pets, most GSMDs will view them as part of the family. If encouraged to make canine friends from puppyhood, most will grow up to be dog friendly.

HOW much exercise?

Adults need a long daily walk, and will benefit from activities such as agility. However, this is a slow-maturing breed, and great care should be taken not to

Character Trait	Poor	Average	Good	Excellent
Attitude toward other dogs				
Quietness				
Not destructive				
Protective behavior				
Not likely to stray				
Good with children				
Ease of training				

Original purpose: Cattle herder, draft animal, watchdog
Male height: 25.5-28.5 in (65-72 cm)
Female height: 23.5-27 in (60-69 cm)
Weight: 80-130 lb (36-58.9 kg)
Lifespan: 7-10 years

overexercise youngsters to prevent the possibility of damage to growing joints and ligaments.

HOW easy to train?

Like most cattle herders, GSMDs are independent, strong-willed dogs who are not the easiest to train. They are also intelligent and willing to please, so persistence, consistency, and reward-based training methods (using treats and lots of praise) will eventually produce the desired results. Don't expect quick results—the slow-maturing GSMD can be a hooligan for the first two or three years of his life.

WHAT good points?

Loving, alert, intelligent, active, eager worker, protective, family oriented. With sensible owners, the GSMD is generally good with people and gentle with children.

WHAT to be aware of?

Large dogs

Strong-willed; extended rowdy puppyhood; a barker; socialization vital to prevent wariness of strangers developing into fear/aggression; does not like being left on his own.

WHAT medical problems?

Hip and elbow malformation (dysplasia), epilepsy, eye problems (entropion, or inturned eyelids requiring surgery; and distichiasis, or extra eyelashes), epilepsy, shoulder problems (osteochondritis), and prone to bloat. Breeding stock should have hip and elbow certificates.

● *Thought to be the oldest of the Swiss Mountain dogs, nevertheless the GSMD was not formally recognized as a breed in its native Switzerland until 1910.*

Doberman Pinscher

Created in the 1880s by German magistrate Louis Dobermann as his ideal guard dog, the Doberman has become one of the most popular working breeds, serving as police and military dog and also a superb companion in the right hands.

Dobermans achieved fame as the "devil dogs" of the U.S. Marine Corps in World War II and, like other powerful guard breeds, have often had their softer side ignored. They do need proper socialization and training—an untrained or abused Doberman is a liability and can be a genuinely dangerous dog. This is an intelligent, sensitive, and versatile breed that can be trained to a high standard, but also strong-minded, dominant, and capable of walking all over an inexperienced handler —not a dog for the novice. He needs activity, both physical and mental, plenty of company, and attention, and is not a dog to be left to his own devices.

WHAT colors?

Black and tan, blue and tan, brown and tan, fawn (isabella) and tan. A controversial strain of white, blue-eyed Dobermans has been in existence since the 1970s, but this color is not recognized by the AKC.

WHAT grooming does the coat need?

The smooth, short coat needs minimal care; a weekly once-over with a hound glove or stiff bristle brush will keep it in perfect order.

HOW suitable are they as family dogs?

A well-trained Doberman makes a wonderful family dog, but a lot of work needs to be put into training. Affectionate and protective, he enjoys being part of family life. Adolescents are rowdy and need constant supervision to ensure that they do not play too roughly with children. The breed is not recommended for inexperienced homes with vulnerable young children.

● *Always ready for action— intense, alert, and energetic.*

WHAT type of home?

A big, active dog, the Doberman needs space and is unsuited to apartment life or a home without a secure yard. Whether he lives in the city or country, he should have access to land where he can enjoy some free galloping every day as well as walks.

WHAT type of owner?

Not a breed for novices, nor for couch potatoes, the Doberman needs an experienced, strong-willed, active, and patient owner with plenty of time for him. He also needs company and should not be considered if he is to be left alone for long periods. A suitable owner will be able to provide confident leadership and plenty of affection for this strong yet sensitive dog.

HOW compatible with other pets?

Dobermans are good with other pets in the same household if raised with them, but be careful about introductions. Strange cats are likely to be regarded as fair game. Socialization with other dogs is essential, as males can often be aggressive with other males.

HOW much exercise?

A great deal. These active, energetic dogs need at least two walks plus an hour's free running

Character Trait	Poor	Average	Good	Excellent
Attitude toward other dogs		▓		
Quietness	▓	▓		
Not destructive			▓	
Protective behavior			▓	▓
Not likely to stray			▓	
Good with children			▓	
Ease of training				▓

Original purpose: Guard
Male height: 26-28 in (66-71 cm)
Female height: 24-26 in (61-66 cm)
Weight: 65-90 lb (29.5-40.9 kg)
Lifespan: 10-12 years

a day, as well as exercise for their minds in the form of interesting, challenging training.

HOW easy to train?

They are highly intelligent and highly trainable, but need calm, confident leadership. They are quick to learn, full of initiative, and often one step ahead of the handler. A confrontational approach will lead to problems. Owners need to earn respect with a firm but sympathetic approach, using reward-based training to motivate the dog to want to learn.

WHAT good points?

Intelligent, loyal, bold, alert, responsive, protective, courageous, versatile, affectionate, playful.

WHAT to be aware of?

A dominant dog that needs responsible ownership. Over-popularity has produced some neurotic and aggressive strains— only buy from responsible breeders who make good temperament a priority.

WHAT medical problems?

Dobermans have a regrettably high incidence of inherited disorders, including heart defects, lack of thyroid hormone (hypothyroidism), cataracts, von Willebrand's disease (a bleeding disorder), Wobbler syndrome (spinal malformation leading to swaying gait with eventual paralysis of hindquarters), and hip malform-ation (dysplasia). All breeding stock should be hip scored. They are also prone to gastric torsion (bloat).

Large dogs

● *An undeserved reputation for savagery owes more to unsuitable owners than to the Doberman's true nature. In the right hands, he is a loving, reliable friend.*

Irish Setter *Other names: Red Setter*

His glorious color and elegant, distinctive lines make the Irish Setter a real eye-catcher, and his zest for life makes him a stimulating companion. Good-tempered as well as good looking, he is a fun-loving, affectionate dog who likes people, is reliable with children, and gets along well with other animals—a superb family dog in the right home. He does need plenty of exercise, firm, sensitive training—and an owner with a sense of humor. A big, boisterous dog who can clear a coffee table with one sweep of his tail and bowl visitors over with his exuberant greeting, he has boundless energy that needs to be sensibly directed.

Setters developed in the age of falconry to find and mark the position of gamebirds, performing the same task later as gundogs that accompanied huntsmen. Today they are popular companions, but avoid pups from working bloodlines, which are usually too active for pet homes.

WHAT colors?

The rich red coat, ranging from chestnut to mahogany, is a hallmark of the breed. A touch of white on chest, throat, chin, or toes is acceptable.

WHAT grooming does the coat need?

Moderate. Daily brushing is required to keep the coat healthy, with meticulous combing behind the ears and through the feathering. Ears need to be kept clean, and some owners tie them back in a headband at mealtimes to avoid sponging dog food from ear fringes.

HOW suitable are they as family dogs?

A well-raised, well-exercised Irish Setter makes a wonderful dog for active families with older children—small children are at risk of being knocked over by an overboisterous playmate. Families who want a well-behaved dog should probably look elsewhere, as in youth (and this is a slow-maturing breed with an extended puppyhood) Irish Setters can be quite a handful.

WHAT type of home?

Ideally this is a dog for a country home, but he will adapt to city life if enough exercise is provided—and this must include off-leash running in a secure area away from traffic. A securely fenced, fairly large yard is essential. An Irish Setter is not suited to apartment life or to small rooms because of his size and high activity level.

WHAT type of owner?

Owners need to be firm, patient, energetic, and ready to appreciate an exuberant dog who can be a real clown. Don't consider this breed unless you enjoy long walks and have plenty of time to spend with your dog. Irish Setters suffer if left alone for long periods and can become highly neurotic if denied the company they need.

HOW compatible with other pets?

His friendly nature extends to other animals as well as people, but smaller animals run the risk of being accidentally flattened.

HOW much exercise?

This is a highly energetic dog that needs plenty of daily exercise—long walks, free galloping, and active play such as retrieving games. He is not always easy to control off leash so training a reliable recall is a high priority. If denied the exercise he needs, he may become destructive and certainly will not be happy.

HOW easy to train?

Irish Setters have a reputation for being hard to train, which is not fully deserved. The breed's original

Character Trait	Poor	Average	Good	Excellent
Attitude toward other dogs			●	
Quietness		●		
Not destructive	●			
Protective behavior		●		
Not likely to stray	●			
Good with children				●
Ease of training			●	

Original purpose: Locating and retrieving game
Male height: 26-28 in (66-71 cm)
Female height: 24-26 in (61-66 cm)
Weight: 60-70 lb (27.3-31.8 kg)
Lifespan: 12-14 years

...unction means they are geared to range far ahead of their owners and use their own judgement, so they are not primed for rigid obedience work. However, patience, understanding, and positive reinforcement will result in a well-behaved dog who is eager to please

● *This dog is an enthusiast—energy on four legs!*

WHAT good points?

Very affectionate, fun-loving, good-tempered, intelligent, kindly, energetic, high-spirited, sociable, good both with children and other animals.

WHAT to be aware of?

High commitment in terms of time and exercise. Bouncy and exuberant, especially when young. Tendency to suffer from separation anxiety. Will bring mud and water into the house. Puppies can be destructive.

Large dogs

WHAT medical problems?

Hip malformation (dysplasia), weakness of the muscle that propels food down the gullet (megaesophagus), degeneration of the light receptor cells in the eyes (PRA), epilepsy, skin allergies, and thyroid problems occur in this breed. Prone to gastric torsion (bloat)—safer to feed two or three small meals during the day rather than one big one.

The largest of Japan's native breeds, the powerful, handsome, and dignified Akita is a truly impressive dog but not one for the novice. He is a dog of strong character and a natural guard, who needs a close relationship with his owner and confident handling, as well as plenty of socialization to prevent his natural dominance and aloofness from turning to aggression. In the right hands, he is a wonderful dog, intelligent, loyal, and versatile

Originating at least 350 years ago as a hunting dog in the Akita prefecture, the Akita was introduced to the U.S. after World War I, and reached the U.K. in the early 1980s. Japanese and American bloodlines diverged so much that they are now considered separate breeds in Europe. From 2006, the Kennel Club in England terms the bigger, heavier American-style dog the "Akita" and the Japanese dog the "Japanese Akita-Inu." The AKC considers them all as "Akitas."

WHAT colors?

Any color, including white, red, black, silvery gray, pinto (any color and white), and brindle, with or without a dark mask.

WHAT grooming does the coat need?

The thick, coarse coat needs thorough grooming at least twice a week, using a firm bristle brush, with daily attention during the heavy twice-yearly molt.

HOW suitable are they as family dogs?

In experienced hands, the Akita can be a much-loved family member, but such a dominant and powerful dog is not an ideal choice around children. He can be very good with youngsters from their own family but he has a low tolerance for mistreatment and may not care for other people's children. Many individual Akitas may be trustworthy, but it is not worth taking risks.

WHAT type of home?

The Akita is suitable for either a city or a country home. He is too big to be accommodated comfortably in an apartment, and needs a yard with a high fence—he is a great jumper. In the country, his hunting origins mean he must be closely supervised around livestock.

WHAT type of owner?

Only owners with experience of large, dominant breeds should consider this beautiful but challenging dog. Potential owners should have plenty of time for a dog who needs sensible socialization and training, well-supervised exercise and a great deal of company—bored Akitas have a tendency to turn to destruction to pass the time.

HOW compatible with other pets?

Be very careful. Akitas are highly dominant and can be aggressive toward other dogs. They will often live peacefully with a dog of the opposite sex, but same-sex rivalry is common. Cats and other small pets should not be considered safe in their vicinity.

HOW much exercise?

The Akita will enjoy as much exercise as you care to give—think in terms of a minimum of two half hour walks a day, with no upper limit. His strong hunting instinct means that he should not be exercised off-leash anywhere he might come across livestock, while owners should also be conscious of other dogs in the vicinity. If is challenged by another dog he comes across, there is a strong risk that he will react aggressively.

Character Trait	Poor	Average	Good	Excellent
Attitude toward other dogs	■			
Quietness		■		
Not destructive	■			
Protective behavior			■	
Not likely to stray			■	
Good with children		■		
Ease of training		■		

Original purpose: Hunting
Male height: 25-28 in (63.5-71 cm)
Female height: 23-26 in (58.5-66 cm)
Weight: 80-130 lb (36-59 kg)
Lifespan: 10-14 years

HOW easy to train?

These highly dominant and strong-minded dogs are not particularly easy to train. Handlers need to be just as strong-minded and very patient. The Akita will not be bullied and needs to be motivated to cooperate by a firm but kind, reward-based approach with plenty of variety to keep his interest going. Training should start early while he is still a puppy and open to new ideas. Early socialization in puppy classes is strongly recommended. An unsocialized Akita is a liability!

WHAT good points?

Dignified, courageous, loyal, calm, intelligent, protective, adaptable, people oriented, loving companion.

WHAT to be aware of?

Large dogs

A challenging breed. Diligent socialization, training, and discipline essential. Can be very destructive if bored.

WHAT medical problems?

Inherited disorders include eye problems (progressive retinal atrophy), inward-turning eyelids (entropion), hip malformation (dysplasia), kneecap dislocation (patellar luxation), autoimmune disease and skin disorders. All breeding stock should be hip scored and have current eye certificates.

● This majestic dog is revered as a National Monument in Japan, where he is described as "tender in heart and mighty in strength."

Afghan Hound *Other names: Tazi, Baluchi Hound*

One of the most glamorous breeds, the Afghan Hound looks like a fashion accessory but is a demanding pet with all the needs of a big hairy hound. He needs a lot of exercise and time-consuming grooming, as well as sensible discipline to control his chasing instincts. Independent, aloof, and difficult to train, the Afghan is not a dog for everyone. In the right home, however, he is a sensitive, playful companion, devoted to family and friends but regarding himself as an equal, not a subordinate. He has a great sense of fun and can be a real clown —not a dog for obedience enthusiasts!

This elegant sight-hound developed in Afghanistan to hunt large game such as antelope and leopard. In the West, where he arrived in the late 19th century, breeding for the show ring has developed a much heavier coat, but the Afghan remains a tough, powerful hunting dog.

WHAT colors?
All colors, including black, red, gold, blue, brindle, cream and black, and tan, with or without a black mask or "domino" lighter mask. White markings are frowned upon in the show ring.

WHAT grooming does the coat need?
The Afghan hound is noted for its thick coat of long silky hair. The coat requires hours of grooming each week to maintain its beautiful appearance. A daily brush through should be backed up by a thorough weekly grooming.

HOW suitable are they as family dogs?
For the suitable family, the Afghan can be a valued family member, but this is not a breed to take on lightly. Afghans are good with considerate children, though care will have to be taken with toddlers, who can easily be bowled over by a big, boisterous hound. Adolescent Afghans can be a very demanding handful, and may be a problem in a busy family without the time and patience.

WHAT type of home?
Although the Afghan needs access to space for exercise, he can adapt to apartment life provided he has daily long walks. He will, however, appreciate a reasonably sized yard, which must be securely fenced. In some ways he may be more safely kept as a city dog—country dwellers will need to be very careful to prevent livestock chasing, as the Afghan's chase instinct is very strong and it takes a great deal of patience to condition him to obey a recall.

WHAT type of owner?
Afghan owners need to appreciate a dog of independent character and must be prepared to devote considerable time and attention to the dog every day, including walks in all weather. Plenty of patience is needed to instill the basic training that will make this dog a treasured member of the family. An untrained underexercised Afghan is a nightmare to live with.

HOW compatible with other pets?
Normally the Afghan gets along well with other dogs and, if brought up with other household pets, the Afghan will consider them part of the family. However, his high prey-drive means that he should never be trusted not to chase other people's pets or livestock.

HOW much exercise?
Afghans need a great deal of exercise—at least two long walks a day plus the opportunity for off-leash galloping. However, it is essential that free exercise takes

Character Trait	Poor	Average	Good	Excellent
Attitude toward other dogs				
Quietness				
Not destructive				
Protective behavior				
Not likely to stray				
Good with children				
Ease of training				

Original purpose: Coursing hare and gazelle
Male height: 27-29 in (68.5-73.5 cm)
Female height: 25-27 in (63.5-68.5 cm)
Weight: 50-60 lb (23-27 kg)
Lifespan: 12-14 years, often more

place only in safe areas, as most Afghans tend to keep running and do not respond to a recall.

HOW easy to train?

Afghans score very low on trainability, which means that training is difficult but not impossible. Firm but kind and consistent training will achieve a degree of cooperation. Harshness and lack of patience will produce a resolute stubborn lack of response.

WHAT good points?

Proud, brave, affectionate, faithful, protective toward owner, gentle, sensitive, playful, easygoing.

WHAT to be aware of?

A very demanding breed. Puppies can be slow to housetrain, adolescents may be obtrusive and very hard to control, and a bored Afghan can be quite destructive. Early socialization is essential, as youngsters left to their own devices can become quite wild.

Large dogs

WHAT medical problems?

Afghans are generally a healthy breed, although hip deformity (dysplasia), juvenile cataracts, lack of thyroid hormone (hypothyroidism), and enzyme deficiencies have been reported. The breed is sometimes prone to tail injuries and is sensitive to anesthesia.

Newfoundland

Majestic in appearance, sweet-tempered, and with an admirable record of saving human lives, the Newfoundland has a well-deserved reputation as a loyal companion. The breed originated in Newfoundland as draft animals and water dogs who carried fishing nets and ships' lines ashore and rescued men and equipment that fell overboard. Modern Newfies also adore water and still serve as water rescue dogs. This is a kindly dog, intelligent, reliable, and trustworthy with children, and also very adaptable to various lifestyle

However, he is not a dog to take on lightly. He takes up a lot of space and is expensive to feed and like any big, active dog, he needs training or he can become a liability. He is not one for the hou proud, as he is a champion drooler, sheds hair everywhere, and his love of water extends to carrying a great deal indoors or his coat and feet.

WHAT colors?

Black or brown (chocolate or bronze), with or without a splash of white on chest, toes, and tail tip. Landseer dogs (regarded as a separate breed in Europe) are white with black markings, ideally comprising a black head with narrow white blaze, saddle, rump, and upper tail.

WHAT grooming does the coat need?

The dense coat needs regular brushing and combing, at least twice weekly, with extra attention when molting. It is important to groom right down to the skin—combing the topcoat only will look good on the surface, but will leave dead hair clogging the undercoat and eventually form mats.

HOW suitable are they as family dogs?

This is a wonderful family dog for families who have the space and

● *The gentle giant of the canine world, the Newfoundland is happiest in the heart of his family.*

time. The Newfoundland is gentle, loving, and exceptionally good with children if raised with them. Supervision is important to ensure that children do not take advantage of his good nature. Never allow youngsters to attempt to ride their giant friend, as this may injure his back.

WHAT type of home?

This giant breed is not suited for apartment living, as he needs lots of room and a large fenced yard. Newfoundland owners need a big house to accommodate this giant breed. His heavy coat makes him susceptible to overheating, so he will not be comfortable in a home where the heat is always turned up high.

WHAT type of owner?

This is a breed for people who expect to treat their dog as part of the family and can give him the time and attention he needs. He loves to be part of family activities and is ideal for people with young children who want a trustworthy family dog and have the space for a giant breed. Owners do need to be capable of handling and training a physically powerful dog.

HOW compatible with other pets?

Most Newfoundlands get along well with other animals if raised with them and sensibly socialized. They are big dogs, however, so

Character Trait	Poor	Average	Good	Excellent
Attitude toward other dogs				■
Quietness		■		
Not destructive			■	
Protective behavior		■		
Not likely to stray				■
Good with children				■
Ease of training			■	

Original purpose: Draft dog, water dog
Male height: 27-29 in (68.5-73.5 cm)
Female height: 25-27 in (63.5-68.5 cm)
Weight: 110-150 lb (50-68 kg)
Lifespan: 8-10 years

...are needs to be taken to protect small pets from being trodden on.

HOW much exercise?

Moderate. Newfoundlands are not hyperactive but they do need regular exercise to keep fit— at least half an hour a day. Puppies under 12 months should not be overexercised as this can cause joint problems later in life. Adults will enjoy activities such as swimming and carting as well as being happy to play with children and other dogs.

HOW easy to train?

The Newfoundland is willing to please and responds well to training. This needs to start early, so that by the time he achieves his full size, he is fully under control. Despite his size, he is a sensitive dog who responds better to encouragement than to heavy-handed tactics.

WHAT good points?

Gentle, docile, sweet-natured, reliable, intelligent, responsive, adaptable, devoted to his family, companionable.

WHAT to be aware of?

Demanding in terms of upkeep; does not take well to being left alone; not for the house proud; susceptible to overheating.

WHAT medical problems?

Hip and elbow malformation (dysplasia) and other joint problems, heart disease, infections of the lip fold, eyelid disorders.

Large dogs

● *The Landseer takes its name from animal painter Sir Edwin Landseer, who portrayed this color.*

Mastiff *Other names: English Mastiff*

Descended from ferocious guard and fighting dogs, the modern Mastiff is a gentle giant. Not many homes have room for a Mastiff: This powerfully built dog is among the heaviest of all dog breeds. Calm, dignified, and loyal, he is gentle with his own family but retains all the protective instincts of his ancestors. He is a sensitive dog who just loves to please and wants to be with his owner all the time, so he is not suited for the role of outside guard dog—in fact, within his own family he is a big softy. However, because of his size, careful socialization and training are essential to ensure that he is not aggressive toward people or other dogs.

Breed historians trace the Mastiff back to ancient times, but the word "mastiff" in old texts referred to any large dog. The modern breed probably descends from medieval heavy hounds.

WHAT colors?
Apricot-fawn, silver-fawn, fawn, or dark fawn-brindle. Muzzle, ears, and nose black with black around orbits and extending upward between them.

WHAT grooming does the coat need?
The short, close coat is low maintenance, needing only a weekly brushing to remove dead hairs.

HOW suitable are they as family dogs?
The Mastiff's calm, loving nature makes him a suitable companion for families who can accommodate a giant breed. He is patient and long-suffering with children, but his size should always be kept in mind. He should not be left unsupervised with youngsters, as he can easily knock over toddlers, and a blow from his tail is painful even to an adult.

WHAT type of home?
Mastiffs need space—a large house with a fenced yard, preferably in the country. This is not an ideal urban dog and totally unsuitable for apartments or small houses.

WHAT type of owner?
Owners of this breed should be experienced, physically strong, and with both space and time enough to keep a Mastiff happy. Mastiffs are not for busy people, nor for the house proud (Mastiffs unequivocally mean mess), nor for those who specifically want a guard dog, an unsuitable role for an animal who needs to be a family dog.

HOW compatible with other pets?
Mastiffs are naturally good-nature and will get along well with other pets if raised with them. Because of their size and strong protective instincts, early socialization with strange dogs is essenti Males especially can tend be aggressive with other males if they are not properly trained.

HOW much exercise
Mastiffs are often quite happy to lead a sedentary life, b they do need moderate exercise —at least half an hour's walk dail A fit adult will enjoy walking for miles, but avoid exercise in the heat: this breed overheats easily. Puppies under two years must no be overexercised, which is likely t cause damage to growing bones.

HOW easy to train?
Sensitive but stubborn, the Masti is not the easiest breed to train, but with a dog this size training is essential. Keep training sessions

Character Trait	Poor	Average	Good	Excellent
Attitude toward other dogs				
Quietness				
Not destructive				
Protective behavior				
Not likely to stray				
Good with children				
Ease of training				

Original purpose: Guarding, hunting
Male height: 27.5-30 in (70-76 cm)
Female height: 27.5-30 in (70-76 cm)
Weight: 175-190 lb (79-86 kg)
Lifespan: 8-10 years

short, frequent, and fun. Pile on the praise when he does right, and keep any possible disappointment low key when he doesn't to avoid negative associations with training.

WHAT good points?

Affectionate, loyal, protective, dignified, quiet, clean, undemanding, good-natured, intelligent, not excitable.

WHAT to be aware of?

High running costs (food, veterinary bills, etc.). Puppies need special diet designed for giant breeds to ensure growth at the correct rate without stress to bones and joints. Adults need soft bedding to prevent callused elbows. Not a dog for the fastidious: his snoring, drooling, and tendency to break wind are also on a giant scale. Socialization essential to prevent aggression.

WHAT medical problems?

Hip malformation (dysplasia) and joint problems, prone to gastric torsion (bloat), some eye defects, heart problems, lack of thyroid hormone (hypothyroidism), arthritis. Like other giant breeds, short life expectancy.

Large dogs

● Mastiffs should be fit and athletic like this, not slow, lumbering, and overweight.

Greyhound

The ultimate canine athlete, the Greyhound is the fastest of all dogs, with a top speed of 45 mph (72 km/h). He is famous world-wide as a racer and still used in some countries for coursing game. However, his gentle, affectionate, and surprisingly adaptable nature also makes him a wonderful companion and family dog. Much as he loves to run, he actually needs less exercise than many sporting breeds and is content to spend much of the day curled on the sofa. Ex-racing greyhounds, usually retired at three to five years old and always available for rehoming, make excellent house pets who appreciate the comforts of home life when their racing life has come to an end.

Long-legged hounds of Greyhound type have been valued since Old Testament times. In medieval and Renaissance Europe they were the favorites of the aristocracy, in the 20th century the heroes of popular sport on the racetrack and, throughout the ages, loving companions.

WHAT colors?

Black, white, red, blue, fawn, fallow (pale reddish-yellow), brindle, or any of these shades broken by white.

WHAT grooming does the coat need?

Greyhounds are naturally clean dogs and the fine close coat requires minimal grooming. A daily rubdown with a hound glove to remove dead hairs will be appreciated and keep the coat in perfect condition.

HOW suitable are they as family dogs?

The average Greyhound's ideal lifestyle is to be a member of a loving family with a spare sofa and a good heating system. These gentle, sensitive dogs want to please, will adapt to family routine, and are generally very good with children. As puppies they can be boisterous and mischievous, and families with young children may prefer to avoid this stage and adopt a retired racer.

WHAT type of home?

This is an ideal country dog, but he will live happily in the city, even in an apartment, as long as he has adequate exercise and adequate company. He does need access to a park or similar secure area where he can safely enjoy an off-leash gallop.

WHAT type of owner?

A gentle, sensitive owner who will appreciate the Greyhound's undemanding companionship and who is happy with a routine of short twice-daily walks. Greyhounds like company, so owners who are regularly out for more than a couple of hours might do well to consider having two dogs—little more trouble than one.

HOW compatible with other pets?

Greyhounds are generally friendly with other dogs. However, they are bred to chase, so care needs to be taken with cats and other small pets (including small dogs). Organizations that rehome ex-racers will advise whether individual dogs are suitable to house with other pets.

HOW much exercise?

Moderate. Given two 20-minute walks a day and the opportunity to run free, most Greyhounds are happy to spend the rest of the day relaxing—although they will enjoy

Character Trait	Poor	Average	Good	Excellent
Attitude toward other dogs			●	
Quietness				●
Not destructive			●	
Protective behavior	●			
Not likely to stray	●			
Good with children			●	
Ease of training		●		

Original purpose: Hunting, racing
Male height: 27-29 in (68.5-73.5 cm)
Female height: 26-28 in (66-71 cm)
Weight: 60-70 lb (27-32 kg)
Lifespan: 10-13 years

In the Middle Ages, Greyhound ownership was reserved for nobility. We are more fortunate today!

longer outings if these are offered. Owners need to be aware of the Greyhound's chase instinct and never trust them off leash in the vicinity of livestock —they can reach top speed in two strides, which is faster than their owners' reaction time.

HOW easy to train?

Moderate again. Greyhounds have a reputation for low intelligence, which is undeserved. Few members of this breed are offered the opportunity to use their brains. They are not naturals for obedience work, but are willing to please and ready to learn. Teaching a reliable recall is essential with a dog with such a strong chase instinct, although it is not necessarily easy.

WHAT good points?

Easygoing, gentle, affectionate, loving, mild-mannered, calm, quiet, dignified, polite with people and other dogs.

WHAT to be aware of?

With his thin coat and low body fat, the Greyhound really feels the cold and needs a coat in cold weather. His desire to chase may be a problem if he is allowed to run off-lead unchecked, and most Greyhounds will kill small animals if they catch them.

Large dogs

WHAT medical problems?

Greyhounds are generally a healthy breed with few hereditary risks, although eye problems (progressive retinal atrophy and lens dislocation) have been reported. They are sensitive to anesthetics and may be vulnerable to gastric torsion (bloat). Some may develop sores from lying on hard flooring. Racers are prone to fractures of the leg and foot bones.

Great Pyrenees *Other names: Pyrenean Mountain Dog*

For centuries this magnificent white giant guarded flocks against wolves and other predators in the Pyrenees of France. In the 17th century his imposing appearance attracted the attention of French nobility, and he became known as "the Royal Dog of France." In modern times he became mainly a companion breed, but he retains his working instincts and today is employed as a livestock protector by ranchers and farmers all around the world.

As a companion, the Great Pyrenees is built on too large a scale for the average home, and his dominant nature and strong guarding instinct make him unsuitable for any but experienced owners. He is a dog who needs space and a job to do, as well as ongoing socialization to manage his protective drive. In responsible hands, he is a calm, confident, sensible presence, devoted to his family, affectionate and gentle with children, and a superb watchdog.

WHAT colors?

White, or mainly white with wolf-gray, badger, or pale yellow markings on head, ears, or base of tail; a few markings permissible on body.

WHAT grooming does the coat need?

The dense, weatherproof coat needs brushing down to the skin at least twice a week, taking care not to strip out too much undercoat. Daily grooming is essential during the twice-yearly heavy molt. If neglected, the coat mats—and smells quite strongly. Clipping the fur short is not advisable, as the coat serves as insulation against both heat and cold.

HOW suitable are they as family dogs?

Great Pyrenees are good family dogs as long as their needs for space, employment, and confident leadership are met. They have a natural affinity with children, although they are simply too big for the comfort and safety of the very young. Supervision is needed to ensure that they are not overprotective, putting family friends and visitors at risk.

WHAT type of home?

The ideal home for a Great Pyrenees is a farm where he can guard livestock. He is better housed in the country; in the city, he needs a large, secure yard, and is certainly not suitable for an apartment. He loves the outdoors, provided he has plenty of company. He enjoys the comfort of the indoors, but is too big to be comfortable in the average home and may overheat if the home is kept too hot.

WHAT type of owner?

The Great Pyrenees needs an experienced owner who is both physically strong and able to take on the role of leader. Owners must have the space to accommodate a giant breed and plenty of time for socialization, training, exercise, and grooming. The ideal owner will also have to be able to provide suitable employment for a working dog—a flock of sheep is recommended!

HOW compatible with other pets?

Other pets in the household will be regarded as part of his family, and his protective instincts will come to the fore. He is strongly territorial and will chase off strange dogs and cats on his property. Early socialization is essential to prevent aggression toward other dogs.

HOW much exercise?

Laid-back to the point of lethargy, adult Great Pyrenees don't demand a great deal of exercise,

Character Trait	Poor	Average	Good	Excellent
Attitude toward other dogs				
Quietness				
Not destructive				
Protective behavior				
Not likely to stray				
Good with children				
Ease of training				

*Place of origin: **France***

Original purpose: Livestock protection
Male height: 27-32 in (68.5-81 cm)
Female height: 25-29 in (63.5-73.5 cm)
Weight: 85-119 lb (38.6-54.1 kg)
Lifespan: 10-12 years

out they certainly should be exercised daily. Long walks will do them good, and they can take as much exercise at their ambling pace as their owner wishes—many enjoy backpacking and hiking. Puppies under 12 months need restricted exercise to prevent damage to growing bones.

HOW easy to train?

Dominant, independent, and stubborn, the Great Pyrenees is not the easiest breed to train, but his size and strength make it essential that he is under his owner's control. Start early and establish firm but kind leadership to win his respect —harsh or heavy-handed handling will lead to recalcitrance. This breed requires a patient, consistent approach.

Large dogs

WHAT good points?

Dignified, loyal, affectionate, protective, confident, intelligent.

WHAT to be aware of?

Barking and territorial aggression if bored. Guard instincts need careful handling. Intermale aggression likely.

WHAT medical problems?

May suffer from hip and elbow malformation (dysplasia), kneecap dislocation (patellar luxation), spinal problems, cataracts and inward-turning eyelids (entropion), and bleeding disorders.

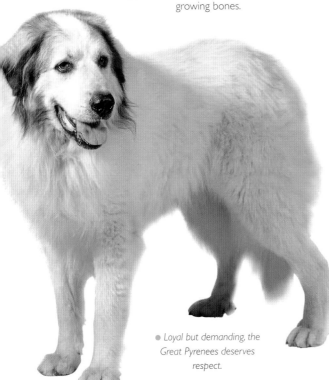

● *Loyal but demanding, the Great Pyrenees deserves respect.*

St. Bernard
Other names: St. Bernhardshund, Alpine Mastiff

St. Bernards take their name from St. Bernard's Hospice in the Swiss Alps, where these powerful dogs have been kept since the 17th century and became famous for rescuing lost travelers and avalanche victims. Today the Saint is a devoted companion, good-natured, child-loving, and highly protective. However, his sheer size can be a problem. This a massive dog who simply will not fit into many homes and lifestyles. He is costly to feed, very messy (a heavy molter and champion drooler) and, like any giant breed, he needs plenty of socialization and training. The 1992 hit film *Beethoven* starring a cute St. Bernard, tempted many people to buy a Saint without considering the commitment needed. The breed deserves better.

Saints come in two coat varieties, rough and smooth. The original dogs were all smooth coats; rough coats were developed in the 19th century, when a Newfoundland outcross was introduced to combat inbreeding.

WHAT colors?
Basically a red and white dog. The red ranges through orange, mahogany-brindle, and red-brindle; white patches include muzzle, facial blaze, collar, chest, forelegs, feet, and tail tip; black shadings on face and ears.

WHAT grooming does the coat need?

Smooths need only a weekly brushing, but roughs need grooming daily, combing right down to the skin. Combing the topcoat only may look good on the surface, but leaves dead hair clogging the undercoat and forms mats. This breed sheds heavily, and extra work will be required during the molt.

HOW suitable are they as family dogs?
For those who have the space and time, this gentle dog makes an excellent family dog. The Saint is gentle, loving, and famously good with children. For his size, he is amazingly careful with the little ones. He loves to be part of family activities (or inactivity—he is quite happy to doze at his owner's feet), and can become distressed and destructive if left to his own devices.

WHAT type of home?
This giant breed is happiest provided with plenty of room and a large fenced yard. They enjoy the outdoors, but are much happier living as one of the family. Relatively inactive indoors, they can adapt to apartment life if enough exercise is provided. They are susceptible to overheating so will not be comfortable in a home where the heat is always turned up high.

WHAT type of owner?
This is a breed for people who expect to treat their dog as part of the family and can give him the time and attention he needs. He loves to be part of family activities and is ideal for people with young children who want a trustworthy family dog and have the space for a giant breed. Owners do need to be capable of handling and training a physically powerful dog.

HOW compatible with other pets?
In general, St. Bernards are good with other dogs if sensibly socialized in puppyhood and also with cats if raised with them. They are big dogs, however, so care needs to be taken to protect small pets (including smaller dogs) from being trodden on.

Character Trait	Poor	Average	Good	Excellent
Attitude toward other dogs			✓	
Quietness		✓		
Not destructive			✓	
Protective behavior				✓
Not likely to stray			✓	
Good with children				✓
Ease of training		✓		

Original purpose: Guard and mountain rescue
Male height: 28-36 in (71-91cm)
Female height: 26-36 in (66-91cm)
Weight: 110-200 lb (50-91 kg)
Lifespan: c.9 years

HOW much exercise?

The Saint's exercise needs are moderate for his size. An adult should walk a couple of miles a day. However, he can enjoy longer walks and off-leash exercise. This breed overheats easily and should not be exercised in hot or humid weather.

Puppies under two years should be limited to short walks and play sessions to prevent joint problems.

● *The quintessential "gentle giant."*

HOW easy to train?

Moderate. The Saint is willing to please, but can be slow to respond —not a dog for obedience enthusiasts. With a dog of this size, training needs to start early and to be patient and consistent, so that by the time he achieves his full growth he is fully under control.

WHAT good points?

Steady, kindly, intelligent, courageous, trustworthy, protective, notably good with children, affectionate, loyal.

Large dogs

WHAT to be aware of?

Expensive upkeep; does not take well to being left alone; not for the house proud; susceptible to overheating.

WHAT medical problems?

This breed has some major health concerns, including joint problems (hip and elbow dysplasia), inturned eyelids (entropion), and heart defects. Only buy from reputable breeders who screen all breeding stock.

Great Dane   *Other names: Deutsche Dogge, German Mastiff*

A giant breed of great nobility and elegance, the Dane is nicknamed "the Apollo of dogs." His ancestors were fierce boarhounds. For generations now he has been bred for the role of companion, with a gentle, kindly temperament. This is a dog who conjures up images of baronial halls, and prospective owners need space on a fairly baronial scale to accommodate a dog who, when full-grown, may weigh as much as a man.

Owners also need considerable commitment to socialization, training and companionship—such huge dogs need teaching and supervision to fit in with modern life, and they are sociable creatures who will not thrive without company.

Despite the name, the Great Dane is a German, not a Danish, breed. It was in 18th- and 19th-century Germany that giant hunting mastiffs were polished into the breed we know today. Since 1876 he has been Germany's national dog.

WHAT colors?

Fawn, brindle, black, blue or harlequin (white, irregularly patched with black or blue). Some countries also accept mantled, or Boston, Danes (black or blue with white shirt front and socks). Merle Danes (typically gray or fawn with dark marbling) occur, but are not recognized by any kennel club.

WHAT grooming does the coat need?

The smooth, short-haired coat is easy care, needing only regular brushing with a firm bristle brush or hound glove to remove any accumulation of dead hairs.

HOW suitable are they as family dogs?

Danes are happy with family life if treated with consideration, but not all families will be happy with a Dane. They are good with children if raised with them, but small children are easily knocked over or trodden on. Youngsters (up to about three years old) are likely to be a hazard in households with young children or frail elderly people, as they are boisterous and clumsy.

WHAT type of home?

This giant breed needs plenty of space and a large fenced yard. Danes don't belong in small apartments or in houses with small, cluttered rooms.

WHAT type of owner?

Dane owners should be experienced and physically strong to cope with a powerful, strong-willed, and sometimes stubborn dog. They must have time to spend with him. Danes are surprisingly sensitive and need kind, stable, confident handling. They are not ideal for the house proud, as they molt and slobber—and accidental breakages tend to follow in their wake.

HOW compatible with other pets?

With proper socialization, Danes are generally good with other animals. However, because they are so big they can accidentally injure smaller animals simply by stepping on them. Although adults are generally gentle, young Danes don't know their own strength and may damage smaller dogs in play.

HOW much exercise?

Danes need a moderate amount of exercise, at least one long walk a day and the opportunity for free running—although if you have large grounds, they will largely exercise themselves. They will enjoy longer walks if that fits in with your lifestyle and can enjoy athletic activities such as agility and flyball. However, puppies under a year old must have their exercise limited to prevent damage to growing bones.

Character Trait	Poor	Average	Good	Excellent
Attitude toward other dogs				
Quietness				
Not destructive				
Protective behavior				
Not likely to stray				
Good with children				
Ease of training				

Place of origin: **Germany**

Original purpose: Boar hunting
Male height: 30-34 in (76-86 cm)
Female height: 28-32 in (71-81 cm)
Weight: 100-180 lb (45-81.6 kg)
Lifespan: 7-10 years

HOW easy to train?

Danes are highly trainable but can be stubborn. Training needs to start early—never allow a cute puppy to get away with behavior such as jumping up at visitors, which will be unacceptable when he weighs as much as you do. This is a sensitive breed and training needs to be based on encouragement and praise. Harsh methods are counterproductive.

WHAT good points?

Friendly, gentle, intelligent, dignified, affectionate, easygoing, noble imposing appearance.

WHAT to be aware of?

Early socialization essential to prevent shyness or aggression. Some individuals are very territorial and dominant. Despite the elegant appearance, Danes are prone to slobbering and flatulence.

WHAT medical problems?

Danes, like other giant breeds, are prone to health problems and often short-lived. Medical problems include joint disorders (hip and elbow dysplasia), heart defects, gastric torsion (bloat), tumors, lack of thyroid hormone (hypothyroidism), von Willebrand's disease (a hereditary bleeding disorder), eye problems, and tail injuries. Breeding stock should be hip tested. Buyers are advised to seek pups from long-living breeding lines.

Large dogs

● *Usually thought of as dignified, Danes can also be clowns at home—inspiring the creation of two cartoon favorites, comic strip character Marmaduke and Hanna-Barbera's renowned Scooby-Doo.*

Borzoi *Other names: Russian Wolfhound*

This powerful Russian sighthound was bred to course wolves, but today is a gentle companion and glamorous show dog. As a house pet, once past the puppy stage, he is calm, dignified, and well mannered. He is deeply attached to his family and very sensitive to their moods. However, he retains his chasing instincts and loves to run, which can be a problem for homes not geared to a sighthound's needs. Although happy to lounge around restfully between walks, he needs regular exercise and free galloping. Early socialization is vital to prevent his natural suspicion of strangers escalating into shyness, and with all his virtues this is not really a dog for the novice.

As a breed, the Borzoi dates back to at least the 16th century, with the first written standard appearing in 1650. It was introduced to the U.K. in the 1860s, and to the U.S. in the 1890s, with instant impact.

WHAT colors?

Any color acceptable, including red, white, brindle, and tri-color. White with colored markings is the most common.

WHAT grooming does the coat need?

The silky coat will mat and tangle if neglected, but requires less maintenance than many long-haired breeds to keep it in good condition. A brush and comb through every few days will suffice, except during the molt, when quite a bit of extra work will be required.

HOW suitable are they as family dogs?

The Borzoi is not the ideal pet for the average family because of his high exercise needs, strong chasing drive, and high-strung, sensitive nature. He is better suited to the role of companion to adults. He is good with sensible children if raised with them, but he dislikes rough handling and is very touch sensitive, tending to snap if startled.

In Csarist Russia, Borzois were favorites of the nobility. After the 1917 Revolution their fortunes went into decline in the USSR.

WHAT type of home?

A Borzoi needs space, so a home with a large secure yard is best. He can cope with city life if enough exercise is provided, although he is unsuited to apartment living. He does need access to areas where he can run free without danger to himself (i.e. no dashes across busy roads) or to local livestock—farmers will not welcome unleashed Borzois near their animals.

WHAT type of owner?

This is a breed for an active person with access to land where a Borzoi can run free, who will appreciate the needs of this sensitive dog, and has the time and patience for socialization and training. Not a good choice for anyone who favors strict obedience.

HOW compatible with other pets?

Borzois are generally good with other dogs, especially other sighthounds. They can be good with cats within their own household if raised with them. However, their natural instinct is to chase and kill anything that looks like prey, so they should not be trusted with small pets or livestock.

HOW much exercise?

A great deal. Borzois need at least an hour's walk every day, plus free running. However, their strong hunting drive and deafness to the recall mean that areas where they can be trusted off leash are hard to find. Many owners find that the answer is to join a lure coursing club, where hounds pursue an artificial hare.

Character Trait	Poor	Average	Good	Excellent
Attitude toward other dogs				
Quietness				
Not destructive				
Protective behavior				
Not likely to stray				
Good with children				
Ease of training				

Original purpose: Hunting
Male height: 29 in (74 cm) minimum
Female height: 27 in (68.5 cm) minimum
Weight: 75-105 lb (34-48 kg)
Lifespan: 11-13 years

HOW easy to train?

Difficult. The Borzoi is independent, stubborn, and not naturally obedient—not the breed for obedience enthusiasts. Nonetheless, careful socialization and training are essential to make him a pleasant companion. Training must be gentle, patient, and consistent. Borzois are very sensitive to stress and respond badly to harsh treatment.

WHAT good points?

Dignified, gentle, quiet, loving, independent, calm, faithful, alert, sensitive, graceful.

WHAT to be aware of?

Strong hunting drive; hard to recall when off leash. High-strung and does not react well to stress. Early socialization vital to prevent shyness.

WHAT medical problems?

Borzois are generally a healthy breed, although like other deep-chested breeds they may be prone to bloat. Hip malformation (dysplasia) and progressive retinal atrophy (degeneration of the light receptors in the eyes) have been reported. Sensitive to anesthesia.

Large dogs

Irish Wolfhound

This impressive giant is the tallest breed of dog, and not one to take on lightly. They are a major commitment in terms of time, space, exercise, and food costs. Given a home that meets his large-scale needs, he is a loving companion. Despite his huge size, he is gentle and friendly, good-natured with children, and very affectionate toward his owners. With a dog this size, who may weigh as much as his owner and is extremely powerful, good socialization and training are essential. Although adult Wolfhounds are generally mannerly, pups (up to two or three years old) are boisterous and mischievous and can be hard work before they mature.

The Wolfhound harks back to the great Celtic hounds of pre-Roman times, which served as war dogs as well as hunters. However, the breed was almost extinct by the 17th century, and the modern Wolfhound is largely an effort of 19th-century reconstruction.

WHAT colors?

Gray, brindle, red, fawn, wheaten, and steel gray. Solid black and pure white are also recognized colors but rarely seen today. Puppies may change color as they grow their adult coats.

WHAT grooming does the coat need?

The harsh, shaggy coat is fairly low maintenance, but needs grooming at least weekly with a pin wire brush and wide-toothed comb in order to remove dead hairs and to keep it healthy.

HOW suitable are they as family dogs?

In the right home, where sufficient priority can be given to his needs, the Wolfhound is an excellent family dog. However, a dog this size is not recommended for households with small children, as he can easily knock them over and even a blow from his tail may cause bruising. Young Wolfhounds can often be too rough for children's comfort and safety.

WHAT type of home?

Ideally the Wolfhound is a country dog, but he can adapt to city living if given sufficient exercise. He is unlikely to be comfortable in an apartment. Big dogs need space, and this breed will cause problems in a home with small rooms where he has to maneuver around furniture and needs to be stepped over all the time. He also needs a reasonably sized and securely fenced yard, as well as access to areas where he can run off-leash in safety.

● A gentle giant, but he may not always realize his own strength.

WHAT type of owner?

This is not a dog for owners who have to leave him while they go to work. He needs company and can develop bad habits if bored and lonely. Wolfhound owners need to have time, space, and money to maintain this breed. They need to enjoy daily walks in all weather and, in order to train and control a young Wolfhound, they need to be physically fit and strong.

HOW compatible with other pets?

Wolfhounds are good with other dogs, although they may accidentally injure small or fragile breeds simply by treading on them. They will generally get along well with cats

Character Trait	Poor	Average	Good	Excellent
Attitude toward other dogs				
Quietness				
Not destructive				
Protective behavior				
Not likely to stray				
Good with children				
Ease of training				

Original purpose: Hunting and guarding
Male height: 31-35 in (79-89 cm)
Female height: 28-33 in (71-84 cm)
Weight: 90-120 lb (41-54 kg)
Lifespan: 5-7 years

and other pets within their own house-hold, but they have a strong hunting instinct and may not resist the temptation to chase a moving target.

● Giant dogs need space— not the right choice for a small home.

HOW much exercise?

Daily long walks and free galloping are essential for an adult Wolfhound, about an hour's walk a day plus the same amount of off-leash running. Like all sighthounds, this breed needs a lot of work on the recall, as he develops selective deafness once he has built up speed. Puppies under a year old should have restricted exercise to prevent damage to growing bones.

HOW easy to train?

Difficult. Training is essential, as a dog this size must be under control, so start early

and stick to it. Wolfhounds are stubborn, and owners need both patience and persistence. Lessons should be reward based with lots of praise. Physical punishment will simply make the Wolfhound distrust you.

WHAT good points?

Gentle, kind, friendly, powerful, brave, affectionate, dignified, sensitive, not aggressive.

Large dogs

WHAT to be aware of?

Not a breed for everyone. Be sure you can cope before taking on a Wolfhound. Rapid growth rate means puppies need specialized diet. Long tail easily damaged in confines of home, and once injured can be slow to heal. Needs supervision!

WHAT medical problems?

The breed is vulnerable to bloat (gastric torsion), liver, heart problems, and bone cancer (osteosarcoma).

Popular Crossbreeds

In recent years crossbreeds have become fashionable. They are often marketed as "designer dogs," with inflated claims as to their superiority over purebreds; conversely they are equally often decried by critics as overpriced mutts. Both views are unfair. A crossbreed, like a pedigree dog, can be an ideal companion or a neurotic, unhealthy mess—so much depends on the breeder and on the breeding stock.

Bear in mind that the appearance and temperament of a crossbreed will be less predictable than that of a pedigree dog. It may inherit the best of both parent breeds; it may not. The descriptions of popular crosses in the following pages are based on average examples—not all specimens will conform to the average.

Before buying a crossbreed, spend some time on research.

• DON'T believe claims that crossbreeds are automatically exempt from inherited health problems such as progressive retinal atrophy (an eye condition leading to blindness) and patellar luxation (dislocating kneecaps, often requiring expensive surgery). Ask to see breed appropriate health certification for both parents.

• DON'T believe that all "doodles" and "poos" (dogs that have poodle ancestry) are nonmolting and hypoallergenic. Some are, some aren't.

• DO research both parent breeds. Your puppy may have any of the traits of either parent, so make sure both sides are compatible with your lifestyle.

• DO research the breeder. It's important to avoid puppy mills, that churn out unhealthy, unsocialized pups as a cash crop, and also to steer clear of starry-eyed backyard breeders who think crossbreed puppies will be cute, and have never heard of health tests.

• DO take descriptions of any particular cross with a grain of salt. Be prepared to enjoy your dog even if he doesn't turn out quite as expected.

Morkie *Other names: Yorktese*

A cross between two silky-coated toy breeds can be relied upon to produce a small, silky dog, but some will have an appearance midway between the two. Others will resemble one parent more than the other. The Maltese is a lapdog, sweet-natured and responsive, while the Yorkie, despite his toy classification, is a terrier—full of energy and attitude; a Morkie may take after either side of the family. You should also bear in mind that outside the show ring, Yorkshire Terriers vary widely in size and coat, so a Morkie may inherit more size and less hair than expected.

A typical Morkie is a loveable and loving companion, lively and playful. Despite his pretty look, he is a dog, not a doll, and needs to be treated as s[...]. Like all toy breeds, he needs to be well socialized i[...] puppyhood to prevent nervous[...] with strange situations, strange[...] people, and strange dogs.

WHAT colors?
Often black and tan, but white, various shades of brown, and tri-color also occur.

WHAT grooming does the coat need?
The Morkie's long, silky, nonmolting hair is high maintenance. Brush daily to prevent tangles and mats. Many owners have the coat regularly clipped into a puppy trim. Facial hair needs to be trimmed or tied back to protect the eyes. Hair inside the ears may need regular plucking, and the fur under the eyes usually needs to be cleaned daily.

● *"Butterscotch" colored puppies like this one generally fade to a lighter shade as they mature. The dark facial mask also fades, usually disappearing altogether by three or four months.*

and need someone at home during most of the day.

HOW suitable are they as family dogs?
These happy, playful little dogs can be an excellent choice for the family with older, sensible children. Like most toys, they are too fragile for toddlers, especially because some Morkies can inherit the terrier tendency to have a short fuse. Morkies are companion dogs

WHAT type of home?
Small enough for an apartment, lively enough for a country home, the Morkie is adaptable to most environments. His silky coat is perhaps better suited to city life. Although he will enjoy country walks, regular applications of mud and vegetation make for a major grooming commitment.

WHAT type of owner?
This is an attention-loving little do[...] who needs an affectionate owner with plenty of time for him who [...] provide activity, play, entertainmen[...] —and also quite a lot of daily coa[...] care. He can be a devoted companion to the elderly or a live[...] family, but is not suitable for busy people. Owners need to be sensible as well as loving, because[...] Morkies are prone to separation anxiety if care is not taken to teac[...] them to accept being left on thei[...] own occasionally.

HOW compatible with other pets?
With sensible training, Morkies are generally good with other pets, although they will need to be taught that small pets such as hamsters are housemates rather than toys to play with. It is wise to supervise play with bigger dogs to prevent accidents.

HOW much exercise?
One or two short walks a day an[...] plenty of play racing around the

Character Trait	Poor	Average	Good	Excellent
Attitude toward other dogs				
Quietness				
Not destructive				
Protective behavior				
Not likely to stray				
Good with children				
Ease of training				

Place of origin: **Mediterranean/Britain**

Original purpose: Companion
Male height: 6-8 in (15-20 cm)
Female height: 6-8 in (15-20 cm)
Weight: 7-15 lb (3-7 kg)
Lifespan: 12-15 years

house, will keep the Morkie fit and healthy. However, given the option of longer walks, he will revel in them, and they will help to burn off his spare energy. Most Morkies have a lot of energy—remember the terrier element in them—and, if underemployed, they can become quite destructive.

HOW easy to train?

Generally bright and quick to learn, Morkies can also be stubborn and easily distracted. Positive training is a must. Make lessons a treat, with lots of short, fun sessions, plenty of praise, and a reward-based approach. A gentle, patient, and enthusiastic trainer will find this dog highly responsive. Harsh words and punishment will quickly teach him not to cooperate.

A puppy clip, trimming the whole coat short, minimizes grooming needs and ensures the dog's comfort.

WHAT good points?

Loyal, cheerful, playful, affectionate, adaptable, nonmolting, easily transported, an alert watchdog.

WHAT to be aware of?

High grooming commitment. Can be slow to housetrain; prone to separation anxiety; loves to bark; destructive if bored.

WHAT medical problems?

Genetic problems inherited from the parent breeds include cataracts, glaucoma, heart problems, hydrocephalus (fluid on the brain), dislocation of the kneecap (patellar luxation), tracheal (windpipe) collapse, hypoglycemia (lack of glucose in the blood), and liver shunt (a blood circulation defect). As with most small breeds, teeth need monitoring as dental problems are common.

Popular crossbreeds

Yorkiepoo *Other names: Yorkiedoodle*

Cross a Yorkshire Terrier with a Toy or Miniature Poodle, and you can expect a lot of fur and a lot of zoom. The Yorkiepoo's build and temperament are less predictable, as traits from either side may predominate. A typical Yorkiepoo is a lively, affectionate companion who blends the virtues of both parents. Others may be tough, cocky little terriers with extra fur, and others gentle and sensitive (even oversensitive) and dependent lapdogs.

Yorkiepoos are people dogs. They want to be with their family, receiving a generous share of attention. They are fun dogs, playful, clownish, and generally responsive. Despite their cute looks, they should not be regarded as fashion accessories. They crave amusement, stimulus, and involvement in family activities. They are bright and trainable and appreciate the chance to use their brains. They also enjoy walks and the opportunity to get muddy as much as most dogs.

WHAT colors?

A wide range, including black (usually with some white), golden, apricot, black and tan, parti-color and tri-color. Black and tan pups may retain their color or may fade to a silvery shade.

WHAT grooming does the coat need?

Quite a lot. The coat may be curly, wavy, or straight, but it will be long and it will tend to tangle and mat if not groomed on a regular basis. Brush and comb at least every other day. Facial hair, and probably the undercarriage and under the tail, need to be trimmed regularly. Many owners prefer to have the whole coat clipped every two or three months.

HOW suitable are they as family dogs?

Yorkiepoos thrive in the midst of a family with time for grooming and play. They are too small to be safe in the clumsy hands of small children, but thoroughly enjoy the company of older, sensible children.

● *Be aware that tiny puppies may grow up to be bigger than either parent.*

WHAT type of home?

Highly adaptable. The Yorkiepoo is small enough to live happily in an apartment (with at least a short daily walk), and lively enough to enjoy racing around in the countryside. Yards must be secure —although devoted to their owners, most Yorkiepoos have enough terrier curiosity to send them off exploring if there is a gap under the fence.

WHAT type of owner?

Suitable owners are people who want a small but lively companion who enjoy playing with a dog, and who have plenty of time to give and receive affection. They also need to enjoy grooming. The ideal owner will appreciate that even little dogs enjoy the stimulus of walks and training sessions.

HOW compatible with other pets?

In general, the Yorkiepoo will live happily with other pets within the household. Although, if his terrier blood comes to the fore, he may find cat chasing too tempting to resist. Most Yorkiepoos are dog friendly, but it is important that they are properly socialized with other dogs in puppyhood to avoid the risk of fear-based aggression.

HOW much exercise?

These are lively dogs who will adjust to various levels of exercise. They can keep fit on a brisk daily walk around the block, burning off any excess energy in play. Equally, they

Character Trait	Poor	Average	Good	Excellent
Attitude toward other dogs				
Quietness				
Not destructive				
Protective behavior				
Not likely to stray				
Good with children				
Ease of training				

Place of origin: **Britain/Germany**

Original purpose: Companion
Male height: 7-15 in (18-38 cm)
Female height: 7-15 in (18-38 cm)
Weight: 3-14 lb (1.5-6.5 kg)
Lifespan: 10-15 years

can enjoy long country walks and, if you build up their fitness gradually, they will happily run for miles.

HOW easy to train?

These are bright little dogs who can be quick learners; they can also be stubborn, easily distracted, and prone to clowning around. Keep their interest by making lessons fun. Be consistent and don't let them get away with misbehavior by looking cute. Be gentle, because they can be sensitive and easily upset, and aim for a well-mannered companion

rather than an obedience contender. Activities such as mini agility may well appeal to a Yorkiepoo.

WHAT good points?

Bright and bubbly, playful, loving, adaptable, nonaggressive, minimal exercise needs, low or nonmolting coat.

WHAT to be aware of?

Above-average coat care; excitable and attention-seeking; often tend to be yappy; may be prone to separation anxiety.

WHAT medical problems?

Potential inherited disorders include joint malformation (hip and elbow dysplasia, kneecap dislocation), eye problems (cataracts, corneal dystrophy, keratitis, progressive retinal atrophy), underactive thyroid, von Willebrand's disease (a blood disorder), endocardiosis (a heart disease), epilepsy, Legg-Calvé-Perthes disease (hip degeneration), hyperadrenocorticism (overproduction of glucocorticoid hormones), atopic dermatitis. It is therefore essential to look for breeders who undertake health testing.

Popular crossbreeds

Chiweenie

The Chihuahua and Dachshund parents of this cross are both popular small companion breeds, well suited to a range of lifestyles. Both are active little dogs without needing a huge amount of exercise. There is a size difference between the breeds, particularly if the Dachshund parent is a Standard rather than a Miniature, so Chiweenies tend to be larger than Chihuahuas. Many Chiweenies inherit the long back and short legs of the Dachshund. Most are short coated, but some inherit long hair from one or both parents; Wirehaired Chiweenies (from a Wirehaired Dachshund line) are less common.

These are lively, loving little dogs, spirited, playful, adventurous, and devoted to their owners. They are often also busy, bossy, and demanding, with a lot of personality and a tendency to be comedians. As long as they have companionship and plenty of attention, they can adapt successfully to a range of lifestyles.

WHAT colors?

Wide range, including black, tan, white, chocolate, golden, merle, brindle, black and tan, parti-color.

WHAT grooming does the coat need?

Both coat types are low maintenance. A weekly brushing to remove dead hairs is all that is needed, plus a quick comb through every couple of days for long coats to prevent mats from forming (especially behind the ears and in the undercarriage).

HOW suitable are they as family dogs?

A lively young family, with sensible, well behaved children will provide the company and entertainment a Chiweenie requires. If raised with children, these dogs can become very attached to them. Remember, however, that childish clumsiness can easily damage small dogs (and the Chiweenie's long back is particularly vulnerable to injury), and that small dogs are often prone to jealousy and may nip.

WHAT type of home?

Chiweenies are highly adaptable. They can be city or country dogs, and are small enough for apartment life. However, they will be happier with a yard where they can burn off energy safely.

WHAT type of owner?

This is a dog for owners who value personality above strict obedience and who have a sense of humor when it comes to minor canine misdeeds. Once that is taken into account, he is adaptable enough to make a devoted friend for the elderly, or an energetic playmate for a lively family.

HOW compatible with other pets?

Many Chiweenies inherit the Dachshund's hunting drive. They are more likely to tease and annoy than to kill, but cats and other household pets may not enjoy sharing their home. They are usually good with other canines, but puppyhood socialization is vital to teach them respect for strange dogs.

● *These lively little dogs need daily walks and off-leash running. However, avoid any exercise that is likely to stress that long spine, such as jumping, hill walks, or running up and down stairs.*

Place of origin: **Central America/Germany**

Character Trait	Poor	Average	Good	Excellent
Attitude toward other dogs				
Quietness				
Not destructive				
Protective behavior				
Not likely to stray				
Good with children				
Ease of training				

Original purpose: Companion
Male height: 8-9 in (20-23 cm)
Female height: 8-9 in (20-23 cm)
Weight: 5-15 lb (2.5-7 kg)
Lifespan: 10-15 years

HOW much exercise?

Chiweenies are usually active dogs who enjoy walks and energetic play. In fact, they need exercise, about two half-hour outings a day, not only for entertainment but to maintain health. Physical fitness will reduce the risk of damage to the elongated spine. However, short legs and a long back are not suited to roughhousing with the children or to jogging or hiking, so don't overdo it.

HOW easy to train?

Bright but stubborn, most Chiweenies can be quick learners if they find training rewarding, but generally need to be persuaded that having their own way isn't even more rewarding. These dogs don't usually have any inclination toward obedience. Owners need to be patient, persistent, and consistent to achieve results. To neglect basic training is likely to result in a dog with "spoiled brat syndrome."

WHAT good points?

Devoted, playful, energetic, good-tempered, low maintenance, convenient size, adaptable, protective, fun-loving, alert watchdogs.

WHAT to be aware of?

Can be difficult to housetrain; often very vocal; can be bossy and jealous; often not good with other pets.

WHAT medical problems?

A long spine means vulnerability to back problems. Other possible inherited disorders include kneecap dislocation (patellar luxation), hypothyroidism (underactive thyroid gland), epilepsy, diabetes, and eye problems (cataracts and progressive retinal atrophy).

Popular crossbreeds

● *His melting expression and comically bustling ways have established the "Mexican hotdog" as a popular choice since American breeders came up with this mix in the 1990s. The Chiweenie is a lot of dog in a small package.*

Pug-zu

The glamorous Shih Tzu and the chunky, clownish Pug may not seem to have much in common at first glance, but they are both merry, independent, and opinionated dogs with a great deal of character. Cross these two breeds, and you can expect an entertaining, loving, and willful companion with oodles of personality. The Pug-zu is typically a stocky little dog with an expressive face. Size varies, as does coat. Some are short haired, others fluffy, and yet others rough coated with wild tufts and whiskery faces.

Unfortunately, the other feature Pugs and Shih Tzus share is a short face, giving an appealingly human expression but, when taken to extremes (as too often happens), is liable to cause breathing problems, misplaced teeth, and bulging eyes prone to injury. Avoid buying a puppy whose parents have overly flat faces.

WHAT colors?

A wide range of colors, including black, fawn, golden, gray, brindle, and parti-color. Many Pug-zus have the Pug's black facial mask.

WHAT grooming does the coat need?

Short coats need weekly brushing to remove dead hairs; longer coats will need combing through. With scruffy coated, whiskery dogs, wipe clean beards and mustaches after meals, and keep facial hair trimmed away from the eyes.

● *Most Pug-zus inherit their color from the Pug parent—fawn with black mask, or all black. Shih Tzu colors and patterns also occur, but are less common.*

HOW suitable are they as family dogs?

Much depends on the family. Cheerful, playful, and always ready to join in with activities, a Pug-zu can be a happy choice for a less active family with considerate older children but is not really suited to an energetic lifestyle, nor is he robust enough to cope with pre-schoolers.

WHAT type of home?

Small and not overly energetic, a Pug-zu will find plenty of play space in an apartment, with a daily walk to keep him fit and stimulated, and will be equally happy in a country home with a secure yard. At heart he is usually more of a city-dweller than a country dog, being a sociable creature who enjoys meeting people more than taking long strenuous walks.

WHAT type of owner?

The Pug-zu is best suited to owners who prefer fun, quirky dogs over impeccably obedient ones. He needs company, affection, and appreciation, plenty of playtime, and full involvement in his owner's activities. He also needs a sensible owner who will not allow amusing willfulness to degenerate to spoiled behavior.

HOW compatible with other pets?

Pug-zus will generally get along well with other household pets, although, like all dogs, they won't understand how to behave with other dogs without effective socialization in puppyhood.

HOW much exercise?

A daily half-hour walk is recommended—the Pug-zu will be happy to work off any surplus energy in playing. He is not designed for long hikes, and many Pug-zus need firm encouragement to take sufficient exercise to keep them healthy. Be aware that, like other Pug crosses, he may easily overheat, so avoid exercise in hot weather.

HOW easy to train?

The typical Pug-zu has a disinclination toward formal obedience, but he is an amiable

Character Trait	Poor	Average	Good	Excellent
Attitude toward other dogs				
Quietness				
Not destructive				
Protective behavior				
Not likely to stray				
Good with children				
Ease of training				

Original purpose: Companion
Male height: 8-12 in (20-30 cm)
Female height: 8-12 in (20-30 cm)
Weight: 8-16 lb (3.5-7 kg)
Lifespan: 10-15 years

creature who is usually willing to cooperate up to a point, especially if food rewards are involved. It should not be difficult to teach him basic good behavior, especially if training is fun, firm, and consistent. He will happily learn tricks if he finds them entertaining, but he is unlikely to win any obedience awards.

WHAT good points?

Sociable, outgoing, affectionate, playful, entertaining, nonaggressive, even-tempered, people oriented.

WHAT to be aware of?

Strong-willed; can be very demanding; tendency to snuffle and snore; some molt quite heavily; may be slow to housetrain.

● Crossbred puppies can take after either parent, or inherit a combination of their qualities, in both appearance and temperament.

WHAT medical problems?

Possible inherited disorders include hip malformation (dysplasia), kneecap dislocation (patellar luxation), epilepsy, respiratory problems (collapsing trachea, pinched nostrils, elongated soft palate), eye problems, dental problems (watch out for severely undershot jaws). All breeding stock should be certified as clear for hip dysplasia and patellar luxation and should also hold current eye certificates.

Popular crossbreeds

Lhatese *Other names: Kyi-leo, American Lamalese*

The Lhasa Apso-Maltese cross is known as the Lhatese and American Lamalese. Strictly speaking, the term Kyi-Leo is reserved for a multi-generation strain dating back to 1960s San Francisco, whose Californian breeders chose the name in 1972 and have aimed to breed to a standard ever since. However, it is sometimes adopted by modern breeders to apply to any Lhasa-Maltese crosses.

From both parents, this little dog inherits a flowing coat, an affectionate nature, a lively personality and, despite his decorative appearance, the need to be treated like a real dog rather than a plaything. Playful, adaptable, and intelligent, he loves company and becomes deeply attached to his owner—often too much, as he is prone to separation anxiety. He is usually an enthusiastic watchdog, and early socialization is important to counterbalance his innate wariness of strangers.

WHAT colors?

Black and white is the most common combination; also black, gold, white, or cream with or without colored markings. The Kyi-Leo strain is normally black and white, occasionally fading to silver/gray and white.

WHAT grooming does the coat need?

The long, dense, silky coat needs brushing (use a soft wire slicker brush) and combing at least every other day to prevent tangles and mats. Some Lhatese are low to nonmolting. Others are not, and will need extra attention during the twice-yearly molt.

HOW suitable are they as family dogs?

For a gentle family with someone at home most of the time and with older children, this cross can be a great choice. He is neither too boisterous nor too fragile to be an ideal playmate for sensible

● *A puppy clip is a practical solution to the Lhatese's grooming needs, making life easier for dog and owner.*

youngsters. However, the unpredictability and sudden movements of younger children can worry him, and he is vulnerable to clumsy handling.

WHAT type of home?

Like most small breeds, this cross is adaptable to most environments, as long as he has his place in the heart of the family or close to his chosen companion. He will live happily in an apartment, but would prefer a home with a yard where he can enjoy playing outdoors. Many of

these little dogs are enthusiastic diggers, so fences need to be thoroughly secured at the base.

WHAT type of owner?

Owners who want around-the-clock companionship, enjoy daily stroll rather than a hike and like grooming will find this cross great fun to live with. He is not a dog for full time workers or for busy people who have no time for cuddles. However, as long as his grooming needs are fully appreciated, his sweet nature and willingness to please make him a suitable choice for the novice.

HOW compatible with other pets?

Most Lhasa-Maltese crosses will live in harmony with other domestic pets, although they should be supervised with bigger dogs who could accidentally injure them, and also with small pets like guinea pigs or hamsters, which might be perceived as dog toys.

Character Trait	Poor	Average	Good	Excellent
Attitude toward other dogs				
Quietness				
Not destructive				
Protective behavior				
Not likely to stray				
Good with children				
Ease of training				

Place of origin: **Tibet/Mediterranean**

Original purpose: Companion
Male height: 8-12 in (20-30 cm)
Female height: 8-12 in (20-30 cm)
Weight: 9-14 lb (4-6 kg)
Lifespan: 11-15 years

HOW much exercise?

These little dogs will satisfy most of their exercise needs through play, but they still need a daily walk of at least half an hour, and some off-leash running time in a safe area. They will also enjoy longer walks, although they were never meant to be long-distance jogging companions.

HOW easy to train?

These dogs are usually bright, eager to please, and respond well to gentle, consistent training, especially if lessons are fun. Training should start in puppyhood and should include regular socialization with both humans and other dogs to establish confidence.

WHAT good points?

Affectionate, loyal, adaptable, lively, gentle, cuddly, playful, generally quick to learn, alert watchdog.

WHAT to be aware of?

Heavy grooming commitment; can be clingy and prone to separation anxiety; can be destructive if lonely and bored; wary of strangers; tendency to bark.

WHAT medical problems?

Generally healthy and long-lived; inherited problems include dislocating kneecaps (patellar luxation), prone to pancreatitis; various digestive disorders and dental issues. They are also vulnerable to ruptured discs in the neck and spine.

● *The Lhatese is a cute little dog, but he is attentive and alert and makes a great watchdog.*

Popular crossbreeds

Jackadoodle *Other names: Jackapoo*

Poodles and Jack Russell Terriers are very different dogs, both in appearance and temperament. Mix them together and the only certainty is that their offspring will be small, lively, and overendowed with personality. What most people expect from this cross is a terrier-shaped dog with a scruffy Poodle coat, and with Poodle sensitivity balancing terrier fieriness. This is one type of Jackadoodle, but others look like rough or smooth coated terriers, while others have full curly Poodle hair. Temperament may also lean toward one parent or the other.

That being said, this cross is becoming increasingly, and deservedly, popular. The typical Jackadoodle is a fun little companion, often described as the choice for people who love Jack Russells but would prefer a less intense version.

WHAT colors?
Solid black, brown, chocolate, golden, white or cream; white with colored markings, often in terrier patterns.

WHAT grooming does the coat need?
Terrier-type coats need only a brisk weekly session with a bristle brush. Poodle-type coats need a daily comb through to prevent matting and may be clipped for ease of management. Most will need at least regular trimming of the hair around the eyes.

HOW suitable are they as family dogs?
Most Jackadoodles make loveable pets for reasonably active families and can be great companions for older children. Families with younger children should think twice, bearing in mind both that small dogs are vulnerable to clumsy handling and that some may inherit terrier reactiveness to toddlers' shrieks, squeals, and sudden movements. Not suitable for full-time workers —these dogs need company.

● *These happy, outgoing little dogs are always ready to join in family activities— or to get into some mischief!*

WHAT type of home?
These little dogs will fit into a city apartment provided they have regular walks and free-running playtime. They will be even happier in a home with a secure yard, although keen gardeners may not appreciate their landscaping work. They are also well suited to country life and long rambles full of interesting smells to investigate.

WHAT type of owner?
Moderately active owners who expect to spend a lot of time with their dog and are looking for a merry companion will suit a Jackadoodle. He needs a lot of human company, both for his own comfort and for his owner's peace of mind—a bored and lonely Jackadoodle will make his own amusements, usually of the destructive type. He is generally too active for couch potatoes or people seeking a lapdog.

HOW compatible with other pets?
Unpredictable. If the temperament leans toward the Jack Russell parent, expect a keen hunting drive that bodes ill for small furry pets, plus a tendency toward dog aggression, which demands lots of early socialization. However, you are just as likely to find a sweet-natured Jackadoodle who will readily learn to live in harmony with other pets.

HOW much exercise?
Jackadoodles inherit bounce and energy from both parent breeds, and enjoy an active lifestyle. Aim for at least two half-hour walks a day

Character Trait	Poor	Average	Good	Excellent
Attitude toward other dogs				
Quietness				
Not destructive				
Protective behavior				
Not likely to stray				
Good with children				
Ease of training				

Place of origin: **Britain/Germany**

Original purpose: Companion
Male height: 10-15 in (25-38 cm)
Female height: 10-15 in (25-38 cm)
Weight: 13-25 lb (6-11 kg)
Lifespan: 10-15 years

plus plenty of playtime. These dogs will appreciate longer walks, and activities such as Frisbee chasing and agility training.

HOW easy to train?

Variable. Some Jackadoodles may have an argumentative terrier approach, others may be more eager to please. They are usually bright little dogs with a lot of potential, so patience, consistency, and a positive, fun approach to training will achieve results— probably not to formal obedience level, but generally to the satisfaction of both parties.

WHAT good points?

Energetic, exuberant, entertaining, loving, active, athletic, full of fun, convenient size.

WHAT to be aware of?

Wide variation in size, coat, and temperament. Often excitable and attention-seeking; may be stubborn; needs plenty of

company; may be noisy; if poodle-coated, high coat maintenance.

WHAT medical problems?

Potential inherited disorders include kneecap dislocation (patellar luxation), eye problems (glaucoma, cataracts, progressive retinal atrophy), Legg-Calvé-Perthes disease (deformity of the hip joint), and congenital deafness.

● *Jack Russells vary in type (e.g., short-legged or long-legged), so expect variation in Jack crosses.*

Cockapoo

The Cockapoo has been popular longer than most other crosses, having been bred in the U.S. since the 1950s. He also has a more varied background because his parent breeds, the Cocker Spaniel and the Poodle, both come in three versions. Poodles may be Standard, Miniature, or Toy size. There are three types of Cocker: Cocker Spaniel (small, round-headed, heavy-coated), English Cocker show type (bigger, less coat, longer muzzle), and English Cocke working type (stockier, even less coat, even more energetic).

In addition to first-generation Cocker to Poodl crosses, Cockapoos are also often bred as second-generation, Cockapoo to Cockapoo, and beyond, or crossed back to a parent breed, i.e., Cockapoo to Cocker or Poodle. Sizes, coats, and temperament va Nonetheless, these dogs tend to have a distinctive appearance, with an appealingly shaggy coat and a sweet face framed by long ears.

WHAT colors?

A wide range of colors includes black, white, cream, red, apricot, buff, dark or light brown, parti-color, tri-color, roan, and merle.

WHAT grooming does the coat need?

Whether straight, wavy, or curly, the Cockapoo's coat is copious and fast growing, and needs frequent grooming to prevents mats and tangles. Straight coats need brushing thoroughly every other day; wavy and curly coats need daily attention with a slicker brush and then with a medium-toothed comb to locate and remove mats. Most owners opt to keep the hair under control with regular trims. In any case, the fringe and facial hair need to be scissored away from the eyes on a regular basis to prevent eye ulcers.

HOW suitable are they as family dogs?

Lively, loving and playful, Cockapoos make great pets for families who have time for exercise, training, and grooming. Older, sensible children

● *These adorable black and tan puppies will grow into energetic adults.*

will adore them. However, they can be too rough and rowdy in play for small children.

WHAT type of home?

These dogs can fit in with city or country life, and the smaller Cockapoos make great apartment dogs provided their exercise needs are met outside the home. As city dogs, they need more exercise than some. As country dogs, they are mud magnets whose dense coats absorb water like a sponge.

WHAT type of owner?

Not a dog for couch potatoes, the Cockapoo needs a reasonably active owner with plenty of time for him. He doesn't do well with a owner who is always busy or out great deal, as he needs company t thrive. Potential owners also need to keep his demanding grooming needs in mind.

HOW compatible with other pets?

Generally friendly with other animals, Cockapoos can be too bouncy for the comfort of small furries. They do inherit a tendency to chase and need to be trained i puppyhood not to torment the ca or paw at the hamster's cage.

HOW much exercise?

The Cockapoo thrives on exercise Toy-sized specimens can maintain fitness with a half-hour walk every day, plus energetic playtime. Large Cockapoos benefit from longer walks and free running time, and will thoroughly enjoy country rambles. These are dogs with considerable potential for activitie such as agility and flyball.

Character Trait	Poor	Average	Good	Excellent
Attitude toward other dogs				
Quietness				
Not destructive				
Protective behavior				
Not likely to stray				
Good with children				
Ease of training				

Place of origin: **Britain/Germany**

Original purpose: Companion
Toy height: 10-12 in (25-30 cm)
Miniature height: 11-14 in (28-35.5 cm)
Standard/Maxi height: 15-17 in (38-43 cm)
Lifespan: 11-15 years

HOW easy to train?

Cockapoos are generally responsive to consistent, positive training—they are sensitive dogs who don't cope well with harsh treatment. At best, they combine Poodle brains with Cocker eagerness to please. However, some can be stubborn and easily distracted.

WHAT good points?

Happy, bright, outgoing, lively, playful, affectionate, people oriented, low to nonmolting, choice of sizes.

WHAT to be aware of?

Demanding coat; may be high-strung; prone to separation anxiety; may be a barker.

WHAT medical problems?

They may inherit hip malformation (dysplasia), dislocating kneecaps

Apricot pups with apricot poodle dam.

(patellar luxation), eye problems including PRA (progressive retinal atrophy) and glaucoma, heart disease, liver problems, and epilepsy. They are also prone to ear infections. All breeding stock should be hip scored and have a current eye certificate. They should also be tested for enzyme (PKF) deficiency, a condition causing low energy, muscle wastage, and anemia; and for defective kidneys (familial nephropathy).

Popular crossbreeds

Cavapoo *Other names: Cavoodle*

Crossing a Cavalier King Charles Spaniel with a Miniature or Toy Poodle produces a sturdy little toy-size version of the popular Cockapoo (Cocker Spaniel cross Poodle—see pages 206-207). Some pups will take after one parent breed, with tight Poodle curls or the flat, silky coat of the Cavalier. The favored type of Cavapoo is an appealingly shaggy little dog with the Cavalier's sweet and accommodating nature and a low to nonmolting coat derived from the Poodle.

In size and appearance, the Cavapoo is quite similar to the Cavachon (Cavalier cross Bichon—see pages 210-211), though often smaller, with a narrower muzzle. However, he tends to be a livelier dog—both his parent breeds have sporting origins, and Cavapoos, despite their cute and cuddly appearance, often inherit more energy and stamina than might be expected.

WHAT colors?
A wide range, including black, white, red, golden, cream, black and white, red and white, tri-color.

WHAT grooming does the coat need?
Most Cavapoos have high-maintenance coats that need daily sessions with a slicker brush and wide-toothed comb to prevent mats and tangles. Many owners have the coat clipped regularly into a puppy clip for the dog's comfort and for ease of care. In any case, it is advisable to trim facial hair to protect the eyes, and belly fur and under the tail for hygiene reasons. Puppies need to be accustomed to grooming before the adult coat comes in at about six months.

HOW suitable are they as family dogs?
A Cavapoo can be a great choice for a lively family with children old enough to regard him as a playmate rather than a plaything. The amount of coat care required should be taken into account. Don't pick a Cavapoo if you don't enjoy grooming. Some strains can be too high-strung for a robust family lifestyle, so check out both parents' temperament before buying a puppy.

● This Cavapoo puppy has inherited his black and tan coloration and ginger eyebrows from his Cavalier mother.

WHAT type of home?
A Cavapoo can be happy in a city apartment, if regular walks and playtime are provided and equally happy with a country lifestyle. These are quite active little dogs who will appreciate a yard to play in. However, the company of their humans is more important to them than their environment.

WHAT type of owner?
This happy little dog does best with a moderately active owner who has time, and the inclination, to provide the company, attention, and affection he needs. Owners who enjoy training will get the most out of him. Despite his teddy bear looks and loving nature, he has a brain that needs stimulus and occupation. Cavapoos who are overindulged and undereducated can turn into spoiled brats!

HOW compatible with other pets?
Generally friendly and nonaggressive, the Cavapoo is far more likely to view other household pets as playmates than as prey. All puppies will chase furry friends until they learn not to, so gradual, well-supervised introductions to resident pets are essential. Proper socialization in puppyhood will teach him how to behave with other dogs and build on his natural good nature.

Character Trait	Poor	Average	Good	Excellent
Attitude toward other dogs				
Quietness				
Not destructive				
Protective behavior				
Not likely to stray				
Good with children				
Ease of training				

Place of origin: **Britain/Germany**

Original purpose: Companion
Male height: 11-15 in (28-38 cm)
Female height: 11-15 in (28-38 cm)
Weight: 6-20 lb (2.5-9 kg)
Lifespan: 12-15 years

HOW much exercise?

Cavapoos are rarely couch potatoes. While they are not designed to be hiking companions, these active, lively little dogs do need a daily walk of at least half an hour (and will enjoy more), as well as energetic playtime. An underexercised Cavapoo will have energy to burn and can become a little hooligan.

HOW easy to train?

Only moderately easy to train, but well worth the effort, the Cavapoo benefits from regular, gentle, reward-based training sessions. Once he has discovered that learning is fun, he should be capable of mastering a wide range of exercises and tricks. With his sense of fun and abundant energy, he is more likely to enjoy mini agility than obedience trials.

WHAT good points?

Affectionate, outgoing, playful, nonaggressive, sociable, active family oriented, often has low to nonshedding coat.

WHAT to be aware of?

Size and appearance variable; high-maintenance coat; can be demanding, clingy, and prone to separation

● *Variation in size, coat, and head shape often occurs within the same litter.*

anxiety; essential that Cavalier parent has full health checks.

WHAT medical problems?

Cavapoos may inherit heart defects, malformation of the hip (dysplasia), dislocating kneecaps (patellar luxation), epilepsy, and eye problems. They may also be prone to ear infections and eye ulcers. Breeding stock should have their eyes, hearts, and knees tested before being used.

Popular crossbreeds

Cavachon

Cavachons vary in size and general appearance, but inherit sweet looks and a sweet temper from both the Cavalier King Charles Spaniel and the Bichon Frise. Some Cavachons resemble one side of the family more than the other, but when the two breeds blend equally they produce an endearingly shaggy little dog with the Cavalier's melting expression and a low to nonmolting coat derived from the Bichon.

The desired coat is long, flowing, soft, and wavy, but some Cavachons have the Bichon's soft curls, some Cavalier's silky coat, and some definitely do molt.

Cavachon temperament, however, is less variable and can usually be relied on to be delightful. The typical Cavachon is a lively (but not hyperactive), friendly, and sociable companion who responds well to training and adapts well to a range of possible lifestyles. His good nature and cuddly appearance have made him one of the more popular modern crosses.

WHAT colors?

A wide range of colors. Most common are white, brown (often attractive pastel shades—peach, apricot, and lemon) or white with brown patches, but sable, black and white, and tri-color also occur.

WHAT grooming does the coat need?

The thick, fluffy coat is high maintenance, needing daily combing to prevent mats and tangles. Most owners have the coat clipped regularly to make it more manageable and to keep the dog more comfortable. In any case, the face needs frequent clipping to stop hair from damaging the eyes, and hair inside the ears needs to be plucked to reduce the chance of infections. Puppies need to be accustomed to grooming before the adult coat comes in at about six months.

HOW suitable are they as family dogs?

A Cavachon can make the ideal family dog, as long as the family

● *Many puppies inherit the Blenheim Cavalier head markings, with a white forehead spot.*

bears his grooming needs in mind. Sturdy enough to enjoy playtime with children, gentle enough to suit the needs of an elderly relative, he is a dog who wants to be with his people and does not thrive if left alone. As with all small dogs, he should be introduced to children under sensible supervision to prevent misunderstandings.

WHAT type of home?

Cavachons are small enough and sensible enough to adapt to a city apartment if regular walks are provided and sturdy enough to enjoy life in the country. The company of their human owners more important to them than the immediate environment.

WHAT type of owner?

An affectionate owner who is there to provide cuddles, attention, playtime, and companionable quiet time will suit a Cavachon. He does not like being ignored or abandoned, but will repay the attention he receives many times over. He may not be the first choice for the house proud. Although most Cavachons molt little or not at all, that beautiful coat carries in a generous share of dampness, mud, and dead leaves.

HOW compatible with other pets?

Cavachons are not naturally aggressive and, if properly socialized from the start, are generally just as full of good will toward other household pets as toward people. All puppies will chase furry friends until they learn not to, so

Character Trait	Poor	Average	Good	Excellent
Attitude toward other dogs				
Quietness				
Not destructive				
Protective behavior				
Not likely to stray				
Good with children				
Ease of training				

Original purpose: Companion
Male height: 12-16 in (30-41 cm)
Female height: 12-16 in (30-41 cm)
Weight: 12-18 lb (5.5-8 kg)
Lifespan: 10-12 years

introductions to cats, rabbits, and the like should be made gradually and under supervision.

HOW much exercise?

Daily walks of at least half an hour, plus off-leash playtime, are needed to keep your Cavachon fit and healthy. Most will relish much longer walks, given the chance. These are lively little dogs, but they are quite active indoors and can burn off quite a lot of energy playing around the house.

HOW easy to train?

Cavachons are bright, willing to please, and even more willing to take part in interesting activities. For best results, start training sessions early and make them fun. Like many toy dogs, Cavachons need to learn basic good manners or they can become demanding and stubborn. Time spent training is never wasted.

WHAT good points?

Friendly, affectionate, gentle, family oriented, nonaggressive, lively without being hyperactive, low to nonshedding coat.

WHAT to be aware of?

Size and appearance very variable; high-maintenance coat; may be slow to housetrain; some may be yappy.

WHAT medical problems?

Cavachons may inherit heart defects, malformation of the hip (dysplasia), dislocating kneecaps (patellar luxation), and eye problems. They may also be prone to ear infections and eye ulcers. Breeding stock should have their eyes, hearts, and knees tested before being used.

● *This beautiful coat demands a lot of care.*

Puggle

What do you get when you cross a clownish little lapdog with an athletic hunter? The goal when crossing Pug and Beagle is a small, sweet-tempered companion dog with the Pug's charm, personality, and expressive, wrinkled face, but without his many physical handicaps. The Puggle is a sturdy little dog, typically built like a small, stocky Beagle with a shorter, wider face, wrinkled forehead, and usually, Pug coloration. He is sometimes likened to a miniature Mastiff. However, there is a wide variation in size and also in head shape—some Puggles turn out larger than expected, some are as chunky as Pugs, and some are quite flat faced.

From both parents the Puggle inherits an even temperament and friendly nature. Unfortunately, less desirable traits may also be passed on, such as the Beagle's howl and his tendency to disappear at top speed after a scent, and the Pug's breathing problems.

WHAT colors?

Most common is fawn or tan, with or without a black mask; black, white, and tri-color also occur.

WHAT grooming does the coat need?

The short dense coat molts steadily and needs weekly brushing to strip out loose hairs. Facial folds and wrinkles should be checked and cleaned each day to prevent soreness and infection.

HOW suitable are they as family dogs?

A Puggle can be an ideal family dog. This is a companion who needs to be involved in family activities and social life. He is small enough to fit in anywhere but robust enough not to need coddling. Good-natured, affectionate, playful, and cuddly, he will enjoy a great relationship with children old enough to act sensibly with a dog.

WHAT type of home?

A Puggle can be happy in the city

● *Puggles are said to be the most popular of all the crossbreeds.*

or country. He will do well in an apartment with regular walks, but even better in a home with a yard where he can burn off some of his abundant energy by running around and playing. His Beagle ancestry means that the yard should be very secure to prevent him from disappearing after an interesting scent.

WHAT type of owner?

This is a sociable dog who will not thrive without company. He needs an affectionate owner with plenty of time for him. Puggle owners need to be moderately active. Puggles have abundant energy and enjoy walks and dashing around the home but are not designed for physically demanding exercise such as jogging or hiking.

HOW compatible with other pets?

Most Puggles will extend their sociability to include other household pets. However, half this dog's heritage comes from a hound breed with a strong chase instinct, so small pets like rabbits and hamsters may need protection.

HOW much exercise?

At least half an hour's walk each day, plus playtime, is essential to the Puggle's well-being. These dogs have a lot of energy to burn, but they lack the stamina of their Beagle parent. Owners need to ensure that they don't overdo exercise. Some individuals can manage regular long walks, but the typical Puggle is geared for Pug-style shorter spells of activity. Be aware that Puggles easily overheat, so avoid exercise in the heat of the day.

HOW easy to train?

On the one hand, Puggles don't inherit a strong obedience drive from either parent. On the other,

Character Trait	Poor	Average	Good	Excellent
Attitude toward other dogs				
Quietness				
Not destructive				
Protective behavior				
Not likely to stray				
Good with children				
Ease of training				

Original purpose: Companion
Male height: 13-15 in (33-38 cm)
Female height: 13-15 in (33-38 cm)
Weight: 12-30 lb (5-13.5 kg)
Lifespan: 10-15 years

they do inherit greediness and can be motivated to cooperate by food rewards (but don't overdo this approach—like the Pug, most Puggles try really hard to become obese). They can be stubborn, clownish, and easily distracted, but short, consistent sessions of reward-based training will have a positive effect.

WHAT good points?
Friendly, loving, playful, lively, good-tempered, adaptable, nonaggressive, people oriented.

WHAT to be aware of?
Stubborn, greedy, rather vocal, sheds hairs constantly, susceptible to overheating, prone to separation anxiety; may be slow to housetrain.

WHAT medical problems?
Possible inherited disorders include hip malformation (dysplasia), kneecap dislocation (patellar luxation), epilepsy, respiratory problems (collapsing trachea, pinched nostrils, elongated soft palate), eye problems, dental problems (watch out for severely undershot jaws). All breeding stock should be certified as clear for hip dysplasia and patellar luxation and should also hold current eye certificates.

● Many Puggles inherit the curled tail of the Pug parent, but usually as a simple single curl.

Goldendoodle *Other names: Groodle*

In the 1990s, Australian and American breeders started crossing Golden Retrievers and Standard Poodles. The goal was to produce a larger version of the popular Cockapoo, combining the Golden's kindly nature with a nonshedding (or at least low shedding) coat. Later, Miniature and even Toy Poodles were used, so that today Goldendoodles come in three sizes: Large Standard, Small Standard, and Miniature.

Given a reputable breeder, most Goldendoodles are friendly, cheerful, intelligent dogs with an enthusiastic approach to life. They can make good family dogs and also good workers. There are Goldendoodle guide dogs, service dogs for the disabled, sniffer dogs, and search and rescue dogs. Many have "shaggy dog" appeal, although the coat is not always predictable. Some are flatcoated, some wavy, and some curly. Some molt and some don't.

WHAT colors?
Golden, red, apricot, white, cream, black, and even parti-color. The coat often lightens with age.

WHAT grooming does the coat need?
Coats vary, but are generally high maintenance. Retriever-type coats need daily combing to remove dead hairs and a weekly thorough brushing. Nonmolting shaggy coats are more demanding, needing daily combing and pin brushing right down to the skin to prevent knots and mats. Most owners prefer to have the coat regularly clipped to keep it in order. At around nine to 12 months, the change from puppy to adult coat often requires a short clip, as molting puppy fur tends to mat into felt.

HOW suitable are they as family dogs?
Goldendoodles make a great choice for families with time for exercise and grooming. They are people oriented, generally good

● *Some Goldendoodles have the nonmolting curls of the Poodle parent.*

with children, and love to be part of family activities. As youngsters, they may be too boisterous for a family with small children.

WHAT type of home?
The Goldendoodle is suited to city or country life, but he is too active, and often too big, to be comfortable in an apartment. He needs a home with a secure yard, and access to a park where he can run. As a country dog, he is not the best choice for wet, muddy walks, unless you are happy to spend a lot of time removing mud and vegetation from his fur afterward.

WHAT type of owner?
Not a good choice for couch potatoes, the Goldendoodle needs a moderately active family who enjoy walks and will make use of his intelligence and responsiveness with stimulating training sessions. He also needs plenty of company, as he may develop separation anxiety if left alone too much. The fanatically house proud should look elsewhere, as he may molt and will certainly be a mud magnet.

HOW compatible with other pets?
Goldendoodles are generally good with other household pets, though they may be too bouncy and playful for the comfort of small furries.

HOW much exercise?
These moderately active dogs will do well with three half-hour walks a day, but they will also enjoy longer walks and as much off-leash playtime as you can fit in. They are athletic and trainable enough to enjoy activities such as agility.

Character Trait	Poor	Average	Good	Excellent
Attitude toward other dogs				
Quietness				
Not destructive				
Protective behavior				
Not likely to stray				
Good with children				
Ease of training				

Original purpose: Companion
Large St. height: 20-24 in (51-61 cm)
Small St. height: 17-20 in (43-51 cm)
Miniature St. height: 13-20 in (33-51 cm)
Lifespan: 11-15 years

HOW easy to train?

With a gundog background, Goldendoodles are usually highly trainable, eager to please, and quick to learn. Patience is required, because they may also inherit the Poodle's zany sense of humor and enjoy playing the fool. Keep training sessions fun and reward based for the best results.

WHAT good points?

Friendly, sociable, active, intelligent, patient, stable, lively, fun-loving, companionable, adaptable.

WHAT to be aware of?

Heavy grooming commitment; can be clingy and prone to separation anxiety; coat type unpredictable.

WHAT medical problems?

Hip malformation (dysplasia) and eye problems (cataracts, progressive retinal atrophy) are problems with both parent breeds, so all breeding stock should be hip scored and have current eye certificates. Other inherited disorders include thyroid problems, von Willebrand's disease (a hereditary bleeding disorder), and vulnerability to bloat, ear infections, and skin disorders.

Popular crossbreeds

● *This beautiful "golden fleece" is highly prone to mats, especially in the armpits, behind the ears, and under the tail. To reduce daily grooming needs, many owners favor clipping the coat to about 1.5 in (4 cm) long all over.*

Labradoodle

In the 1980s, Australian guide dog breeders crossed Labrador Retrievers with Standard Poodles in an attempt to produce hypoallergenic dogs for blind people. The Labradoodle has since become highly popular, and now comprises many variants—first crosses, multigeneration crosses, Medium and Miniature sizes (bred from Miniature and Toy Poodles), and Australian Labradoodles, whose ancestry includes a dash of other breeds, including spaniels. And of course, there are varying coats. Some dogs have the desired low molting, wavy "fleece coat"; others a more Poodle-type nonmolting, curly "wool coat"; and yet others a Labrador-style molting "hair coat."

With all these possible variations, a Labradoodle from a responsible breeder is a boisterous, athletic, and very good-natured companion with an appealing scruffy appearance and the intelligence of his parent breeds.

● Whichever coat type, there is no guarantee that any Labradoodle will be hypoallergenic, so don't make this your main reason for choosing this particular crossbreed

WHAT colors?
Any Poodle color, including white, cream, brown, apricot, black, silver, blue, and parti-color.

WHAT grooming does the coat need?
Straight coated dogs need weekly brushing (more often during the molt) to remove dead hair. Fleece and wool coats are dense and mat easily, requiring grooming with a slicker brush and wide-toothed comb at least every other day to remove tangles. Most owners of dense-coated Labradoodles opt to have the coat clipped every six to eight weeks for ease of management and for the dog's comfort and hygiene. A full-coated dog is undoubtedly a major daily grooming commitment.

HOW suitable are they as family dogs?
A Labradoodle can be a very good choice for those who want a dog to participate fully in family activities, and who have time for exercise, training, grooming, and play. These dogs want to be in the midst of things and among company. They are generally good with children, though in adolescence they can be too bouncy for little ones.

WHAT type of home?
Lifestyle is more important than area. City or country will do, provided enough exercise and entertainment is available, although larger Labradoodles are really too big and bouncy to make good apartment dogs. These are active dogs who will appreciate a yard to play in.

WHAT type of owner?
Labradoodles are not part-time dogs. Owners who have the time and inclination to build up a close, loving companionship are needed. Potential owners should also enjoy regular walks and playtime and have time for grooming and training. Most Labradoodles are mud magnets and enthusiastic diggers, so keen gardeners and the house proud should probably not apply!

HOW compatible with other pets?
Most Labradoodles should be good with other dogs and household pets, although as exuberant puppies they will need to learn good manners and that cats are not to be bounced on or chased. Canine socialization in puppyhood is always advisable.

Character Trait	Poor	Average	Good	Excellent
Attitude toward other dogs				
Quietness				
Not destructive				
Protective behavior				
Not likely to stray				
Good with children				
Ease of training				

Original purpose: Companion
Standard height: 21-24 in (53-61 cm)
Medium height: 17-20 in (43-51 cm)
Miniature height: 14-16 in (35.5-41 cm)
Lifespan: 10-15 years

HOW much exercise?

These are active, energetic dogs who, as adults, will need at least an hour's daily walk, plus lively playtime and free running. Mental stimulus via training is important too. A bored Labradoodle is often destructive and noisy. They are well-suited for active sports such as agility and flyball.

Both parent dogs are water loving, so most Labradoodles will relish the opportunity to swim.

HOW easy to train?

Labradoodles are often highly intelligent, responsive, and quick to learn, although as puppies they can be

● Labradoodles have become too popular for their own good, so beware of unscrupulous breeders who don't health-test.

wild and distractible. It pays to start training early and to make it a fun, rewarding activity. A pup who looks forward to training sessions becomes a dog who is easy to teach.

WHAT good points?

Intelligent, friendly, energetic, affectionate, nonaggressive, people oriented, fun-loving.

WHAT to be aware of?

Coat may be high maintenance; needs lots of company; tend to be chewers and diggers. They are often water lovers who consider a walk incomplete if not soaked and filthy.

Popular crossbreeds

WHAT medical problems?

Inherited disorders include hip and elbow malformation (dysplasia), epilepsy, thyroid problems, eye problems including progressive retinal atrophy, and von Willebrand's disease (a bleeding disorder). All breeding stock should have hips and eyes screened.

Alusky
Other names: Huskamute

Crossing the fastest sled dog, the Siberian, with the strongest sled dog, the Alaskan Malamute, could produce an all-around draft dog. In practice, Aluskies may be midway between the two breeds in build, or may resemble one parent more closely, and they tend to be favored as strong, active companions rather than working draft dogs. From both parents they inherit high energy levels, friendliness toward humans, stubbornness, and a high prey drive.

Athletic, affectionate, and demanding, these are dogs who need plenty of mental and physical stimulus. They are not an ideal choice for full-time workers or novices. Potential owners should look beyond the striking appearance and consider how such a dog will fit into their lifestyle. In the right hands, the Alusky is an affectionate, tireless and outgoing companion. In the wrong hands, chaos on four legs.

WHAT colors?
All colors, including black, white, red, silver, gray, brown, with or without white markings. Eyes may be blue, brown, parti-color, or one blue and one brown.

WHAT grooming does the coat need?
The dense coat needs a thorough grooming with a stiff bristle brush at least weekly, with daily grooming during the heavy twice-yearly molt. Avoid baths unless absolutely necessary. Frequent baths damage the coat by stripping its natural oils, which can also lead to skin irritations.

● *Alert and watchful, Aluskies are nonetheless too friendly to be watchdogs.*

energy to meet the demands of this type of dog.

HOW suitable are they as family dogs?
Aluskies are great family dogs as long as their own needs are met. They are usually good with children. However, as youngsters they are often too rough and rowdy for the safety of younger children. Parents of young children are unlikely to have the time and

WHAT type of home?
Sled dogs were never designed for city life or small living spaces. They need access to a large yard or paddock, with secure high (6 ft/1.8 m) fences that they cannot dig under, jump over, or simply demolish. They also need to live near open spaces where they can burn off energy (on leash, for

the safety of livestock), and may no be popular in urban areas because of their tendency to howl.

WHAT type of owner?
Only active, outdoor types with plenty of time for a dog and an interest in strenuous activities such as hiking, agility, or Canicross will enjoy life with an Alusky. These dog need a lot of everything— company, exercise, training, and grooming. Like other Snow Dogs, many Aluskies end up in shelters and rescues because their owners loved their looks but failed to think about their lifestyle.

HOW compatible with other pets?
Not a good choice. Aluskies have a high prey drive, so cats and other small pets are vulnerable. If raised with cats and/or smaller dogs, most Aluskies will accept their household companions, but should not be trusted with other people's pets. These are pack dogs who are happiest with a canine companion (or several), ideally of their own

Character Trait	Poor	Average	Good	Excellent
Attitude toward other dogs				
Quietness				
Not destructive				
Protective behavior				
Not likely to stray				
Good with children				
Ease of training				

Place of origin: **Alaska/Siberia**

Original purpose: Sled dog; companion
Male height: 21-26 in (53-66 cm)
Female height: 20-24 in (51-61cm)
Weight: 60-100 lb (27-45 kg)
Lifespan: 10-15 years

...ype. Some Aluskies may be same-sex aggressive.

HOW much exercise?

A great deal. These dogs need at least a 60-90 minute brisk walk every day, and will benefit from scootering, towing a sled or wheeled rig, Canicross (running exercise), agility, and similar work. Many Aluskies can never be trusted off leash, especially near livestock. Puppies from six to 18 months should have exercise sessions built up gradually to prevent damage to growing bones.

HOW easy to train?

Moderately difficult. Aluskies are bright, but not programmed for obedience. Owners need to be kind but firm, patient, and very persistent to get the message across. However, training is essential to teach basic good manners in and outside the home, and is also valuable to keep this dog's mind occupied.

WHAT good points?

Affectionate, people oriented, great activity companion, good with children, minimal "doggy" smell.

WHAT to be aware of?

Very high-energy; high prey drive; fairly high-maintenance coat; heavy shedder; often escapologists; very destructive if bored or lonely; loud howler.

WHAT medical problems?

Inherited disorders include hip malformation (dysplasia), entropion (inward-turned eyelids), cataracts, glaucoma, bloat, and skin irritations. All breeding stock should be hip scored and have current eye certificates.

Popular crossbreeds

● *Handsome but demanding, this dog needs real commitment.*

Wolf look-alikes

People are fascinated by wolves, but wild canines, and most wolf-dog crosses, do not make good pets. About 30 years ago, some British breeders decided to develop a type of dog with wolflike appearance but no actual wolf blood, which they named the Northern Inuit. Subsequently, breeders in the U.K., Finland, and the U.S. have pursued different lines, including the Utonagan, the Tamaskan, the Alaskan Noble Companion Dog, the Anglo Wulfdog, and half a dozen others.

The basis of most is a mixture of German Shepherds, Siberian Huskies, and Alaskan Malamutes. Some have added other breeds into the mix, and there is ongoing debate as to whether some have introduced wolf blood, either directly or via the Czechoslovakian Wolf Dog. The goal for each type is to achieve a true breeding line that could eventually achieve formal recognition as a breed.

WHAT colors?

Wolflike colors are aimed for. Northern Inuits: white, shades of sable from gray or apricot to black; dark masks and white on legs and feet permissible. Utonagans: gray, silver, black, white, buff. Tamaskans: wolf gray, red gray, and black gray.

WHAT grooming does the coat need?

Coats vary in length but are typically dense, requiring thorough grooming weekly or more frequently with a firm bristle brush to remove mats and tangles, plus extra attention during the molt.

HOW suitable are they as family dogs?

It is hard to generalize about such a wide variety of types and breeders. The declared goal of breeders is to produce a family friendly, nonaggressive dog, and many of the wolf look-alikes are just that. However, it would not be safe to make assumptions. In any case, these are big, energetic dogs who can bowl over toddlers and would

● *The Utonagan (above and bottom right) takes its name from a Native American guardian spirit, "the Spirit of the Wolf" of the Chinook tribe.*

not be the best choice for a family with small children.

WHAT type of home?

These dogs need space and are unsuited to city life. An ideal home would have a large, secure yard with room to run, access to suitable land for long, stimulating walks, and someone at home most of the time. These are not dogs to be left alone for long periods. Yards need high fences, secured at the base to prevent tunneling.

WHAT type of owner?

Not for the novice, not for couch potatoes, not for full-time workers and not for dedicated gardeners! These dogs need a lot of attention, a lot of physical and mental exercise, and a reasonably experienced trainer. Active owners who enjoy stimulating training sessions and canine sports such as agility will be the best match.

HOW compatible with other pets?

Be careful. Many breeders claim that their dogs are good with other household pets, but these dogs have sled dog blood and some individuals will inherit a strong prey drive. They are also big, strong dogs very bouncy in puppyhood, and could accidentally injure smaller pets. Early socialization with other dogs is essential to ensure that they are dog friendly.

HOW much exercise?

Lots. Two daily walks of at least 45 minutes, plus free running time should be viewed as the minimum.

Character Trait	Poor	Average	Good	Excellent
Attitude toward other dogs				
Quietness				
Not destructive				
Protective behavior				
Not likely to stray				
Good with children				
Ease of training				

*Place of origin: **Various (see text)***

Original purpose: Companion
Height: 23-30 in (58-81 cm)
Weight: 55-110 lb (25-50 kg)
Lifespan: 10-15 years

with no real maximum. These energetic dogs will enjoy hiking, Canicross, and similar activities.

HOW easy to train?
Variable. In the right hands, these dogs can often be trained to a high standard, but they will do best with experienced trainers. They can be stubborn and challenging.

They generally need firm but kind and consistent handling, starting at an early age.

WHAT good points?
If from an ethical breeder, should be friendly, nonaggressive, intelligent, responsive, and a loving companion.

WHAT to be aware of?
Demanding of exercise and company; prone

to separation anxiety, and may be destructive if bored and lonely; temperaments vary widely; it is essential for new owners to research ethical breeders.

WHAT medical problems?
Different bloodlines may be prone to various problems. In general, however, hip malformation (dysplasia) and cataracts are known to occur, and all breeding stock should be hip scored and have current eye certificates.

Popular crossbreeds

Index

Note: Page numbers set in *italic type* refer to pictures and/or captions; page numbers set in **bold type** indicate the main entry for the breed.

Picture Credits

The publisher wishes to thank the individual photographers and picture libraries who have contributed photographs for this book. Their pictures are credited here by their page number. Any pictures that are not listed below come from Interpet Publishing's own photographic archive. Note: t = top, c = center, b = bottom.

David Dalton: 28t, 39t, 59b, 77t, 92t, 97t, 142c. **John Daniels:** 5 (large), 21b, 27b, 30t, 39b, 42b, 43b, 48c, 55b, 56t and c, 57t and c, 63b, 76t, 77b, 82t, 83b, 96t, 98c, 99b, 128t and c, 129t and b, 134c, 135b, 136c, 137t and b, 139b, 144t, 145t and b, 154c, 155t and b, 158t and c, 159t and b, 161t, 162c, 163t and b, 164c, 165t and b, 169b, 173t and b, 174t, 175b, 176c 177b, 182c, 183b, 184b, 185b, 187b, 189b, 190c, 191b. **Dreamstime.com:** 210t (Tjkazimer). **Kim Fearheiley Photography** 203b. **Flickr/Creative Commons:** 198b (Melinda). **iStockphoto.com:** 200t (Margotpics). **Laura Kalbag:** 218t and c (Oskar). **The Kennel Club Picture Library:** 29t (David Dalton), 38b (David Dalton), 42t, 43t (David Dalton), 58t, 76b, 78t 79t and b (CA Johnson), 142t (Colin Seddon), 191t. **Frank Lane Picture Agency:** 26c (Mitsuaki Iwago, Minden Pictures) 82c (Mitsuaki Iwago, Minden Pictures), 83t (Gerard Lacz), 143t (Foto Natura, Alice van Kempen).
Shutterstock.com: 3 (Eric Isselée), 5 (small – Dorottya Mathe), 5 (popular crossbreeds – RTimages), 7t (Tatyana Vyc; npine), 7b (Eric Isselée), 10 (Ermolaev Alexander), 12bl (Marina Jay), 12tr (Halfpoint), 13b (Susan Schmitz), 14t (Nikolai Tsvetkov), 15t (Patrick Foto), 17 (Julia Remezova), 28c (Dorottya Mathe), 29b (Dorottya Mathe), 30c (Erik Lam), 31t (cynoclub), 31b (Anna Furman), 34t (Eric Isselée), 46b (Julia Remezova), 47t (Jagodka), 58c (Eric Isselée), 60t (vertraut), 7 (leungchopan), 72c (Jagodka), 73t and b (otsphoto), 92c (Eric Isselée), 93t and c (Eric Isselée), 94t (Susan Schmitz), 94c (Erik Lam), 95t (mj007), 95b (Erik Lam), 96b (Eric Isselée), 97b (Eric Isselée), 110t (Lee319), 110c (Chantal Ringuette), 11 (Eponaleah), 111b (Susan Schmitz), 112c (cynoclub), 113t (nenad vojnovic), 114b (Eric Isselée), 115t (WilleeCole Photography), 148c (Eric Isselée), 149b (Eric Isselée), 151b (Marina Jay), 166t and c (Erik Lam), 167t and b (Erik Lam), 18C (mikeldray), 181b (Eric Isselée), 188c (Jagodka), 192 (Erik Lam), 194t and c (JStayley401), 195t (JStayley401), 195b (Jim Vallee), 196t (Tom Feist), 196c (JStayley401), 197t (JStayley401), 198t (Anna Hoychuk), 199b (Susan Schmitz), 201t (Eric Isselée), 204t (JPagetRFPhotos), 206t (dragon_fang), 207t (RTimages), 208t (Ross Stevenson), 209t (Quayside), 210c (JStaley401), 211t (JStaley401), 212t and c (Anna Hoychuk), 213t (Stuart Monk), 214t (Lee319), 214c (Hannamariah), 215 (Laaonnoi), 216b (Joca de Jong), 216c (Erik Lam), 217t and b (Erik Lam), 219t and b (Eric Isselée), 220t (Targn Pleiades), 221t (absolutimages). **Lucinda Tennant:** 202t and c, 203t (Baloo). **Warren Photographic:** 1, 5 (medium), 6 all, 9, 10-11, 1 15b, 17, 19b, 23b, 25b, 33b, 35b, 41b, 44c, 45b, 47b, 48t, 49t and b, 51b, 53b, 54c, 60b, 64c, 67b, 69b, 71b, 81b left and right 85, 86c, 87b, 88t and c, 89b, 91b, 100t and c, 101b, 103t and b, 105b, 106c, 107b, 108c, 109t and b, 115b, 116c, 117b, 119 122b, 123b, 125b, 132b, 133b, 140b, 141b, 143b, 144c, 147b, 150c, 152c, 153b, 157b, 160c, 161b, 168c, 170t, 171b, 178c, 179b, 186c, 188t, 189t, 197b, 200c, 201b, 204c, 205 t and b, 206c, 207b, 208c, 209b, 211b, 213b, 215b, 220c, 221b, 222t and b, 223t. **Wikipedia/Creative Commons:** 199t (Cgoodell).